PLAIN OF BOROA. (P. 305.)

THE ARAUCANIANS;

OR,

NOTES OF A TOUR

AMONG THE

INDIAN TRIBES OF SOUTHERN CHILI.

BY

EDMOND REUEL SMITH,

OF THE U. S. N. ASTRONOMICAL EXPEDITION IN CHILI.

NEW YORK:

HARPER & BROTHERS, PUBLISHERS,

FRANKLIN SQUARE.

1855.

TO

LIEUT. JAMES M. GILLISS, U.S.N.,

COMMANDER OF THE U. S. N. ASTRONOMICAL EXPEDITION IN CHILI,

This Volume is respectfully Dedicated

BY THE AUTHOR.

PREFACE.

In the year 1849 the United States government authorized an Expedition, under the command of Lieutenant James M. Gilliss of the Navy, for the purpose of making astronomical and other observations in Chili. Deeming the opportunity an unusually favorable one for visiting a country somewhat removed from the ordinary route of tourists, I made application to the Secretary of the Navy, and received an appointment as a member of the expedition.

On arriving in Chili a permanent observatory was established at Santiago, the capital. It is not my object to treat of the nature of our observations, to give a scientific description of the country, or even to introduce the reader to the refined and agreeable society which gave a charm to our long residence at the seat of government. Such subjects have been left to the abler pen of one whose high position in the scientific world will give to his opinion a degree of authority that could never be attached to any thing contained in the present volume. Suffice it to say, that so confining was the nature of our work, that at the end of three years, when the Expedition was ordered home, we had enjoyed but few opportunities of going beyond the limits of the city in which we were stationed.

Unwilling to return to the United States without first becoming somewhat acquainted with the country in which we had so long resided, I tendered my resignation, and set out on a tour through the central and southern portions of Chili.

After several weeks spent in traveling through parts of the country that have frequently been described by others, I reached Concepcion, from which place I subsequently started to visit the Araucanian Indians, who form the subject of the following pages.

At a time like the present, when so general an interest is felt in every thing relating to the aboriginal races of America, I feel that no apology will be expected for the publication of any information in regard to a tribe of Indians who are but little known and rarely visited, though they have won for themselves an enviable reputation, by successfully resisting the encroachments of the white man for more than three hundred years.

My object has been to give such an account of the manners, customs, religion, and present condition of the Araucanians as may be interesting both to the student of ethnology and to the general reader.

The narrative of my journey, from the time of leaving Concepcion until I entered the Indian territory, may perhaps be considered irrelevant; but I have thought proper to include it, in order to give the reader some idea of the character and life of the frontier inhabitants of Chili, who are themselves nearly related to the aborigines of the country.

CONTENTS.

CHAPTER I.

CHAPTER II.

CHAPTER III.

CHAPTER IV.

CHAPTER V.

CHAPTER VI.

CHAPTER VII.

CHAPTER VIII.

CHAPTER IX.

CHAPTER X.

CHAPTER XI.

CHAPTER XII.

CHAPTER XIII.

CHAPTER XIV.

CHAPTER XV.

CHAPTER XVI.

CHAPTER XVII.

CHAPTER XVIII.

CHAPTER XIX.

CHAPTER XX.

CHAPTER XXI.

CHAPTER XXII.

CHAPTER XXIII.

CHAPTER XXIV.

CHAPTER XXV.

CHAPTER XXVI.

CHAPTER XXVII.

CHAPTER XXVIII.

CHAPTER XXIX.

LIST OF ENGRAVINGS.

THE ARAUCANIANS.

CHAPTER I.

Leave Concepcion.—The Bio-Bio.—Gualqui.—The Posada.—Maté.—The Arriero.

It was on the 4th of January, 1853, that, impelled by the love of adventure, I started from Concepcion to visit that classic field of Chilian history—the land of Araucania.

I had been disappointed about horses, delayed in procuring the requisite outfit, and at the very eleventh hour my servant deserted me, terrified by the warnings and entreaties of his friends, who represented a journey among the Indians as fraught with every danger. But determined to be detained no longer, I picked up a guide who agreed to accompany me to Los Angelos, and though the day was already far advanced we immediately set out.

Leaving the city we came upon the Bio-Bio, along which our road wound for several leagues. The shores are undulating, and generally finely wooded, and though the current is rapid, the surface of the water is beautifully tranquil. This river is broad and deep; it is the largest in Chili, and its whole appearance reminded me much of the Potomac near Washington.

A ride of a few hours brought us to Gualqui, a miserable hamlet. The place offered little attraction to the traveler; but night was approaching, the skies were darkly overcast, and prudence forbade our proceeding further. We accordingly halted, and after some trouble discovered a hovel where, according to a board nailed upon the wall, entertainment could be procured for both man and beast. This was the "posada" (inn), and was a fair sample of those generally found throughout the rural districts.

The usual magnificent declaration that we could be accommodated with whatever we desired, dwindled down to the never-failing jerked-beef and chicken broth, the latter of which was ordered; and thinking that wherever chickens were procurable eggs might also be had, I asked the old woman who seemed to be the presiding genius, to fry a few for our supper. Her answer was singularly characteristic—"*Aqui, S'ñor, los huevos andan a caballo!*" ("Eggs ride on horseback here, Sir!") meaning that they were scarce and dear. Not exactly comprehending her meaning, as the expression was new to me, I made some foolish reply, much to the amusement of the old lady. The explanation that I was an "Ingles" did not satisfy her, and soon after I overheard her in earnest conversation with the servant. Being assured that I was really a foreigner, she was more than ever surprised. "*Benaiga sea Dios, S'ñor,*" she exclaimed, "*pero be' Usted que habla per-fau-ta-mente como nosotro' mesmo'!*" ("The Lord be praised! Well! if he don't talk as well as we do ourselves!") The compliment was a doubtful one.

The "posada" was built of cane, plastered over with mud and thatched with straw. It contained two rooms, the one occupied as a green-grocery for the sale of tobacco, candles, jerked-beef, etc., the other intended for guests. The latter was about fifteen feet square, with no other floor than the ground. The walls were without whitewash, and overhead there was no ceiling, but the bare rafters were begrimed with soot and festooned with dusty cobwebs. The low door alone admitted light; and furniture there was none, except a rude frame in one corner, covered with a bull-hide, and intended as a bedstead.

On entering the house we were struck by a peculiar and rather unpleasant odor that arose from the grinding of toasted wheat, a process which a strapping fellow was carrying on in the middle of the room. He knelt upon the floor, bending over a flat stone about two feet long and one broad, the end of which, nearest to him, was raised at such an angle as to allow the meal to slide down freely into the sheepskin placed beneath for its reception. At his side lay a pile of wheat, from which he fed his mill; then grasping with both hands a small stone roller, he propelled it briskly backward and forward with a rolling motion, which allowed the ground meal to escape, and brought a fresh supply of grain continually under the grinder. Judging from the torrents of perspiration that flowed from the fellow's forehead, it was no easy work.

Every now and then some dirty little imp, with

more or less of an apology for a shirt on, would rush in, grab a handful of the meal, stir it up in a cup of water, and drink it off. This beverage, called "ulpo," is much used by the poorer classes throughout southern Chili as a substitute for bread, which at a distance from the towns is seldom met with.

In a small shed outside, the wheat was being toasted in an earthen dish over a hot fire; a ragged girl, squatting on her haunches among the ashes, was briskly stirring the grain to prevent it from burning.

Our supper was a real "casuela de ave"—the best dish that can be had in Chili—and one which, I verily believe, can be had nowhere else. A chicken broth with such a savory mixture of onions, potatoes, and other things too numerous to mention, it never entered into the head of a "gringo" to imagine. The only drawback is the delay of at least two hours which the hungry man is always obliged to endure.

My pack-saddle and boxes were converted into table and chairs; spread there was none; neither did the establishment boast such a thing as a plate, but the huge dish was accompanied by an iron spoon, and nothing more was necessary.

That we might not be in utter darkness, our landlady brought a candle. As there was no candlestick, we were at loss to know where she would put it; but dexterously tipping the soft tallow dip, and letting the grease run down one side for a moment, she dabbed it suddenly against the rough mud wall, and there it stuck. The flare of the unsteady light disclosed, in all directions, spots of grease, drippings, and waving lines of smoke upon the wall, showing that the lady's feat, however surprising, was nothing new.

The supper was followed by "maté." As this beverage is peculiar to South America, the method of preparing it deserves a description. A pan of burning charcoal was brought in, and on it water was set to boil in the "tacho," a small copper jug. The hostess followed with a tin box having two partitions, the one containing sugar, the other filled with the "yerba" (Paraguay tea). A small gourd and a "bombilla" (a tin tube with a perforated bulb) completed her armament.

Sitting down upon the floor, the old woman fans the fire with her petticoat until the water boils; a live coal is dropped into the sugar to burn it; the bombilla is placed in the gourd; a handful of the tea follows; a lump of burnt sugar is thrown in atop; and over all is poured the boiling water. After a pull at the bombilla to see if all is right, the beverage is passed to the person of most importance present. If you have ever sucked a sherry cobbler through a straw, you will soon get in the way of drinking "maté;" but, while yet a novice, beware of scalding your mouth!

Maté is universally used in the country; but among people in better circumstances much more decorum is observed in its preparation, and the utensils are generally of silver, often of the most aristocratic pretensions. In the cities, tea and coffee are entirely supplanting the more national maté in wealthy circles, yet many of the old school still cling to it "sub rosa."

The Paraguay tea has many properties in common

with the Chinese plant, and when well prepared is a very agreeable substitute.

Whoever travels through the interior of Chili must always carry an "almofrer," which is essential alike to comfort and respectability. The "almofrez," is a leather sack, large enough to hold a mattress and bedding (which are not to be had at the country inns), with smaller articles useful on the way. It is easily packed upon the mules, protects the bedding from rain, and serves at night as a temporary bedstead. It is true the room, in this case, contained something that was evidently made to sleep on, but it had a very suspicious look, suggestive of vermin, and I much preferred making up my bed on the ground.

The candle still stuck upon the wall, and, half dozing, I lay watching its countless freaks. It would flash up and then burn low, flare, flicker, sputter, and almost expire; then suddenly blaze up again. What with the greasy stalactites on the wall, the varying shadows of the sooty cobwebs hanging from the dingy roof, and the continual drip, drip, drip, of the tallow on the floor, like trickling waters, I could almost fancy myself dancing through some subterranean cavern, led by a "will o' the wisp." Suddenly there was a grand flash, flare, sputter, spit, and blaze, like the finale of an opera or the winding up of a display of fire-works, and all was darkness.

My guide slept outside in the open air, in company with a couple of "arrieros" (muleteers), who, with their troop, were on the way to Concepcion.

The hardiness and perfect system of these travelers by profession makes them worthy of study, and in nothing more so than in their dispositions for the night. At the end of a day's journey their first care is for the animals; then they arrange their packs, with a view not only to the safety of the goods but also to their own comfort. The most heavy and unwieldy articles are piled up so as to form a scientific barricade and a protection against the wind, while smaller packages are placed within reach of the men, who always lie about in such positions that every thing is under somebody's eye.

If the arriero is fortunate enough to get a supper, he gorges himself, like the anaconda, uncertain when he may have another meal; if nothing is to be had, and his saddle-bags furnish no remnants of the last repast, he tightens up his sash, smokes a cigarito, and is content.

For a bed he never wants. The native saddle is composed of about a dozen sheepskins, one half of which are placed over a rude tree, and the other half beneath. These skins, spread upon the ground, form a soft resting-place; the tree is the pillow, and wrapping himself in the never-failing poncho, his only blanket, the wearied rider, with pantaloons and boots on, stretches himself out with no other canopy than the blue sky.

Is there the slightest noise during the stillness of the night—does a footstep approach, he is on the alert in an instant, and his formidable "machete" (a long knife) is always at hand.

With the first rays of the morning he is up. He has no dressing to do, no toilet to make—that is to say, he does not make it—but starts in search of his animals, and is soon ready for another day's march.

CHAPTER II.

The Coast Range.—The Lunatic.—Treatment of the Insane.—Chilian "Sleepy Hollow."—The Frenchman.—A live Yankee.

LEAVING Gualqui the road strikes off over what is usually known as the "coast range." To the northward the mountains composing this range are divided into parallel ridges with extended intervening plains; but in this latitude they are all blended together. Continually you are engaged in winding and climbing, ascending and descending a wilderness of hills, whose very confusion produces a monotony irksome alike to body and mind. Gazing from some lofty point you feel lost amidst the interminable disorder of ups and downs, with no clew by which to ascertain the points of the compass. Even the occasional view of finely-wooded summits and smiling valleys, or the glimpse of some little stream dancing along noisily toward the sea, could not relieve the tedium of the journey.

The soil is red, and appears to be composed almost entirely of disintegrating granite—so friable, that with each heavy rain it washes down, leaving huge gullies in the hillsides. In many places we found yawning chasms, two or three hundred feet in depth, stretching up on either side, so as to leave barely room for a horse to pass, and threatening with the next shower to swallow up the road itself.

This frequently happens, and the traveler, unacquainted with the "changes of the times," will sometimes find all further advance cut off by a vast gulf gaping before him, on the other side of which the road winds on toward his destination.

Near a house by the roadside a large cross, some fifteen feet high, attracted our attention. While conjecturing what it might mean, a powerfully-built young man, with the hair of his head cropped unfashionably short, came running out, entreating us to aid him in annihilating certain Jews, Turks, infidels, and heretics that were endeavoring to overthrow the true religion.

He accompanied this request with an attempt to possess himself of a huge dragoon sword which my trusty squire carried by his side. We anticipated some difficulty; but the heretics and Turks, half a dozen in number, came to the rescue, and bore the religious enthusiast away.

They had forced him nearly to the house when, bursting from them, he ran to the cross, embraced it for a moment, and then turning, showered a volley of kicks and blows upon the persecuting unbelievers.

The last we saw of the poor lunatic, the whole party had thrown him to the ground, and were pommeling him to their heart's content.

This method of curing madness brought to my mind an incident that happened at a small country village in another part of Chili. The wife of the innkeeper at whose "posada" we stopped had become crazed, and, among other things calculated to trouble an affectionate husband, would occasionally manifest a disposition to sit in the lap of perfect strangers.

The landlord was a coarse, burly man, with no very pleasant expression, and apparently morose; but under the soothing effects of a maté (at our expense), his heart would soften, and he loved to dwell upon his numerous afflictions, the principal of which was the melancholy condition of his wife. "But," he would conclude, lifting his eyes devoutly, "this is but one of the many crosses which, in this world, we are all destined to bear!" There was a solemnity in his air, implying patient endurance under suffering, that impressed us deeply.

A chuckle-headed fellow, who happened to be present, ventured to recommend to mine host various curatives, declaring that he had known a lunatic, in his own parish, to receive great benefit from the application to his cranium of a mixture of *ass's milk, and the blood from a mare's ear!*

"No, Señor!" exclaimed the afflicted saint, turning indignantly upon the intruder. "I have tried every thing; there is but one course to be pursued. *Dé le penca, Señor; es un santo remedio!*" ("Give her a sound drubbing, Sir; it is an infallible remedy.")

When it is remembered that the "penca" is a heavy lash of braided hide attached to the reins of a horse, and intended not only as a whip, but also as an effective weapon, the excellence of the cure can not be doubted.

Until very recently there was no separate provision in Chili for the insane. Some few were admitted to the hospitals; but they were treated with so much harshness, and allowed to live in such a filthy manner, that it may well be doubted whether their condition was bettered or made worse. Incorrigible maniacs, if belonging to wealthy families, were sent to the mad-house in Lima—if poor, they were frequently chained in the prison.

On one of the principal streets of Santiago is still pointed out a window, six feet or more from the pavement, closely grated, and covered with a wire screen. Within is a small room where, for several years, a raging madman was confined. His food was thrown to him through the iron bars, as to a wild beast; egress was denied him; he became more and more furious, and finally died in this den, amidst the filth accumulated during his long confinement.

Once, as a woman was passing, he climbed to the window, extended his arm, and catching hold of her braided locks, hauled her up to the bars, where she hung struggling and screaming until cut down, when she ran off, glad to escape with only the loss of her hair.

Thanks to the spirit of the age, these relics of mediæval barbarism are fast disappearing. There now exists in the capital an Insane Asylum, conducted like similar institutions in Europe; may it prove the precursor of other establishments equally useful. The blind, the deaf, and the dumb, are still uncared for; nor can the present government in any way more highly justify its claim to an enlightened liberality than by establishing such charitable institutions as are wanting, and thoroughly remodeling those which at present exist.

We crossed several brooks, the principal of which was the Quilacoga, passing through a fine estate of the same name. Further on we came to the Gomero, a small streamlet running through the fertile valley of Talcamavida, described by the poet as

> "Valle de Talcamavida importante,
> De pastos y comidas abundante."

Night was now coming on—the roads were dangerous to travel after sunset—we were tired, and we determined to halt and beg lodgings on the neighboring estate. The place itself is unusually inviting; for, in addition to its pleasant appearance, it bears a "Sleepy Hollow" reputation peculiarly attractive to weary travelers.

Not far from here it was, according to Ercilla, that a haughty Indian chief performed the wonderful feat of sleeping for three nights and two days on a stretch. After describing the arrival of the chieftain from the wars, the poet goes on to state that he ordered a supper to be prepared, and retiring to his couch, remained

> "Deep buried in a slumber so profound,
> As though a thousand years he had been dead,
> Until the sun three times had journeyed round
> The earth, when, rising from his bed—
> 'What ho, ye slaves! bring forth my garments,' said he,
> 'And tell me, is the meal I ordered ready?'
> The servant answered—'If I may be bold, Sir,
> Your dinner after cooking has got cold, Sir!
> For you have slept, without as much as winking,
> Full fifty hours, forgetful of your toils,
> Taking no care for eating or for drinking,'" etc.

On receiving this information, the Indian expressed no surprise, but stated that during fifteen consecutive days he had not closed his eyes, for reasons all of which are faithfully recorded by the garrulous old chronicler.

The overseer of the estate proved to be a Frenchman. He was overjoyed to find some one that could converse in his own tongue, and invited us to spend the night at his quarters. Some tough jerked-beef, with an omelet of my own cooking, made a tolerable supper.

The meal was washed down with some bad wine, and a good deal of worse French—for I was getting sadly rusty. In spite of every precaution a Spanish word would occasionally slip in with just sufficient change to give it a Gallic jingle, and cheat me for a moment into the idea that I was speaking the true Parisian. These blunders the Frenchman charitably overlooked in his anxiety to hear the news from Europe, and it was a late hour before I could get away from him to my bed, which had been made up on a hide in the store-house, amidst a confusion of bags of grain, barrels of beans, wine-jars, and jerked beef.

Next morning when pay was offered to the overseer, he refused it as only a Frenchman could; but, in the same breath, hinted that a few rials might prove acceptable to the cook. She did not decline.

This cook, by the way, was evidently the overseer's wife—or ought to have been—and was about as low and dirty a specimen of the common class as he could well have selected. He did not seem ambitious to raise her to his own level; on the contrary, he was fast sinking to hers. It is not uncommon for other foreigners to form such alliances, but they generally strive to elevate their mates. Not so the French, who usually fall from their own position, and seem to assimilate with their inferiors in manners and refinement more rapidly than any other people.

Riding along we were struck by the appearance of a small house, which, though humble, was as un-Chilian as possible. The walls were whitewashed; the windows were glazed, and actually provided with blinds; a row of brightly-scoured tin pans were glistening in the sun, and hard-by grunted a fat porker, tied to a stake in the ground.

A fair-haired child, neatly dressed and wearing a sun-bonnet, came running out of the house, followed by a tidy, rosy-cheeked woman, also wearing a sun-bonnet. There was something so characteristic about them, especially the sun-bonnets, that I felt convinced they must be Americans, and was half inclined to stop and inquire.

A little further on we came to a flour-mill. Out of the second story window protruded a long, shrewd face. A profusion of yellow locks was tucked behind the ears, while a tall, shapeless white beaver was cocked back at a sufficient angle to display a high, expansive forehead. A pair of lank arms and long bony hands completed the picture of one who was unmistakably engaged in some deep calculation.

He was evidently the owner of the house we had passed, and turning my horse I rode up to the mill and addressed him in Spanish. His reply was very characteristic—"*Me no intendy.*" Dropping the Spanish, I continued, "I guess you ain't a Yankee?" The head popped in with an exclamation, "Wal, I ain't any thing else!" and in a moment he was down stairs at the door.

The poor fellow was delighted to meet a fellow-countryman, and pressed us to stop for dinner.

"My wife will be glad to see you," he said, "and I'll give you such a dish of corned-beef and cabbage as you haven't seen for many a day."

The invitation was a tempting one, but as the guide had gone on, and the mule-bell was sounding faint in the distance, I was obliged to decline.

I felt proud of my country as I shook the honest Yankee by the hand. Far away from home, cut off, as it were, from the world, his lot seemed a hard one; but unless the man's looks very much belied his character, a few years would produce great changes in his circumstances; in shrewdness and energy he possessed the elements of success; in the burden of a family he had both an incentive to exertion and a solace.

To the young foreigner who seeks by the labor of his hands to acquire wealth upon this coast, it is all-important that he should come accompanied by a partner alike willing and able to share his toils and comfort him in adversity. He must have a home and society that will render him, in a measure, independent of the world Many bright hopes have been dashed for want of such resources.

The stranger arriving poor and friendless, will look in vain for that society to which he has been accustomed at home. Only by time and patient industry can he acquire a social position. If of a generous and impulsive nature, the want of that sympathy so necessary to the human heart, added to the feeling of pride that leads us to contemn those by whom we deem ourselves neglected, may induce him to form unworthy associations, and ere he is fully aware of the danger, he may be drawn into some entangling alliance, which will continually drag him down, and prevent his ever attaining that high standing in society which he might otherwise have gained.

CHAPTER III.

Yumbel.—The Valdiviano.—Volcanic Sand.—The Recruiting Station.—Rio Claro.—Singular Embankment.—Search for Lodgings.—Distant View of Antuco.—Falls of the Laja.

After a ride of four or five hours we reached an elevated point, where a magnificent view burst suddenly upon our sight.

Before us lay the great central plain of Chili; beyond rose the lengthened Cordillera, where proudly domineered the snowy Chillan, sublimely beautiful with its graceful dome, and the rugged Sierra Velluda, with the neighboring cone of Antuco wrapped in clouds. While to the north and south the pinnacles of Loncair, the truncated Descaberado, and the peaks of Santa Barbara, with other summits distant and more dimly visible, rose like islands above the blue horizon of the plain, rolling onward like the sea.

It is true that the highest mountains in this part of Chili are far inferior, in actual elevation, to many of those at the north; in fact the whole range of the Andes gradually lowers as it runs toward the south, until swallowed up in the ocean at Cape Horn; but the prominent southern peaks are by far the more striking in appearance; they tower more above the general mass, their greatness appeals to the eye, while that of their more northern brethren addresses itself to the understanding.

Descending into the plain we soon reached Yumbel.

This town is laid out in regular squares, with one-story houses, built of sun-burnt brick, and roofed with tile. It has an "alameda," or promenade, and boasts a "plaza de armas," or public square, faced on two sides by the church and barracks, and on the other two by stores and dwellings. There is doubtless a convent, and probably a chain-gang to repair the streets. In a word, it is—like all other towns in the country—a small edition of Santiago. But though the capital of the province of Rere, its general appearance was in no way prepossessing.

We inquired for the "posada," but were informed that though there was once a "café" in the place, it had been given up for want of custom; and the prospect was that we should be obliged to ride on dinnerless until night.

Half hoping somebody might be found hospitably disposed, I rode into several of the best houses to make inquiries, but received no greater satisfaction than a shrug of the shoulders, accompanied by the polite regret that the town could not furnish any accommodations for strangers.

At last a lady, more considerate than the rest, suggested that, at the further end of the street, some poor people might be found, who would be happy to cook us a meal for a few rials. The hint was a valuable one, and was of course taken.

Just on the outskirts there was a collection of miserable huts, and we succeeded in ferreting out an old woman, who was willing and able to provide for our wants.

The hovel was dirty enough, and having no desire

to spoil my appetite by seeing the cooking done, I started for some apple trees which stood near by, and throwing down my poncho in the shade, composed myself for a siesta. After an hour's sleep dinner was announced, and entering the house I found a box which appeared to be a bushel measure, spread with a dirty towel and crowned by a steaming "Valdiviano."

The "Valdiviano," which is a national dish with the Chilenos, is made of jerked beef, cooked up into a hash with a variety of vegetables, the most essential of which is the onion. This savory mess is easily made, and extremely palatable to the hungry traveler. To a delicate stomach it might prove repugnant, but a ride of some twenty miles over a rough road, on a hard trotting horse, is an unfailing cure for fastidiousness.

The table scarcely reached to my knees, as I sat upon the high bench that ran round the room; but after inviting each person present in true Spanish style to partake of the meal—an invitation which was, of course, declined—I fell to without further ceremony. A huge horn tumbler full of wine, and a plate of olives followed.

The olive in Chili is seldom eaten green and in pickle, as it comes to us from Spain, but ripe and in the oil; it is a fruit of which most persons become fond when once accustomed to its use, though there are but few strangers who relish it upon first trial.

Leaving Yumbel, we started in a southeasterly direction to visit the Falls of the Laja.

The road for most of the way lay over a plain composed of a black, almost impassable volcanic sand, that shifts about with the wind, and is piled up at short intervals into small hillocks.

This sandy waste is a feature of unusual geological interest, especially when considered in connection with the vast layers of tufa and scoria found in other parts of the same plain.

The traveler, however little acquainted with science, can not fail to be deeply impressed by these great records, so clearly indicating a comparatively recent period of vast volcanic activity. The frequent spasmodic tremblings of the earth, driving the frightened inhabitants from their houses, and sometimes strewing their cities in the dust—the occasional faint smoke from distant and almost extinguished craters—the unmistakable evidences presented by the coast that the country is still being uplifted from the sea, all prove that the internal fire is not yet extinct; but when we compare its present feeble efforts with former achievements, in piling up the majestic Andes like Pelion on Ossa, till they reached the very skies, they seem like the struggles of a dying giant, crushed beneath the vast mass raised by his own once powerful hand.

The plain was scattered with coarse stunted bushes, over which twined innumerable creepers bearing a large red flower, lighting up with a smile the surrounding desolation.

In the midst of this wilderness of sand we came upon a rude tent, with a flag flying in front, and a sentinel under arms. As we approached, a fierce-looking character with red pantaloons, a handkerchief tied round his head, and a sabre dangling in his hand, stepped forth and eyed us for a moment. A number of tatterdemalions, all very red from exposure to the sun, were lying about with guns and swords, but without uniform of any description.

The inscription upon the flag told the whole story. The officer—for such was the man with the red pantaloons—was recruiting for the cavalry, and had posted himself here as a place where he would be likely to pick up vagabonds fit food for gunpowder.

The whole group had more the appearance of banditti than of soldiers, and brought forcibly to mind the renown of this spot, which, according to popular tradition, was once infested by lurking desperadoes as wild and untraceable among these shifting hillocks as the roving Bedouins amidst the sands of the desert. Whether the stories we heard ever had any other foundation than the gloomy impression which such solitudes are apt to produce upon the minds of an imaginative people we did not stop to inquire, but believed implicitly in the famed "montaneros" of the "Arenal," willing to credit any thing that could throw a tinge of romance around the journey

The traveling through the sand was heavy and tiresome to the horses and unpleasant to the rider, owing to the clouds of impalpable dust rising with every puff of wind. This continued until we reached the Rio Claro, a small, clear stream (as the name implies), running over a wide bed, and frequently changing its channel.

Running continuously along the brink of the northern bank of this river, was a singular mound of sand, thrown up to the height of twelve or fifteen feet with a precision and regularity that gave it much the appearance of an artificial fortification. It was probably a freak of contending winds blowing over the plain and up the bed of the river.

The river was not deep, and we forded without difficulty. The sun was setting when we reached the Laja. As the plain was a dead level, we saw no indications of the river until we stood upon its very brink, except a few trees and the spray wreathing up from the falls.

The road passes within a quarter of a mile of the falls; but so slight is the curiosity of the people about such matters, that, of the numbers that travel this route, few turn aside to see one of the finest natural objects in Chili, and almost the only one of the kind. My squire, though he had frequently crossed the river, did not know there was any thing there to be seen, and grumbled when I proposed stopping over night.

We did not see the falls until actually standing upon the rock overhanging the abyss into which the river plunges. The last rays of the setting sun threw a bright bow over the spray, which rose like smoke from the surface of the stream; beneath, all was dark —but a sullen roar told of the fierce struggles going on beneath our feet, and gave, perhaps, a more sublime impression than if we had caught our first view in the broad light of noonday.

A few rods from the river stood a small, rude mill, and near by two or three "ranchos," up to which we rode in search of lodgings.

In an open door-way sat a rather good-looking woman, who, on being asked if we could pass the night there, answered, eying us suspiciously, "*Quien sabe!* the master of the house is not at home."

"Can you give us any thing to eat?"

"I think not, Señor!"

"Have you no chickens?"

"No, Señor."

"No beef?"

"No, Señor."

"No vegetables?"

"No, Señor."

Now it so happened that certain feathery things, looking very gallinaceous, were roosting near at hand, while the small garden-patch behind the house seemed to be well-stocked with onions and potatoes. There was here a strange discrepancy between facts and statements; but having been similarly situated before, I well knew what to do, and ordering the servant to unload the mule, and turn the animals into the "corral," I sat down patiently to await the coming of the "dueño de casa."

The damsel shrugged her shoulders but said nothing. Inhospitable she could not have been, for the lower class of Chilenos never are; but she probably dreaded the jealousy of her lord, and feared the responsibility of extending any attention to strangers.

The man of the house, who, with his family, had been off farming in the neighborhood, soon made his appearance driving a dumpy, little, solid, wheeled ox-cart. He received us very hospitably, assuring us that we were welcome to the best his house could afford. He was communicative, intelligent, more independent in his opinions than most of his class, and afforded me both amusement and information.

On asking him about the volcano of Antuco, then in a state of eruption, he informed me that it was plainly visible, and offered to lead me to a spot from which a good view could be obtained.

At a short distance from the house, where there were no intervening trees, the volcano burst upon us in full blast.

The night was dark, the mountains were enveloped in clouds, but we could plainly see the flames playing about the vent, and occasionally shooting high in air; while a lurid stream of lava, like a river of molten iron, poured down toward the plain. At intervals it would flash and writhe like a snake, as, with some new eruption, fresh materials were added to the burning mass; and the overhanging canopy of clouds would glow with a glare like that of the distant lightning which is seen, in summer evenings, flashing about the horizon.

The grandeur of the effect produced was heightened by the roar of the Laja—singularly in unison with the scene—and I stood lost in admiration, until my host hinted at the cold wind that swept down from the snowy cordillera, and proposed that we should return to the house.

A smoking "casuela" awaited us, into whose composition, strange to say, entered nearly all the numerous articles whose very existence the lady had so flatly denied.

The next morning was spent in examining the falls.

FALLS OF THE LAJA.

The plain here is covered with a thin overlying cloak of compact lava, which, at a comparatively recent geological period, must have flowed from some vent in the chain of the Andes—probably from the volcano of Antuco, at a time when much more active than at present. The Laja, in two shallow branches, runs over this stratum, and at its termination plunges down a depth of about seventy feet—wearing narrow and deep channels, for several miles, until the various streams reunite, and flow on, in one broad river, until lost in the Bio-Bio.

Accompanied by mine host, I descended into the bed of the river, to a spot from which could be seen both falls of the northern branch, which, at this point, is divided by a small island. One of these has a horse-shoe form, and the effect of the two taken together is not unlike Niagara upon a small scale.

Just below the island the waters of the two falls unite and rush through a narrow channel worn in the rock, seething and boiling in a space so contracted that I was almost tempted to leap across. A good English hunter might have cleared it with ease.

With the camera lucida I managed to take a pretty accurate sketch, which I painted roughly on the spot with water-colors that I carried rubbed upon a plate. The whole operation caused considerable surprise to the "*native*," who thought that I was prying into the hidden mysteries of nature. He asked whether I had discovered treasures in the depth of the river; and wanted to know if the blueness of the water did not indicate the presence of gold. I tried to make explanations, but he looked incredulous, and, though too polite to express them, evidently had his suspicions.

Upon the southern branch of the Laja, there are also two falls—not so high as those on the northern branch, but followed by a succession of wild rapids, and well worth a visit.

CHAPTER IV.

Fording Rivers.—Hanging Bridges.—The Donkey "wot wouldn't go."—Getting across.—Scenes on the Road.—Politeness of the Natives.

SOME distance above the falls we found the Laja broad and shallow; and, though the current was strong, we forded without difficulty.

Most of the rivers in the interior of Chili are crossed in this manner; but, as their descent to the sea is rapid and their velocity great, the passage is often attended with difficulty and danger.

The stranger, on reaching one of these rivers, should always engage the services of some of the natives, who, by constantly crossing and recrossing, become skillful pilots. The merest boy, living near the ford, will lead you safely through the swollen stream. At the word, he begins operations in an off-hand way that proves how perfectly he understands his business.

He approaches a horse and slips into his mouth a halter, to serve as bit and bridle; a lasso is thrown about the neck of the bell-mare, then, rolling up his wide drawers, he swings himself by the mane upon the horse's bare back, and plunges in, dragging after him the unwilling mare. First he tacks up the stream, then down, now straight for the opposite shore; then, describing a curve, he proceeds slowly, looking carefully about, noting each stone and every curling eddy.

As he sits upon the startled horse, amidst the white foam of the torrent—his bare legs dangling in the water, a red *poncho* around his waist, his breast and shoulders naked, and his matted locks blowing about his face, while his black eye glances cautiously around—he would form a striking picture for an artist.

The mules, in single file, follow warily in the course of their leader with the tinkling bell, and the "arrieros" ride close behind, urging them on by shouting and the whizzing of their lassos.

Lift your feet upon the back of the saddle, and, pressing firmly with your knees, keep close to the guide. Though ready to jerk him up in case of a stumble, let your horse have pretty much his own way, and, if an old stager, he will move on cautiously, never bringing down his foot until sure of the ground. In this manner you will get over safely. But when amidst the deafening roar of the waters and the crash of large stones tumbling about and dashing against each other, you will understand the perils of these fordings, and credit the stories so often heard of travelers who, stunned by the din and dizzied by the whirl around them, fall from the saddle, and are swept away by the impetuous flood.

Permanent bridges, with the exception of a few near Santiago, are unknown in the country; but when the rivers become impassable, from the rains of winter or the melting of the mountain snows, suspension bridges are generally erected. These "puentes de cimbra" (shaking bridges), as they are appropriately called, are extremely rude both in material and construction.

The narrowest part of the stream is selected. Upon

the bank a couple of strong poles are planted in the ground; two heavy cables, made of raw hide firmly twisted, are attached to these poles near the earth and carried across to the opposite shore, where they are securely fastened to other poles. On these cables a floor of cane and brush is laid. From the tops of the poles are stretched other cables, that help to strengthen and support the floor, by vertical thongs at short intervals.

So soon as this primitive structure is completed and properly braced, the transit commences, and continues until the bridge is broken down or swept away by some freshet.

Occasionally it happens that, by the breaking of the cane flooring, an animal's foot goes through, and,

HANGING BRIDGE.

in the struggle to extricate himself, the ropes give way, precipitating him into the raging torrent.

I shall never forget my first crossing one of these crazy structures.

It was a stormy day when two of us reached the Cachapoal. The bridge swayed and creaked violently in the strong wind, and it was not without some forebodings that we asked the toll-gatherer if we could pass. He answered, dubiously,

"Yes; I think you can pass over; but it won't hold out much longer."

This was not very consoling—but the river was impassable by fording, and we had no alternative.

First a horse was started over. Being an old traveler, he got along very well, and the others were induced to follow, one by one. It was not easy to make them face the bridge; but once started, they went safely over, picking their way carefully, as though fully aware of their danger. When we came to the last mule he was obstinate.

After being bullied and beaten into starting he went half way over; then, like the ass that he was, he lay composedly down and began treating himself to a succession of fresh rolls, amidst a tremendous crashing of the baggage intrusted to his care. As he was heavily laden, it was unsafe to approach him. Shouting, howling, and showers of stones were unavailing, for he would not move. The case seemed a hopeless one, and I began to solace myself by humming the old ditty:

"If I had a donkey wot wouldn't go,
D' ye think I'd wollop him? Oh no! no!"

But the two muleteers seemed to be of another mind;

for, losing all patience, they sprang upon the bridge and laid hold of Mr. Donkey in the most summary manner.

One caught the brute by the ears, which he jerked incessantly, while the other seized the tail, which he began pulling and twisting as though drawing the cork out of a bottle. To this treatment was added an accompaniment on the offender's ribs, by two pair of boots, until, at last, even mulish endurance was forced to yield.

The hooting and laughter of the by-standers, the curses and kicks of the muleteers, the obstinacy of the mule, the tossing of the bridge, and the wild roar of the foaming river, all conspired to produce a scene of confusion seldom equaled.

Next in order came our turn to go over on foot. As you commence walking upon one of these light structures a vibratory motion is imparted to it, running from end to end like the movements of a snake; and you have, at each step, a lateral rolling, tossing you from side to side, and making you pitch like a ship at sea. Add to this the sight and sound of the river surging and roaring beneath your feet, and the variety of sensations produced makes the passage of a "puente de cimbra" no easy matter.

Many persons are affected by the motion with giddiness to such an extent as to disable them from proceeding, and they have to be carried across.

Some of the larger streams are crossed in launches; but few of the rivers have a sufficient depth to allow of their employment.

We were now upon the central road, connecting all

the interior southern towns with the distant capital—the great thoroughfare over which passes most of the internal trade of the country.

The plain, upon either hand, parched for want of rain during the long dry season, looks sombre and uninviting; but the road itself presents much that is interesting to the stranger in the frequent groups of country people bearing their produce to market.

A noise is heard like the approach of a railroad train, and a long file of mules comes jogging by, loaded with lumber. Half a dozen boards or joists are tied on to each animal, the ends in front projecting far beyond his head; while behind they drag and clatter along the ground. As they pass, give them a wide berth if you do not wish to be unhorsed. These donkeys are great sticklers for the right of way, and make no allowance for the convenience of others.

Again your ears are saluted by a screeching, like that of a hundred wheel-barrows; and turning, you see a yoke or two of oxen coming slowly along. It is only when nearly abreast that you catch sight of the cause of so much creaking. A clumsy pair of solid wheels, hewn from transverse sections of a tree, and without tire, are working ungreased upon a rude axle, to which are fastened a couple of saplings projecting some distance behind, and joined in front so as to form a tongue. This tongue is strapped to the yoke, which, resting on the back of the oxen's necks, is tied to their horns with leathern thongs. The body of the cart is simply a hide laid upon the saplings, and rests about a foot from the ground.

CHILIAN CART.

These dumpy little vehicles are common throughout the country, and when laden to their utmost capacity, with a driver on top stirring up the team with a long pole, their appearance is grotesque in the extreme.

Another troop of mules approaches. Those swollen sheep-skins are the "*bottles*" of which we read in the Scriptures, and are filled with the famed wines of Concepcion.

The horsemen that follow close behind are unlike the others you have met. They do not wear the high Guayaquil hat and the wide drawers that are so common at the North, neither do they use the more military cap generally worn by the people of the South. Their heads are surmounted by a conical blue bonnet;

instead of the European jacket they wear a loose garment of coarse woolen homespun or blue cottonade, not unlike an under-shirt in form, and cut down to a point both in front and behind; their legs are encased in overalls of undressed hide, and their feet are covered with moccasins of the same material. To an experienced eye there is something peculiar even in the color of their ponchos.

These men are Maulenos, as the people are called living near the river Maulé and its tributaries. They are rather uncouth in appearance, and their loud voices and red faces seem to justify the common idea that wines transported in this manner become watery, and lose much of their fine flavor before reaching their destination. But however noisy, they do not forget as they pass to lift their hats with the salutation, "*Adios, Señor!*" "*Buen viaje, amigo!*" "God be with you, Sir!" "A pleasant journey to you, my friend!"

This innate politeness is every where met among the Chilenos, in all their actions, from the most important business down to the lighting of a cigarito.

CHAPTER V.

Arrival at Los Angelos.—Birth-days and Saint-days.—Watching an Angel.—Los Angelos.—Manufacture of Ponchos.—Start for the Volcano of Antuco.

Arriving at Los Angelos, I repaired immediately to the house of the Intendente, Don José Erasmo Jofré, with the letters with which the Governor of the province had kindly furnished me, stating my objects, and recommending me to the attention of the authorities.

The Intendente received me with assurances that every assistance should be rendered me in the prosecution of my designs. As there was no "posada" in the place, he invited me to take pot-luck with him in his own narrow quarters; saying, at the same time, that, if I preferred, he would request some family in the town to give me lodgings where I could be more comfortable.

Knowing that it was necessary to be a burden upon somebody, I accepted his hospitable invitation in preference to being quartered on any family; for a request from the Intendente, in whatever terms it might have been couched, would probably have been construed into a demand, and complied with as such.

As my host had official business to occupy his time, he handed me over to the care of a young gentleman, whom he requested to entertain me for the evening;

and I was accordingly taken to a house in the neighborhood, where we found quite a large party assembled.

The object of this gathering was to celebrate the birth-day of the lady of the house, or rather her saint's-day.

It is an almost invariable rule in Chili to name a child after the saint upon whose day it happened to be born, even though the saint chance to be a woman and the child a man, or *vice versa.* Hence it is that we meet with so many Franciscas, Joséfas, and Pablas among the women, and so many Marias among the men. They all celebrate their nativities as their saints come round; but many of the latter are movable in the calendar, and often a Chileno is at a loss to know the real day of his birth.

I had hoped to enjoy the privilege of looking on quietly without taking part in the festivities—for after a hard ride, a seat in one corner would have been far more agreeable than violent dancing; but my friend insisted on introducing me to every one, giving me a string of titles that was perfectly alarming, and I soon found myself in the awkward and embarrassing position of "the lion of the evening." No excuses would be heard; I was stuffed with cakes and sweetmeats; partners were selected for me, and, in spite of my drowsiness, I danced away polkas and waltzes, quadrilles and zamacuccas until two o'clock in the morning.

The ladies were many of them pretty and finely formed; all of them were well dressed and agreeable in their manners; they were vivacious and (though without much education) intelligent, and possessed a degree of refinement not to have been expected in an unimportant place so far removed from the capital. The young men were real country beaux, with considerable pretensions to elegance, and dressed in the extreme of fashions somewhat out of date. This was not the first opportunity I had of observing—as every stranger in Chili must—the unaccountable superiority, both intellectual and physical, of the women to the men.

Returning from the party at a late hour, I had an opportunity of witnessing festivities of quite a different character.

Passing in front of a small house, my attention was attracted by loud singing and shouting within. A woman, who stood in the open door-way, seeing me pause, invited me to enter.

"What is there going on?" I asked.

"*Estamos velando un angelito de Dios*" ("We are watching an angel of God"), she replied.

Such an unintelligible answer only excited greater curiosity, and I entered.

The room was filled with a collection of men and women of the lower class, engaged in drinking and clapping their hands to the music of two females who sat on the floor, guitar in hand, singing a drawling ditty, the burden of which was the happiness of somebody or something in heaven.

But the most prominent object was a kind of altar, set round with lighted candles, and ornamented with tinsel flowers. In the midst of these sat the figure of an infant, of the size of life, profusely painted with red and white, dressed in tawdry finery, and adorned with gauze wings. "It is only the image of some saint," I thought, and was turning away; but a second glance convinced me that there was something unusual about the figure. The hair looked very natural; those eyes were strangely vacant and filmy; even the finger-nails were perfectly formed. There seemed to be "too much of art for nature, yet too much of nature for art;" and I approached to scrutinize it closely. It was *a corpse!*

"What is that?" I asked of a by-stander.

"*An angel, Sir,*" he replied.

"A what?"

"*A dead child.*"

I hurried away in disgust.

A refined sentiment may induce the bereaved mother to strew the bier of her infant with fresh-blown flowers —emblems of youth, beauty, and innocence; but this display of tinsel and paint, this maudlin profanity, this midnight debauchery in the presence of the dead, is revolting.

I was informed that these "watchings" are very common thoughout the rural districts, and that frequently they are continued with music, dancing, and drunkenness, night after night, until the corpse becomes too offensive for endurance.

Los Angelos, though laid out with much regularity, has no pretensions to beauty. There are no public buildings, unless the unfinished barracks may be so called; and the church, which is a large cane hovel, plastered with mud, and thatched with straw, is rather the worst house in the town. The stores and dwellings are mostly ill-built, though some few of the latter are well furnished. Strange to say, the "alameda" (public promenade), the great ornament of all Chilian towns, was here wanting, though the planting of one was contemplated by the Intendente.

These "alamedas" are wide avenues, planted with from four to six rows of the Lombardy poplar—a tree which in this climate grows with great rapidity, and gives a dense shade. The long, cool alleys are furnished with benches. These promenades are frequented on Sundays, feast-days, and warm summer evenings by rich and poor; the youth, the beauty, and the fashion, all in their best attire; they also serve as parades, where the militia are regularly drilled and reviewed.

Los Angelos, like most of the towns in Chili, seems not to have sprung up from any natural advantages of location. Its importance is owing rather to the fact of its being a military post. In the early settlement of the country the province was frequently ravaged by the Indians, and the inhabitants were often obliged to seek refuge in the old Spanish fort, whose massive adobe walls and deep fosse still remain, though fallen to ruin. The place is still essentially a military station; the tap of the drum may be heard through the day, and the "alerte" of the sentinel through the night.

For commercial purposes and facility of communication with the coast, San Carlos and Santa Fé, both of which are upon the Bio-Bio, present much greater advantages, and would seem to have been more appropriate seats for the capital of the department. But governments, as a rule, are not fortunate in locating towns, and deciding where commerce shall and shall not go; for a shrewd commercial spirit, and speculative industry among the people, can alone develop the resources, and appreciate the natural advantages of a country. Yet the town was said to be flourishing, and was evidently improving.

A considerable trade is here carried on with the Indians, in the exchange of cloths, knives, wines, and trinkets, for cattle and wool; the surrounding districts furnish large quantities of wheat to extensive mills in the neighborhood; but there are no manufactures of any description, if we except the few ponchos, and other articles of the same nature, made by the poorer people.

While rambling about, I came across a house where several girls were engaged in weaving ponchos of various kinds. They sat upon the bare ground, or on very low stools, working at looms of the rudest construction.

Permission to enter was readily granted, but the work, out of politeness, was immediately dropped, and with difficulty could they be persuaded to resume it.

I was surprised to learn that the colors, so often admired by strangers for their brilliancy, are not dyed by the natives, whose dyes are mostly sombre—generally indigo and browns. The scarlet and other bright wools used in ornamenting their ponchos are obtained by raveling out fine English or French flannels, and the threads thus separated are spun into yarn suitable for their work.

There was one "chamanta," as those ponchos are called which are entirely composed of stripes of different colors, which particularly struck me, on account of the fineness of the texture and the beauty of the work. It was making to order; the owner having selected the pattern and furnished the materials. Its market value would be about thirty-four dollars. The poor girl expected to be occupied on it from three to four months, and was to receive twelve dollars for her labor when finished. Never before had I so fully realized the immense revolution caused by steam in human labor. And yet it is a singular fact, that with all the appliances of modern science, the most celebrated looms of Europe have not been able to equal fabrics produced by the aid of the most primitive machinery. Not only do the shawls of the East remain unrivaled, but even the South American blanket has not been successfully imitated.

The English manufacturers send great numbers of ponchos to Chili, but they never can be mistaken for the native article; though of finer texture and more chaste colors they do not wear so well, and on exposure to the rain are easily drenched, while those made in the country, on being slightly moistened, become compact and stiff, shedding rain like a roof, and keeping the wearer perfectly dry.

I had reason to regret not having left Concepcion a week earlier, for the Intendente informed me that he had but just returned from a visit to the volcano of Antuco, accompanied by several officers, and an English gentleman, from Valparaiso, with whom I was acquainted.

Their object had been to ascertain if any grounds existed for the fear generally entertained by the people of the province, that the waters of the lake Laja, which had been dammed up by the stream of lava, might burst forth and cause an inundation. The apprehended danger they found altogether imaginary; but the whole trip had proved exceedingly interesting, and I was advised to delay my intended visit as little as possible.

I determined to start immediately. A letter of introduction to the "Cura" (parish-priest), and an order for the services of the "Sub-delegate" of the district, were kindly furnished me by the Intendente, to whose exertions I was also indebted for a guide.

CHAPTER VI.

On the Road.—Lost in the Woods.—The Brazero.—Sunday in Antuco.—Pehuenches.—The Zamacúca.—The Cura of Antuco and the Cura of R——.—Hospitality and Peppers.—Peddling versus Respectability.

THE volcano bears E. by N. from the town, but the road lies more to the northward.

Soon after starting we came upon an extensive grassy plain, interspersed with clumps of fine trees, which grew more numerous as we entered upon the splendid "Hacienda de las Cauteras," an extensive estate belonging to ex-president Bulnes. This estate is said to be one of the best in southern Chili, and like many others hereabouts, was purchased directly from the Indians.

It was understood that the government intended to investigate the titles of estates so obtained, and confiscate such as had been fraudulently acquired, or improperly conveyed; but the title to "Las Cauteras" is not likely to be questioned, so long as it remains with the present owner, though in the hands of one less influential the case might be far different. In the distance we saw the large dwelling-houses of the "Hacienda," but did not approach them.

Further on we came to what appeared to have been formerly the bottom of a lake, and still bears the name of "La Laguna" (The Lake). Through this ran a small stream, following which we entered a gorge winding between hills that rose with sides of almost perpendicular rock crowned by thick groves.

There was something in the sight of these rock-ribbed hills that brought back a pleasant home feeling—these thick groves, stretching far away, looked like the tangled woods of my childhood. I had become tired of the boundless plain—where no tree meets the eye except an occasional orchard or the long rows of poplars by the roadside—and I was glad to exchange the tropical "chaguar," with its gorgeous blue flowers, and the stately columnar cactus, scarlet with the parasitic "quintral," for the modest little strawberries that blushed beneath the grass, reminding me of the hills of New England.

Soon the gorge widened, and the ground was thickly covered with trees and bushes. Here the road was cut up by frequently diverging trails, and having halted to pick a wayside flower, I lost sight of the guide, and inadvertently took the wrong path. I hurried on, but did not overtake him. The sun had gone down, it was getting quite dark, and I wandered about in vain endeavoring to find the road. I shouted, but received no reply; again and again I shouted, but with no better success; and I was beginning to make calculations as to the best way of spending the night in the woods, with the possibility of meeting some of the straggling Indians who travel over this route in their trading excursions to Chillan, when I heard a faintly answering voice in the distance. Riding in the direction from which the sound came, I found, not the guide, but some boys, who, hearing my shouts and comprehending my situation, had made a friendly response.

They directed me by a cross cut which took me on to the main road, and I soon reached the village of Antuco.

When I found the parsonage it was eight o'clock, and the guide had been there for some time, awaiting my arrival and uneasy at my delay.

A bountiful supper awaited us, to which full justice was done. The Cura was a young man of good education and polished manners; his house was the common resting-place of strangers who occasionally visit the neighborhood; and he seemed glad to entertain them, for their society made a break in his usually monotonous existence.

A cheering bottle of *mosto* followed the meal; and pulling out a few choice Havanas, which I kept for extra occasions, we drew up to the brazier of glowing coals, to while away a few hours in conversation.

In Chilian houses, with the exception of a few of more modern construction, fire-places are unknown—though fires are always necessary in winter, and would often add much to comfort during the chill evenings of the spring and fall. Their only means of heating their houses is by braziers of charcoal, which have been allowed to burn in the open air long enough to drive off the greater part of the fumes.

The brazier is set down in the middle of the room under a wicker basket, on which the ladies may often be seen resting their feet, with their dresses spread out so as to get the full benefit of the hot air.

On a disagreeable winter night, when the winds come cold and piercing from the Andes, and the rain pours down in torrents, a whole family will huddle round one of these *brazeros*—the ladies enveloped in shawls, and the gentlemen wrapped in their ample cloaks—fairly toasting their shins, while their backs shiver in the damp chilly air that comes in through doors and windows left open for the escape of the noxious vapors of the charcoal. And yet, if a stranger enters, the Señoritas will congratulate themselves on their delightful climate, laughing at the imaginary sufferings of us poor Hyperboreans—not knowing that it is only in countries where the rigors of winter render every precaution necessary, that warm and comfortable dwellings can be found.

Among the poor the winter must pass cheerlessly; for their miserable hovels afford but little protection from the inclemencies of the season, and the luxury of a fire can be seldom indulged in—at least in northern and central Chili, where fuel is brought from a distance, and is consequently expensive.

The next day was Sunday, and early a tremendous clattering commenced, intended to announce the mass in the small chapel which stood but a short way off. The campanile was a large apple-tree, in the crotch of which was perched a young imp beating lustily with two stones upon a small cracked bell suspended among the branches. The chapel, though small and without ornament, was neat and tasteful within. The audience was large, and partly composed of Indians, who, though probably attracted merely by curiosity, were respectful and well-behaved during the service.

PEHUENCHE INDIANS.

After mass the priest's house was besieged by men and women, with complaints and grievances of various kinds to be redressed. The Cura seemed to be the arbiter of all their disputes, exercising over them a species of patriarchal sway which none of them were inclined to question. Such matters properly belong to the Sub-delegate, a petty officer commissioned by the head of the department; but as in unimportant places the priest, in addition to his sacred character, is usually the person of most intelligence, he easily acquires an ascendency often productive of the happiest results.

During the day there were a number of Indians loafing about the place. They had been on a trading expedition to Chillan, taking cattle and salt for sale, and were now on the way across the Andes to the pampas of Buenos Ayres with the proceeds. They had stopped at this last post on the route for a drunken spree, and bid fair to return to their homes much poorer than they came.

They were dirty, wild-looking, and, withal, noisy; but, though drunk, not turbulent nor quarrelsome. For hours they would sit in a circle, passing the jug from mouth to mouth, while some one of the number kept up a monotonous discourse, copiously interlarded with shouts, to which the listeners answered with guttural grunts of approval.

Their dress was the ordinary costume of the *Gauchos* of the pampas: a poncho thrown over the shoulders or tied round the waist; another tied by a sash and looped up into a kind of Turkish breeches, under which were worn wide white drawers with a heavy fringe. Their feet were cased in horse-skin boots, through which the big toe protruded just enough to allow of its insertion into the small triangular wooden stirrup.

Their hair hung long and unconfined except by a bright cotton handkerchief tied round the head. A few wore their hair partly gathered in a queue behind, and ornamented with silver beads; but generally they know enough to make but little show of wealth when away from home.

These Indians were "Pehuenches" or "Puelches," a general term applied to all those living east of the Cordillera; or, perhaps, among the mountains east of the plain. The name signifies ("*Pepuen*" pines, and "*Che*" people) People of the Pines; probably from the groves of pine which are found at the foot of the mountains.

The word "*Puelche*" is also much used by the common people in Chili in the sense of the East, or the wind which blows from the East.

These Indians are of the same race as the Araucanians, speaking the same language, and differing only in a few peculiarities of manners and customs, growing out of differences of climate, soil, and modes of life.

Antuco is a small hamlet entirely built of reeds, mud, and thatch. The church and the parsonage were the only two houses in the place with any pretensions to whitewash. At the time of our visit the officers connected with the piquet, around which the village has sprung up, were engaged in the seemingly hopeless attempt to bring the crooked lanes into something like military discipline.

In the evening, accompanied by two of the officers, we called on one of the notabilities of the place, and were hospitably entertained. The house was, like all the others, plastered inside and out with mud, and the rafters overhead were bare. The furniture consisted of a few wooden chairs (which, I verily believe, were made in Connecticut), and a small strip of home-made carpet, spread before the seat of honor, where the Señora, flanked by her daughters, sat in state to receive company.

The stiffness of the first introduction quickly wore off, despite this formidable array, and after the usual amount of pressing, excuses, hoarseness, forgetfulness, and coughing, one of the ladies took up the guitar and favored us with a song. A polka followed; but as the performance of rapid gyrations to the music of the guitar over a rough mud floor, and with partners not very *au fait*, was a difficult task, the fashionable dances soon gave way to the more national *Zamacúca.*

The Zamacúca has been very much reviled by foreigners, who have seen it only in sea-port towns, at places of a questionable character; but as danced in good society, or even by the lower classes in the interior, it is no less graceful, and far more modest than the schottishes and redowas of the modern ballroom.

A couple rise and stand facing each other a few yards apart. The guitar strikes up, the song commences, and the by-standers clap their hands, beating time to the music. The dancers advance and retreat coquettishly, circling round, or moving to one side as

THE ZAMACUCA.

caprice may suggest, but always facing each other, and waving their handkerchiefs continually, as they wind through the ever-changing mazes. As neither step nor figure is arbitrary, every one has his own style, which adds much to the beauty and interest of the dance. The music, though a monotonous repetition of a few notes, is soul-stirring; and the verses, if not very poetical, serve to enliven the dance. The following is a fair sample:

> "Dices que no me quires,
> Porque no tengo que darte;
> Enseña me abhorrescerte,
> Porque no sé mas que amarte."

Which might be rendered freely—

"You say that you love me no more,
Because I have naught to bestow;
Then teach me to hate you, I pray,
For to love you is all that I know."

In the best society of the capital, and the seaport towns, the Zamacúca has been "tabooed," from the fact that it is "plebeian;" the same reason has caused the guitar to be entirely neglected, and even held in bad odor by the "upper ten;" but at their balls and parties, after the supper, when all formality has disappeared, the national dances and music generally come back to reassert their lost supremacy, and are always welcomed with enthusiasm.

The Cura at first seemed unwilling to compromise his dignity, and rather held aloof from the sport, but after considerable good-natured bantering he yielded, and tucking up the ends of his cassock, entered heartily into the dance.

There was much about the young priest that I liked; he seemed to be sincere, and have the welfare of his flock at heart, yet there was nothing ascetic nor harsh in his nature; he was an agreeable associate, and did every thing in his power to contribute to the comfort and pleasure of his guests.

Once before I had been thrown upon the hospitality of one of his cloth, whom he knew well; and I related to him the reception I had received. He was much entertained by my story, and though the recital may not prove equally interesting to the reader, I shall take the liberty of here repeating it.

During my wanderings in northern Chili, chance

threw me in company with B——, a young Englishman, who was traveling toward Chillan with a large troop of pack-mules, on some business, the nature of which I never discovered.

It was a cold, rainy day when we arrived at the little town of R——; for several hours we had ridden through the pelting storm, and we were thoroughly drenched; but there was a cheering prospect before us, for B—— brought a letter of introduction to the Cura of the village, who, he had been assured, would receive us with a hearty welcome.

The sight of two white turrets sent a thrill through our bosoms. Trudging wearily through the mud, we had looked forward, with pleasurable emotions, to the snug vicarage; we had conjured up many pictures of the good Padre with his jocund face and

"Fair round belly, with fat capon lined,"

a very model of hospitality and good cheer. Now our dreams were about to be realized.

Turning a sharp corner, there stood the quiet parsonage, a pattern of neatness and comfort, snugly ensconced beneath the shadow of the church; a plot of flowers before the door indicated the presence of some female hand. Every lingering misgiving, if there had been any in our hearts, immediately vanished, and putting spurs to our horses we dashed up to the house, nor did we draw rein until at the very threshold.

The guitar was tinkling merrily, and there was a sound of smothered laughter; but both were hushed in a moment, and a dozen fair faces looked out of the window, and were quickly withdrawn. There came a sound of loosening bolts; the door opened slightly, and out popped a little pug nose, and two very black eyes; there was something bewitchingly impudent in that little pug, admirably in keeping with the eyes that stared at us with a most defiant coolness and inquiring wonder. A pile of noses and eyes were dimly visible behind, all wearing about the same expression of surprise.

Bowing very low, we inquired, "Is the Padre at home?"

"Yes, Sir."

"Can we see him?"

"Not now, Sir; he is sleeping the siesta, and can not be disturbed for an hour yet."

Hereupon B—— dragged out of his pocket something looking like a wet rag, and extended it to the damsel, informing her that it was a letter for the Cura.

She turned it over inquiringly, saying that she would hand it to him when he awoke. "But," cried B——, growing impatient, for the rain poured down in torrents, "It is an introduction; we have come here to lodge!"

"Ah!" said she, with astonishment, "then perhaps you would do well to come in and wait until the Cura rises."

We were shown into a small room which served as the passage-way from the street to the inner court. A window and a door wide open kept up a free circulation, and the temperature was about as disagreeable within as out of doors. A plain deal table, a settee, and two old-fashioned high leather-backed chairs, formed the furniture, and the damp brick floor was uncovered by carpet or mat.

We felt no surprise at finding such a room in the country, where the rooms, which often serve as parlor, kitchen, bedroom, and hen-house, are generally no better; but the half-opened door disclosed a snug little parlor, nicely carpeted and furnished, starting in our mind a train of deductions not over favorable to the civility of our fair entertainers.

The ladies looked at us for a few moments, made some remarks about the weather, asked all the questions necessary to satisfy their curiosity, and then tripped gayly back to the parlor to resume their dancing. From the same room, also, came a smell of burnt sugar, a hissing of the kettle, and other unmistakable evidences that the maté was shedding a genial influence over all.

Now this was very aggravating: a seat in that snug parlor would have been delightful; the lively dance would have helped to warm our sluggish blood; but cold, wet, and hungry as we were, to bring the steaming maté palpably before our senses—the maté, that very "calumet" of the Chilian wigwam—and not proffer it to our expectant lips, that was too bad.

B—— thrust both hands into his pockets, and dropping his head upon his breast, burst out in the most furious invectives against the baseness of mankind, and the Chilenos in particular.

As to myself, though hungry, weary, and no little annoyed, this sudden and unexpected destruction of all our fair dreams was so ludicrous, that I could not help laughing heartily and twitting my companion on his excellent introduction. But on that point he was immovable; "what we had suffered was owing merely to the rudeness of a few thoughtless girls, and the good Padre, immediately on waking, would make us extremely comfortable."

An hour—to us an age—had passed, when one of the girls came to tell us that they were about to give the Cura an "esquinazo," to rouse him from his slumbers. Then the whole troop came rushing out like so many bacchanals, and soon we heard, resounding from the distant corridor, the monotonous strumming of the guitar, a loud, laughing chorus, and an alternate rubbing and beating upon the door with a sheep-skin, in imitation of the hissing and explosion of rockets.

The girls came trooping back, took another inquisitive look at us, and then started off through the rain to their homes.

The Cura soon appeared. He was a large, portly man, dressed in the usual black gown of the clergy; over his broad shoulders was thrown a shaggy brown poncho; his feet were cased in *suekos* (clogs), raising him some two inches off the ground; and his head was surmounted by a white night-cap, the tassel of which hung down in front. A large pair of goggles adorned his nose; his lips were firmly compressed upon a paper cigarito, whose smoke curled disdainfully from his nostrils; his broad face was about the color of a dried codfish; even his double chin conveyed no expression of benevolence; and as he stood with his hands in his pockets, eying us askance, his whole air had little in it of open-hearted hospitality.

"I brought you a letter, Sir," said B——, bowing politely.

"Yes, I have read it," was the significant reply of the prelate, as he dropped his portly person into an arm-chair.

Both of us were seized with the same idea—to rush out of the house and seek lodgings elsewhere. But where could we go? The storm raged pitilessly—our servants had started off to pasture with the horses—we knew nothing of the town, and had no means of transporting our luggage. A pause followed; broken, at last, by B——.

"We are very sorry, Sir, to put you *to so much trouble.*"

"Not the slightest in the world, Señor; the house is entirely at your disposal," was the freezingly polite reply.

"At the earliest possible hour in the morning we shall relieve you of the burden."

"Ah!" exclaimed our host, staring at us and at the formidable pile of baggage, as though he thought we had come to spend a month. He evidently felt relieved; and asked, in a somewhat more conciliatory manner, how long we had been upon the road.

"We started early in the morning, not even *waiting for breakfast;*" answered B——, throwing out his elbow in the direction of my ribs, to call my attention to the delicate manner in which the hint had been conveyed. But though both the hint and the elbow struck me forcibly, the good Padre did not seem to notice either.

"Had you much rain upon the road?"

"Yes, Sir, the storm was violent; and what with the wind, we were wet through and chilled."

The elbow again punched my ribs, after this excellent *hit;* but our kind host could not comprehend that either food or fire would add to our comfort, and puffed away at his cigarito in silence.

My poor friend looked the picture of despair. He had been completely outgeneraled, and would have relinquished the attack, had he not perceived an ill-disguised smile struggling for mastery in my face. That re-inflamed his pride; and rousing all his energies, he exclaimed,

"My dear Sir, we are *very hungry; will you give us something to eat?*"

We were assured, with a dignified wave of the hand, that we need feel no uneasiness on that score.

"But, Sir," continued B——, determined to push his advantage, "we are, also, very cold; will you not order for us *some fire?*"

The order was given; and, after a few moments spent in silence, the servant appeared with a huge pan of burning coals. The Padre then went out, leaving us to enjoy the fire.

"What think you now of your excellent introduction?" I asked, as the Cura left the room.

My companion broke out in furious denunciation of all introductions and introducers. He was vehement against all South Americans, especially the Chilenos, and more particularly the denizens of R——, among whom he clearly demonstrated that the padres were the vilest and most unprincipled. But as his wrath expended itself, he fell into a more charitable mood, and discoursed on the advantages of traveling and studying human nature, in a manner that would have done credit to a philosopher.

Another hour had dragged slowly along, when a Señorita entered, and pulling out the drawer began to set the table. This done, she drew up a chair to the fire, and entered into conversation. She was young—or passably so; sprightly, like all her countrywomen, and rather pretty, with a light complexion, rosy cheeks, and bewitchingly black eyes, under whose mild influence we began to mollify, and think that, at her hands, even the bitter bread of unwilling hospitality would be sweet.

She told us that she was the good Cura's niece, and had come to live with him in order to superintend his household, and look after his temporal affairs. We had not asked any questions; but she seemed to think this explanation of her position necessary—for the world is too apt to be uncharitable.

The meal soon came; and it was abundant. There was a huge "casuela de ave," redolent with the fumes of onions; a massive piece of roast beef followed, flanked on the right by a dish of sliced beets, and on the left by sundry bottles of red wine—the rich *mosto* of the South. The worthy Padre (perhaps, rather, the niece) had outdone himself, and rose rapidly in our esteem.

The young lady insisted on sitting at the table to serve us; and, determined to do honor to her kindness, I began by a brimming spoonful of the savory soup. I had forgotten the predilection of the Chilenos for "*aji*" (red peppers); and as I stopped to draw breath,

I felt my whole mouth and throat blistered, as though I had swallowed so much melted lead. The pain was intense; and seizing the nearest thing at hand—a bottle of mosto—I swallowed a full glass; but it was a strong, fiery wine, and felt like liquid flame in my already lacerated throat. I could have screamed in agony; the tears hung trembling in my eyes, and I gazed wildly around, in hopes of finding something with which to allay the burning pain.

The Señorita, perceiving that I wanted something, said, with an angelic smile,

"What do you wish, Sir? Perhaps you would like a little more *aji;*" and, suiting the action to the word, she deposited alongside my plate a *bowl of red peppers!*

I clutched the thing convulsively; and had this aggravation of my misery come from a man, I should have dashed it at his head. But it was done in such a good-natured way, and with such a sweet smile! She, doubtless, thought red peppers the most delightful vegetable in the world. So, choking down my feelings, and endeavoring to look pleasant, I assured her that the soup really could not be improved by the addition of any condiment, and that "it would not have been better, even if prepared by her own fair hands"—a perfectly Spanish compliment; and, unlike most compliments, literally true.

During this scene, I felt afraid to look at B——, knowing that his turn for laughing had at last arrived. But I took a stealthy glance at him; and there he sat, his face red with endeavors to preserve a sober deportment. He had been cautious, and was picking out little bits of chicken very gingerly—carefully avoiding the extras. For the moment, I wished him and his friend, introduction, Padre, peppers and all (except the Señorita), in the very bottom of Tophet.

All further attempts to eat were useless. The Señorita was all sympathy, fearing that I had lost my appetite, or was sick; and for several days after my swollen lips and blistered mouth reminded me continually of the good Cura and his casuela.

Our after-dinner meditations were interrupted by the entrance of two gentlemen, who wished to see our host. In one of them I thought I recognized a certain Major S——, whom I had known in Santiago; nor was I mistaken, for, after scrutinizing me a moment, he rushed forward and shook me violently by the hand, in the manner of persons who wish to appear extremely glad to see you. The Cura stood aghast; he wanted an explanation, and it soon came; for the good Major, seeing that we were imperfectly acquainted, immediately introduced me as the Señor Don Eduardo, a particular friend of his, and an officer in the United States Navy. He then went on to explain, in a novel and original manner, the nature and objects of the Observatory at Santiago, in which he represented me as holding some highly honorable and lucrative post; and finished off by recommending me to the Cura as a distinguished *savant*.

I was overwhelmed by the Major's volubility, and surprised by so much attention from a person with whom I had never been very well acquainted; but, whatever may have been his object, nothing was lost by the encounter. The friends of so distinguished a dignitary as the military chief of the district (for such was the Major), could not be other than persons worthy of high consideration; and from being obscure, unwelcome, and, I fear, suspected strangers, we suddenly found ourselves the intimate friends and cherished guests of the military, civil, and ecclesiastical authorities!

The Cura, when satisfied of our character, became as cordial as he had before been reserved. He did every thing in his power to entertain us; and the next morning, as we were preparing for an early start, he insisted upon our staying for breakfast, and would have persuaded us to remain another day, promising to make the remainder of our visit pleasant; but we declined his hospitality, and determined to push on, promising to call and see him, if possible, on our return.

Just as we were about to leave, the whole secret of our singular reception leaked out; a number of the villagers came to the house, and inquired for us.

"Have you any guitar strings for sale?" asked one.

"No!" was the reply.

"Have you any ribbons?" inquired another.

"No; we have nothing to sell!"

"What, then, do you carry those large boxes for?" said a third, pointing to the heavily-laden mules.

"*They must think that we are peddlers!*" cried B——, indignantly.

"To tell you the truth, gentlemen," said the Cura, laughing, "*I thought so myself at first!*"

Every story has its moral: should the reader ever have occasion to travel in Chili, as he values his respectability, let him beware of pack-mules and superfluous baggage!

CHAPTER VII.

Ballenar.—The Tuvunlevu.—Scoria.—Volcano of Antuco.—Making a Night of it.—Lake Laja.—Inquisitiveness of the Guasos.—Nearly an Adventure.—A pleasant Drink.

THOUGH the town of Antuco is within sight of the volcano, and though the people had been in the greatest trepidation on account of the eruption, I found that not one of the villagers had ventured near it except the Cura, who had accompanied the Intendente. I was, therefore, obliged to fall back upon the orders I had received for the Sub-delegate, and ask the services of the *Capitan dè Amigos* (Indian interpreter), who lived near the volcano, and was acquainted with all the localities. The interpreter was told to hold himself in readiness; and the next morning, about half past five, we started out.

Passing along the valley which borders the Laja, we soon came in sight of the volcano, rising boldly in the air, isolated, and black; forming, in its sombre majesty, a fine contrast with the more immediate landscape, which was romantic and beautiful—the abrupt hills, covered with woods, and the gentler slopes smiling with verdure.

We had been nearly five hours on the road when we arrived at the house of the Capitan, our guide, where we breakfasted and rested our horses.

Near this point is the fort of Ballenar, or rather

the ruins, situated upon a hill of so singular a shape that I, at first, imagined the name, Castillo de Ballenar, to be applied to the hill itself, from a fancied resemblance to a castle with terraces and bastions complete.

The fort was of brick, and, though small, of much importance in the times of Pincheira, as a check upon the Indians, who were wont to sweep through the neighboring gorge in the Cordillera, and lay waste the surrounding country; but it has long since been deserted as a useless precaution. The only bands of Indians that now travel the road are peaceful traders, bound on friendly expeditions, to traffic with the towns which, in by-gone days, they so often made desolate.

About noon we resumed our march, the guide stowing away some two or three yards of jerked beef between the skins of his saddle, and filling his saddle-bags with onions, as provisions for the trip.

As we proceeded the scenery became finer, for we wound through deep ravines, passing and repassing a thundering brook, forming, in one place, a splendid cascade, at whose feet the waters were collected in a basin so pure and crystalline that every bright pebble could be seen twinkling at the bottom.

Soon we began climbing a high ridge, and from the top another view broke upon us perfectly Alpine in its character. I can remember to have seen nothing finer. On the right hand rose proudly the rugged Sierra Velluda, lifting to the skies its dark and craggy pinnacles, crowned with eternal snows; on the left towered other snow-clad summits, all sending down their tribute of foaming cascades, that tumbled over the cliffs, to swell the current of the Laja, here a small mountain stream roaring at our feet. Directly in front, desolate and black, stood the isolated cone of Antuco, capped, it is true, with snows, yet not pure and glistening in the sun, but vailed with a cloak of dust and ashes.

No signs of eruption were visible except a slight cloud of smoke and steam, hanging like a vapory mist over the principal crater.

Descending from this ridge we began to find more frequent evidences of recent eruption in the pieces of scoria and fragments of stone scattered along our track. These became more numerous until we reached the Tuvunlevu, a noisy brook, near which are the remains of a piquet, the last on this side of the mountains. Here we came upon a mass of scoria which in some former eruption had flowed down from the volcano, and after making a circuit of eight or ten miles among the hills, burst into this valley, intercepting the course of the Laja.

It was of a black ashen hue, more resembling, in color and texture, the slag of an iron furnace than any thing else I could recall. It was not compact and homogeneous like lava, with rich veins and variegated colors, but a rough mass, as though the rocks, riven and crushed by violent convulsions, had been acted on by the internal fires enough to allow the fragments to glide freely over each other and adhere on cooling. It had flowed along in tortuous currents, in some places rolled down like water, in others thrown up like a wall. Again it stood cresting and curling over like the foam-caps of a wave, as though some impetuous mountain torrent, bursting suddenly through its icy barrier, had been instantly arrested and petrified in its furious course. Over this we wound cautiously in the rude path worn by the Indians, and soon after arrived at a clump of apple trees growing in a green patch of meadow, where there was a fine turf strewed with ripe strawberries, and a limpid rivulet of cold snow-water gurgling through the long grass. Here we rested for a while, and the guide wished to stop for the night, assuring us that there was no better view, and no pasture equally good for the animals.

The hills that rose abruptly around us were composed of loose volcanic sand and ashes, perfectly barren, with no verdure except a few cedars growing at their feet, and in moist places creeping up their sides. But the volcano stood only a short distance in front; it was only four o'clock, and I was anxious to proceed.

Almost overhanging that side of the volcano on which the recent eruption had taken place, was a high point where could be discovered small patches of green, and the snows around gave promise of water. As it looked near, I insisted on reaching it, and the guide reluctantly consented.

The distance was greater than it had appeared, and overcoming it, more difficult than I had expected. Directly before us lay a vast bed of scoria, that must be slowly crossed by winding about and avoiding rough spots where the animals were liable to injury. There was the river, not deep nor broad, but impetuous, and filled with holes and slippery rolling stones. Passing a deep gully our ascent began. The first hill was composed of loose volcanic sand, ashes, and sharp, angular pieces of scoria, and rose more than three hundred feet, with a declivity so great as to appear almost perpendicular. I ascended for some distance on horseback, by making short zigzag tacks, but the poor brute labored so hard, and got along so slowly, that I soon dismounted and climbed up the rest of the way, frequently obliged to use both hands and feet. The servant also dismounted; but the guide stuck to the saddle, preferring, as he said, laming his horse to laming himself. He clambered up in safety, though I momentarily expected to see both horse and rider rolling down the steep and treacherous bank.

Other rough hills succeeded, covered at intervals with low, stunted bushes, bearing a large berry not unlike the whortleberry; and after a tiresome ride we reached the point which we had seen from the valley. But the sun had set, it was growing dark, and though the scene would probably be fine during the night, there was no pasture; what I had mistaken for grass was only some low, scraggy bushes.

I was in a quandary, and began to deliberate about making up my bed there, and allowing the guide and servant to take the animals to pasture wherever it could be found. But this did not last long. A storm that had been darkly gathering burst suddenly upon us.

The lightning began to play over the mountain-tops, with long reverberating peals of thunder, and the big drops of rain falling thick and fast bid fair soon to wet us through. There was no shelter at hand, nor any to be found without retreating more than a mile to a deep recess among the hills, bordered by a grove of sombre pines.

Here was an opportunity of passing a night amidst all the elements of the sublime. But the thought of a thorough drenching and nothing to eat, to be followed by colds and rheumatism, threw a damper over all my romantic feelings, and off we scampered at a furious rate, over a plain of sand and ashes, interrupted by deep gullies, until we reached a friendly tree, whose low, wide-spread branches offered a shelter for the night. A snow bank, that may have lain there for ages, furnished a trickling stream, around which the grass was green and fresh.

Turning adrift the tired animals, and building a huge fire with the dry branches that lay around, we soon had an encampment worthy of the gipsies themselves.

The Capitan spitted a piece of beef on a stick, and planting it over the fire, before long it made a savory supper, without other seasoning than a little salt and a good appetite. Lying down under the tree, we hacked the meat to pieces with our jack-knives in perfect equality and good-fellowship.

I also cut up some charqui and onions, which I put over the fire, and tried to make some soup. But though the water boiled furiously, neither the meat nor the onions seemed to soften at all. The reflection that at such an elevation the boiling point must be very low, solved the mystery, and I tossed the soup away without venturing a philosophical explanation to my companions.

Our beds were made up under the low, hanging branches of the tree; and with the additional precaution of a poncho spread overhead, we retired.

The rain did not last long. The lightnings and thunder continued, producing a grand effect among the mountain tops; and the black clouds would occasionally flash, giving back a lurid light from the volcano, which was hidden from sight by a projecting hill. But the nasal tones of my snoring companions seemed to possess a greater charm than the echoing thunders; and I soon helped to form a trio, forgetful of all the sublimity of nature.

By daylight we were up. A chilly, piercing wind came down from the ice-fields around us, making our teeth chatter. The ground was golden, in patches, with the yellow "*flor de perdiz.*" The first strawberries were but just blossoming. On the plain, far below, the autumnal grain stood ripe for the sickle; in the near valleys we saw the verdure of summer; here it was but early spring, and but a little way above us winter reigned—an eternal winter!

After a long chase in pursuit of the animals that had wandered off to seek shelter during the night, we went back to the point which we had reached the night before. From this place we clambered up another high hill, which offered a view of the surrounding country.

The scene impressed me with a sense of dreariness and desolation such as I had never before experienced. Gazing in whatsoever direction, not a living thing, no sound of life, no indication of animated existence could be met: all was an uninhabited, uninhabitable waste, given up to the warring elements.

Black and gloomy the vast cone of Antuco rose before our eyes. The snowy summit stretched far away, while the broad base sprang from beneath our very feet. As we hung over the giddy brink, we could see where, hundreds of feet below, the black tide of lava had rolled and surged against the rocky wall of the precipice, blocking up, with a solid barrier of stone, the bed of the Laja, damming in the waters of the lake, which had risen more than twenty feet, but could not yet escape.

The two new vents which had been opened by the late explosion were upon the northern side of the cone, some two-thirds of the distance up, just below the snow line, and about on a level with the spot on which we stood.

The black streams of scoriaceous matter which had rolled down, were spread out at the base of the volcano to the width of about half a mile. Though the eruption had ceased, for the moment at least, wreaths of smoke and sulphureous vapors rose along fiery channels in the principal currents. Occasionally a small jet of molten matter would be projected over the ledge which formed the brim of the crater, or a half melted stone would come wriggling down, with a writhing, uneasy motion.

The booming, cannon-like explosions that we had heard from the village of Antuco had ceased; but there was an incessant rattling noise, as though, deep in the bowels of the earth, the crushed and riven rocks were tossing and grinding together. It was more the sound, on a grand scale, of bar-iron carted through a stony street, than any thing else I could remember. The noise of waters dashing from many a beetling cliff into the lake and valleys below, was the only other sound that could be heard.

To the southwestward of the volcano stands the Sierra Velluda, a lofty, rugged mountain mass, shooting up in sharp pinnacles, wrapped in glaciers and fields of never-melting snows.

In many places arise walls of high, perpendicular crags, on which no snows can rest; forming, with their dark purplish hues, a bold contrast with the white drifts around them. From many of these we could distinguish little silvery threads of cascades descending to swell the current of the river.

To the east of the volcano lies the lake of the Laja, a body of water some seven miles long, and from one to three broad, curving around the base of the cone. As we stood upon the edge of the cliff, a pebble could have been dropped into the water, which lay green, calm, and noiseless beneath. No ripple disturbed the surface—no bird played upon its bosom; and enveloped in morning mist, with mountains rising dark and blue upon the farther shore, so gloomy, so deathlike, it seemed a fit companion for the desolate Antuco, upon whose vast sides not a blade of grass, nor any other sign of life existed.

This lake had been described to me as beautiful; with the bright sunshine lighting up the shores with a joyous smile, and dancing upon the waters ruffled by the breeze. It might be so; but we saw it far otherwise; and it awakened, in my bosom at least, no pleasing emotions.

The impressions caused by the whole scene were of sadness, dejection, and awe. Though interesting as a study of one of the most wonderful agents in the formation of the physical world, there was nothing in the sight calculated to cheer and elevate the mind. It did not seem to be the contemplation of Nature, ever beautiful in her works; but of her black and smouldering ruins—the evidences of her wrath.

If the ascent had been difficult, the descent was none the less so. In some places we could ride, but in others it was impossible. Even the Capitan was convinced that there are some places where it is easier to get along afoot than on horseback; but it was not without considerable grumbling that he dismounted and trusted himself to his own feet.

The old Andalusian song says—

"Para las cuestas arriba
Quiero mi mulo,
Pero las cuestas abajo
Yo me las subo."

But the Chileno is not apt to spare his beast even in going downhill, and the veritable "Guaso" never thinks himself so safe as when on his horse.*

* A young American in Santiago, an enthusiastic Nimrod, was wont occasionally to shoulder his rifle and start off to the mountains in pursuit of game. One of his favorite resorts was the "Dahesa," an estate high up the side of the Cordillera, and he became famous, thereabout, for his clambering propensities and unerring skill in bringing down the swift-footed "guanacos" that frequent the lofty summits, and bound like the chamois from cliff to cliff.

After one of these excursions, Don Manuel, the hospitable propri-

Driving the animals on ahead, we followed in their tracks, which formed for us a path. In many spots they would put their forefeet together and slide. We, too, were more than once treated to a slide, getting along over the loose ashes and scoria in a manner highly detrimental to pantaloons.

We reached the bottom in much less time than it had taken us to ascend; but not without some hard rubs and serious damage to our boots. The horses' feet were cut by the sharp fragments of lava, and one of my animals was so much injured as to be ever after almost useless; his feet remaining so tender that he could never get over stony ground without limping.

I had a great desire to scale the volcano—the top of which, the guide informed me, had never been reached, although some foreigners had ascended the greater part of the way; but it would have required considerable time and expense, and as neither the guide nor the servant could be persuaded to make the attempt, I was obliged to abandon the idea. They both of them seemed filled with a superstitious dread of they knew not what, and on my suggesting an attempt to reach the crater and look into it, they shook their heads and answered, "*Quien sabe, Señor, si no se enoje el volcan!*" ("Who knows but the volcano would get angry.")

etor of the estate came to the city, and called to see us. Warming under the genial influence of a steaming punch, he gave us a glowing description of the hunt and the skill of our Nimrod with the rifle; but what seemed most to surprise him was the hunter's agility in scaling the mountain-sides. "By the Holy Virgin!" he exclaimed, bringing down his glass with a crash, "that young rascal would climb up *afoot* in places where I could not go *even on horseback!*"

I am not sure that they were fully satisfied with the nature and objects of my expedition; they probably connected it in some way with the black art, or the search for treasures; the fact of traveling purely in pursuit of knowledge or pleasure they could not understand.

An amusing incident, illustrative of this feeling among the lower classes, had happened on my journey from Los Angelos to the village of Antuco. We were overtaken upon the road by a countryman, who, riding up, fell into conversation with my servant. As their discourse was of no interest to me, I started on ahead, preferring to be left to my own thoughts; but soon I noticed that they were talking mysteriously in an under tone, interrupted occasionally by exclamations of surprise.

Arriving at a brook I dismounted to drink, scooping up the water in my hand. The countryman immediately came forward, and pulling out a horn-cup offered it for my use.

After drinking I started on again, but he of the cup evidently thought that "one good turn deserved another," for bringing himself alongside he opened on me in real Yankee style. With great dexterity he discovered whence I had come, and whither I went; but not finding me communicative, he began to surmise that there were great quantities of gold in the volcano. I thought not. "Nor silver?" "No." "Nor copper?" "No."

"There are no precious stones in the lake, are there?" he asked, looking very knowing.

"Probably not many."

"*Pero su merced va tra'minar la la'una, S'ñor, por eso trujo la maquina sin duda?*" ("But you are a-going to look through the lake, I guess, or else you wouldn't have brought that machine along?") said he, pointing to the camera-tripod strapped upon the mule.

I could bear it no longer, but putting spurs to my horse hurried on at full gallop to be rid of his company.

As the camera was something he could not comprehend, he had taken for granted that it was some mysterious instrument enabling its possessor to peer into the most hidden recesses of the earth and discover deeply-buried treasures. My explanation, that I had no object but curiosity and pleasure, only served to convince him that his suspicions were correct.

Having reached the valley we turned our faces from the volcano, and started for the village of Antuco. Near the Tuvunlevu we halted, and while the men were engaged in making "charquican" for breakfast, I took a sketch of the volcano, from a spot where the view was enhanced by a pretty little double fall in the foreground.

We left the Capitan at his house, near Ballenar.

When within an hour's ride of Antuco, while passing through a patch of woods, considerably in advance of my servant, I heard a loud shouting, and the sound of horses approaching. Looking down the road, I saw a party of drunken Indians coming toward me.

Near at hand was a path diverging from the road, and thinking that a band of drunken savages might be troublesome in such a place, I turned my horse aside, still keeping my eyes fixed upon the main road. Suddenly I felt a violent jerk upon the throat, and found that I had been taken under the chin by a branch, which, as the horse moved on, was dragging me out of the saddle. With some difficulty I reined back, and an examination showed many hanging branches ahead, stopping further advance, and obliging me to retreat. Just then the Indians came up, saluting me with a loud "Mari! mari!"

"Mari! mari!" I shouted, gathering up the reins at the same time, intending to dash past them. But the manœuvre was anticipated, for checking their horses they formed a semicircle, completely blocking up the road.

As they sat before me, drunk, bloated, half naked, their eyes inflamed, and their faces horribly painted, I felt no assurance of their good intentions, and almost involuntarily slipping a hand under my poncho, I cocked my revolver.

The spokesman, a young, good-looking savage, advancing a little, addressed me in broken Spanish, and inquired if I had not been to see the volcano: I answered that I had. A number of questions were then asked. "Was the volcano angry?" "Had the explosions ceased?" "Would the old road, which ran along the margin of the lake and had been covered by the lava, be soon passable, etc.?" To all these I answered as favorably as possible.

After my answers had been duly interpreted, an old man, evidently the chief, grunted out something, which the spokesman translated, to the effect that they had been a long time in Antuco, behaving themselves very well, and he thought that, in consideration of their sobriety, as *none of them had been drunk*, I ought to give them a real (12½ cents).

The leer and hiccup with which this was spoken, sadly belied the words; but I cheerfully handed the old man a quarter of a dollar, and the moro coming up at the moment, we rode on, as much amused as gratified at the termination of almost an adventure.

Passing the night at Antuco, we left the next day for Los Angelos.

With the volcano, the rugged Sierra Velluda, the mountain brooks, and the foaming cascades so near at hand, I would willingly have remained a week longer at Antuco, rambling about the country with the good-natured priest, and the companionable young officers: but the season was advancing; the grapes were beginning to ripen; the apples were assuming a mellow hue, suggestive of wine and cider, and reminding me that, if bent on an Indian excursion, it were desirable to start before the season of drunkenness should set in.

On the road to Los Angelos I noticed three high crosses erected in a vineyard. One of these had a rude ladder attached, thus serving the double purpose of a charm against the machinations of the evil one, and a watch-tower, from which the vineyard tender could glance over the extended fields, and detect any who might be prowling around to steal the fruit. Small crosses are often seen planted in fields of grain; but this was the first that seemed calculated to serve some useful purpose, though it was a sad union of sacred and profane.

After riding for a long time in the hot sun without meeting any running stream, we spied a farm-house in the distance, and going to it we asked for a glass of water.

"There is not a drop of water within a mile of the house," said an old woman who came to the door, "but we can give you some 'chicha de manzanos' (cider) that is very nice!" producing at the word a huge glass of a greenish, muddy liquid. To call it vinegar would be too high a compliment, and to add that it was flavored with gall, would convey no adequate idea of this abominable stuff, which had been made from the very greenest of green apples; one mouthful sufficed for me, and my first impressions of chicha de manzanos were not favorable; but the guide tossed it off with evident relish.

CHAPTER VIII.

The Policeman's Horse.—Visit to a Hacienda.—Branding Cattle.—Farming in Chili.—Chilian Wine.—The limits of the Polka.—Traveling in Carts.

Early in the morning a gentleman came and invited me to join in a picnic excursion to a neighboring hacienda.

The invitation was gladly accepted, but the question arose—how was I to go? Not only were my horses tired, but they had been sent to a distant pasture: several horses were placed at my disposal, but, like my own, they were all at a distance; an hour or two would be lost in sending for them; the party were all mounted and ready to start. In the emergency I called a "vigilante" (day-policeman), and asked him if he knew any one in the village that had a horse to hire.

"I have an excellent one myself," he answered, and posted off to bring it.

As a "vigilante's" horse is a thing proverbial in Chili, I was not surprised when the animal arrived; he was a good specimen of his race, and might have served as a model for Rosinante. As he stood with his legs stretched out so as to cover the greatest possible surface, with every rib and joint protruding, he appeared like some huge phantom invested with the skin of a smaller brother. His tail was elevated at a remarkable angle; his ears seemed watching for the slightest sound, and his distended eyes rolled about incessantly, as if he felt it incumbent upon himself, as a member of the police, to be continually on the alert.

Though fully aware of the figure I should cut, I immediately struck a bargain, satisfied that the party should be amused, even if at my own expense.

As I shook the reins to arrange them, my charger bounded forward with a vehemence that nearly shot me off behind, and as I drew upon the bit he halted with a jerk, threatening to pitch me over his head. A slight touch of my boot on his ribs would cause him to whirl about, suddenly, in one direction, and an unequal pressure upon the other side would make him twirl back with the greatest rapidity.

At every demonstration of this kind there was a round of applause from the by-standers, and at first I imagined that a vicious brute had been palmed off on me. But five minutes spent in studying his actions made me acquainted with his whole system of tactics: he was merely obeying signals with which every-day practice had made him familiar—the horsemanship of the police being peculiar, and in a great measure telegraphic.

Once understood, there was no further difficulty; he could be managed admirably without whip or spur, for, despite his ill-looks, he was intelligent, and had a good deal of fire still left.

On the road every passer-by would turn to look at the sorry appearance I presented amidst the dashing throng of gay caballeros, most of whom were finely mounted. The history of my steed was plainly written in his every movement, and occasionally some wag would put his fingers to his mouth and salute my ears with an imitation of the peculiar whistle used by the "vigilantes." At that familiar sound my horse started off at full run, and when checked by the bridle, fell back upon his haunches as though he thought I were in the act of throwing the lasso of justice around the neck of some fugitive malefactor.

Arriving at the hacienda we were cordially received by the proprietor. This gentleman, seeing that I was a foreigner, took much pleasure in showing me, as far as the limited time would allow, the extent of his estate, and the method of its cultivation.

Land in Chili is measured by the "quadra" (about $3\frac{3}{8}$ acres). This hacienda, though not considered unusually large, contained over seven thousand quadras. Two thousand of these were pasture lands—some four thousand lying off on the mountains were wood land—about four hundred were planted with wheat, and the rest was principally laid out in vineyards. The different division lines were formed by deep trenches in lieu of fences, and as we gazed in every direction, the estate appeared boundless—hemmed in only by the snows of the Andes and the blue horizon of the plain.

We saw many fine cattle, but most of those belonging to the place were at a distance from the part we visited.

To foreigners who are accustomed to see cattle raised and carefully tended for dairy purposes, the system pursued in Chili is novel. Vast herds, being valued only for their flesh and hides, are allowed to run wild among the mountains, simply with the precaution of a few tenants stationed near the boundaries to prevent the animals from straying away to other estates. From valley to valley they rove, continually ascending as, with the summer sun, the plains parch up and the snows retire, leaving fresh pasturage on the mountain sides. When winter approaches they gradually descend to the plain, though it often happens that they are overtaken by sudden storms of snow, and many perish.

Once a year there is a grand réunion of all the cattle, which are driven down to the "corrals," as the pens are called, where the branding and slaughtering are carried on.

On this occasion, as on all others, when large numbers of hands are required, the labor is performed by the "inquilinos" (tenants), who, for the privilege of living on the estate, are obliged to render a certain amount of service annually to the proprietor.

At this time the Chilian "Guaso," as the country people are called, is seen in perfection. Dressed in his most gaudy apparel, and mounted on his best horse, he scours recklessly over hill and dale, swinging his lasso, and pouring forth a volley of oaths as some refractory animal eludes his pursuit; with his legs cased in overalls of untanned hide, he dashes fearlessly after the stragglers as they fly over rocks and stones, and amidst the clumps of the cactus, armed with formidable spines.

Every one has his station fixed in some part of the circle formed to surround the herds, and strives to drive them to a central point. As the circle contracts the air resounds with shouts and laughter; each feat of dexterity, each narrow escape from the horns of an infuriated animal, is hailed with loud acclamations. All exert themselves to display, to the admiration of their neighbors, their own dexterity, and the fleetness, strength, and beauty of their horses; each one recounts again and again the wondrous deeds which he has performed during the day, not unfrequently drawing upon imagination for details, or weaving into his story all the prodigies of horsemanship and valor that he has heard narrated from infancy.

When collected in some convenient spot the separation of the animals commences.

The yearlings are driven off to one pen. As each one enters he is lassoed and thrown to the ground; the hot-iron hisses for a moment on his side, or the point of a knife cuts some rude cipher on his quivering thigh; he rises bearing the peculiar mark of the estate, and trots off to give place to others. Any of the older animals that may have outgrown their mark, are rebranded,

Another pen is constructed for slaughtering; into this leads a narrow lane, down which the animals are furiously driven. As each one comes in, a man, concealed at the entrance, steps forward, and with an unerring blow hamstrings the passing animal, which plunges and falls upon a hide stretched on the ground for its reception. Forth steps another man, and with the blow of an ax stuns the prostrate victim; a pair of horses, mounted and harnessed, are hooked to the hide, and spring forward under the spur, bearing away the lifeless carcass amidst a blinding cloud of dust.

Another hide is spread with a nice calculation of distance, and the hamstringer stands ready to tumble another victim upon it, by striking at the exact moment, which long experience has taught him.

The carcasses are borne a short distance to where the butchers are at work. The hide is stripped off, stretched out, staked down on the ground, flesh side up, and, with a slight scraping, it is left to dry.

The flesh is taken off in layers as the muscles run, and, with a slight sprinkling of salt, hung up in the open air; by the action of sun and wind, in an atmosphere remarkably pure and free from moisture, it soon becomes dry and hard, forming the jerked beef of commerce. When retailed it is commonly sold by the yard.

The bones are considered valueless; the horns are made into cups and other such articles. These horn cups are used almost to the exclusion of glass among the lower classes, with whom, also, the jerked beef forms the principal article of food.

The animals not intended for slaughter, but reserved for stock, are counted and driven back to pasture.

All these various operations give constant employment to a large number of men for a week or more, and require the supervision of the proprietor, who, as a general rule, spends the greater part of his time in the capital, or in some of the larger towns, visiting his estates, which are left in charge of overseers, only at the busy seasons of slaughtering, planting, harvesting, and vintage.

The immense fields of wheat standing ready for the sickle excited my admiration. The climate of Chili is peculiarly adapted to the cultivation of this grain, and when facilities for irrigation are at hand, the yield is great and the quality excellent. The mode of its culture is of the most primitive kind.

The plow is formed of a log sharpened to a point; a sapling inserted at the proper angle serves as the tongue; a single upright stick answers as a handle, which the plowman grasps in one hand, while in the other he carries a long goad with which to guide the oxen. The point of the plow is sometimes shod with iron, but, even then, the furrow it makes is but a mere scratch upon the surface. The only harrow used is a bunch of bramble bushes, loaded with several large stones, upon which the driver sits.

When the grain is cut it is placed in immense piles in the open air. Around these, at a distance of some yards from the base, a fence is built with an opening on one side. Into the ring so formed, a troop of mares (kept upon every estate for this purpose) are driven by horsemen, who, following in the rear, urge them on at their greatest speed, while from the top of the heap a dozen boys throw down the sheaves of wheat upon the track. After five or ten minutes the mares are let out into an adjoining pen; the grain is raked over and spread evenly upon the course, fresh sheaves are added, and again the mares are driven in.

By this process large quantities of wheat are thrashed in a short time, at a trifling expense, and with much less injury to the grain than might be supposed: as the track soon becomes hard, there is but little admixture of dirt. The greatest objection is the loss of the straw, which is beaten to powder.

The winnowing is performed by simply throwing the grain into the air with shovels, the wind carrying off the chaff while the grain falls to the ground.

The fact that, in this plain, the wind blows with great regularity from certain directions, according to the hour of the day, renders the cleaning of large quantities of wheat by this method, comparatively easy.

Some of the wealthy land-owners in Chili have endeavored to introduce European instruments and methods of cultivation upon their estates, but hitherto with little success. The laboring classes are more inclined to look backward than forward, reverting always to the usages of their fathers, and having an unconquerable aversion to innovations, especially if demanding too much application, either mental or physical. The foreign implements have generally been quickly ruined either through ignorance or malice, and the laborers have returned to their old ways.

A large vineyard rendered this estate complete; for in Chili the three great branches of husbandry are the breeding of animals (principally horned-cattle), the raising of wheat, and the culture of the vine. Other branches, however important, are generally carried on by small proprietors, being either not sufficiently profitable, or too troublesome to engage the attention of capitalists.

When the vintage is small the grapes are trodden out by men, as in southern Europe; but where the produce of immense vineyards is used entirely for making wine, the grapes are placed in large circular troughs and trodden out by horses; the juice runs off into vats, where it is left for fermentation. When fermented, the wine, if not sold, is poured into large earthen-ware jars, six or seven feet in height, which are closely covered and sealed with clay or pitch.

Though the grape grows in Chili in the greatest profusion and of excellent quality—owing to some climatic influence, improper culture, or defect in the after process—the wines do not contain a sufficiently large proportion of alcohol, and will seldom keep without an admixture of spirits, or of wine which has been boiled down.

The "mostos" of the southern provinces are rich, and somewhat like port; but as they are rarely kept for more than a year, one of the chief essentials to good wines—namely, age—is wanting to give them the flavor of the celebrated Europeon brands.

A few foreigners have undertaken to make fine wines in the country, but never on a sufficiently extensive scale to exert any beneficial influence; and though her advantages for the culture of the grape are perhaps unsurpassed, it must be many years before Chili can enter the market in competition with the wine countries of the old world.

"Chicha," as the new wine is called, is consumed in great quantities, and is an agreeable beverage to those somewhat accustomed to its use; but in its crude, fermenting state, it can not be other than injurious to health.

The farm-house, like most others on the estates throughout Chili, was a long, one-story building, constructed of adobes and roofed with tiles: the doors were rudely made of heavy timber; the windows were iron-barred, unglazed, and furnished with board shutters to keep out the wind. In a long, low parlor, the company was drawn up in the old-fashioned way, in two rows, confronting each other across a narrow strip of carpet spread along one side of the room. About a dozen young ladies were present, accompanied by their ever-watchful mammas, and as many of the former played the guitar and sang, we soon had the zamacúca in full blast. Now and then a polka or a waltz would strike up, and a few couples would have the boldness to venture it—no easy work on a narrow strip of carpet (to which etiquette seemed to confine the dancers), spread on a rough brick floor.

I asked a young lady to accompany me in the polka, but she declined: an application in another quarter met with the same result, and I gave up the chase. It so happened that the two ladies were sisters; for finding myself, soon after, seated beside an old lady, she informed me that they were her daughters, and was kind enough to make me an apology for the refusal I had received.

"You will please excuse the girls," she said, "for they *have promised their father confessor not to dance the polka for two months.*"

I was much amused by the old lady's naïveté, and

could not help telling her that I thought the "padre confessor" would have done better had he even prohibited such dances altogether.

About sunset the party broke up; the gentlemen saddled and mounted their horses; but the ladies were furnished with a very different kind of locomotion. A huge cart, drawn by four oxen, came lumbering up to the door. The body of this vehicle was covered with a high arched top, built of cane-work and reeds, perforated at the sides with small barred windows, open at each end, and hung with white and red curtains. The whole affair had the appearance of a small house on wheels. The bottom of the cart was spread with mattresses, pillows, rugs, and cushions; the ladies were lifted in; the guitar struck up, and the whole cavalcade moved off with many adieus.

Some of the gay caballeros rode close behind, conversing with the fair señoritas, whom the fluttering curtains occasionally disclosed huddled together among the rugs and pillows; others kept alongside, gazing through the windows, or joining in the chorus of the song; while a few, who had done full justice to our host's rich vintage, were riding furiously back and forth, racing their horses over the level road.

The oxen did not move very fast, despite the constant goading of an individual who sat astraddle of the cart-tongue, calling them by such names as "Mariposa!" "Golondrina!" (Butterfly, Swallow)—and it was a late hour of the night before we reached the town.

These carts are much used for moving about the

country, and even in Santiago they may be seen lumbering through the streets full of gayly-dressed women. But their use in the cities is generally confined to people of a very low class; for most of the better families keep their own carriages, many of which are very elegant, and even those who do not, would seldom avail themselves of such a conveyance except for some special object.

CHAPTER IX.

Halting-places of the Dead.—San Carlos de Puren.—A pleasant Bedfellow.—Nacimiento.—River Vergara.—Life at Nacimiento.—The Old Lady.—A Scorpion.

At Los Angelos—so near the Araucanian boundary—I had expected to be able to procure every information in regard to the Indians and their territory; but the ideas of most of those whom I met I found to be very vague. No one gave me encouragement; nearly every one dissuaded me; and many assured me that my contemplated expedition would be attended with great risk, both to property and to life. Even the Intendente, though he offered to give me every assistance in his power, thought that I was about to expose myself to danger.

Such being the case, and finding no servant willing to accompany me, I determined to push on to Nacimiento. As that town lies within the Indian territory, I hoped to find there traders or others whom business might lead to Valdivia by the route I wished to pursue, and who would be glad to have an accession to their numbers.

I was accompanied by a *Capitan de Amigos*, who rejoiced in the sounding name of Pantaleon Sanchez. There was really no necessity for an interpreter, since the road between Los Angelos and Nacimiento is short and much traveled; but the Intendente supposed, not without reason, that such a companion would prove useful, and be able to give me more information than could be otherwise obtained, and accordingly gave him instructions to escort me as far as the river Vergara.

Along the roadside we passed many small crosses, planted generally in groups. I had seen many such throughout the southern part of Chili, and had always supposed they were pious mementoes placed over the graves of those slain in the late civil war, or, perhaps, intended to mark the spot where they had fallen; but on questioning my guide, he informed me that the places so designated, were "paraderos de los defunctos" (halting-places of the dead).

In rural districts, where population is sparse, the parishes are large; the churches are distant from each other, and as the burial-places are always near the parish church, it often becomes necessary to carry the dead a journey of one or two days; for no one would ever think of being buried in other than consecrated ground. On such journeys, wherever the pall-bearers stop to rest, they deposit the corpse by the roadside, plant a rude cross of twigs, and repeat a few prayers for the rest of the departed.

In particular spots where, more than at others, it is convenient or necessary to rest, the crosses accumulate, and such places become known by the startling appellation of "halting-places of the dead!"

We noticed that these crosses were more numerous near the river banks than elsewhere; but whether the choice of such locations was in any way connected with the old-fashioned belief in regard to the devil and running water, did not appear.

About two hours after leaving Los Angelos we came to the Duqueco, a small river that was easily forded, though rapid, and in some places deep. An hour and a half later, we reached the little village of San Carlos—a collection of miserable houses upon the banks of the Bio-Bio.

The fact that there is here a military post, and that barges are stationed for the transportation of passengers and merchandise, gives the village its only importance.

The Bio-Bio is, at this place, narrow, but extremely rapid; the barges were whirled about like straws in the current, and reached the opposite shore far below the point from which they had started, requiring to be towed up stream each time before recrossing. But the rapidity of the current was best understood by watching the timber rafts that came shooting past like arrows, darting down the stream, and quickly disappearing at the bend of the river below. Each one of these was formed of half a dozen logs, and manned by two or three men, who ran about perfectly naked, with the exception of a handkerchief at the loins; now pushing with long poles to avoid the rocks; now jumping to one side, now to the other, as the rafts were whirled resistlessly along.

On crossing I was much surprised to find that no toll was taken from us; for our passports—without which no one is allowed to enter the Indian territory—certified that I was in the service of the Chilian government. This was new to me, but as there was no object in gainsaying it, I held my peace.

The southern shore of the river is a low, sandy

plain, while San Carlos, on the northern side, is situated on a high bank overhanging the river, and commanding the opposite shore.

The military post could hardly be called a fort; but it is a strong position, and being surrounded on three sides by a deep ditch, and on the fourth bounded by the perpendicular bank, some eighty feet high, it is impregnable by the Indians, against whom alone it is intended to serve. There was one fine rakish gun —suggestive of long shots—pointing to the south; but from the condition of the carriage, I doubt whether it would have been more dangerous to friend or foe.

The original San Carlos de Puren was built on the southern shore of the river; but it was destroyed by the Indians, and no traces of it now exist.

The patron saint of this place, "Our Lady of Puren," is renowned in the neighborhood for her miracles, which are as numerous, wonderful, and well attested as those of nearly any other saint of greater reputation. Her fame rests principally upon her miraculous restoration to the faithful after a long captivity among the Indians, who had destroyed the town and pillaged her church and shrine: why she should ever have allowed the sacrilegious barbarians to commit such unheard-of outrages is not stated; it appears the greater miracle of the two.

Some six or eight miles beyond the Bio-Bio we came to Badeo, a collection of some half a dozen hovels occupied by Chilenos, who, like Sanchez, hired and cultivated lands in the neighborhood belonging to the Indians. My guide owned a house and generally resided at San Carlos; but, at the time, the whole family had come down to assist in harvesting the wheat.

It was late when we arrived, and after a hearty supper all retired. As the house was filled to overflowing with grown-up people and children of both sexes—to say nothing of the dogs—I preferred sleeping in the open air, and had my bed made up under the "ramada" (shed of brush and cane) just back of the house.

Opening my bed to retire, I perceived something moving between the sheets, and stooping down I saw, by the light of the moon, an enormous spider very deliberately crawling out, and occasionally rearing up on his hind legs, as if disposed to show fight. His body looked as big as a dollar, with legs in proportion, and he was covered with long, coarse hair. Surely traveling makes strange bed-fellows!

Having got rid of this gentleman, and examined very carefully lest another should be snugly ensconced among my linen, I lay down; but it was some time before I could rid my thoughts of the disgusting object I had seen. More than once I started from a nap begun, with a shudder at the thought of something crawling over me; I felt uneasy even at the biting of the fleas, to which I had become so accustomed by long residence in Chili as to consider their company no drawback to a pleasant night's rest. But tired Nature conquered at last, and all thoughts of spiders were drowned in refreshing slumber. Well did Sancho say, "Blessed be the man that invented sleep!"

These huge spiders are found in all parts of Chili,

and are common in the fields during hot weather, when they sally forth from their holes in the ground.

Though so revolting in appearance they are considered perfectly harmless, while a small, round, black spider, also found in the fields, though not formidable in appearance, is said by the natives to be extremely venomous—often biting the reaper while at work, and sometimes causing death.

On the following day I resumed my journey toward Nacimiento.

With Sanchez I had much conversation, and found him more intelligent than the most of his class. He readily comprehended my wishes, entering warmly into my plans, though in many essential particulars he differed from me entirely. A trip to Valdivia he did not think calculated for the accomplishment of my designs; those with whom I proposed to travel usually pass over the route as quickly as possible, having little communication with the Indians; and the road being much traveled, the Indians themselves have laid aside, in great measure, their national peculiarities, assimilating gradually in dress, manners, and customs to the descendants of the Spaniards.

The better plan, he thought, would be for me to join a trading expedition, and penetrate into the unfrequented parts of the interior with the ostensible object of trade—the only one which the Indians comprehend, and view without suspicion.

Finally he proposed, in case I could find nothing to suit my purpose better, to get up a trading expedition himself, with his own available means and the money he could borrow from friends, taking me along as the apparent *patron*, or head of the party, provided that I could procure for him the necessary permission from the Governor. Thus he could at once furnish me entertainment and information, and make, perhaps, a profitable speculation for himself.

This proposition struck me favorably, and I promised to consider it, but did not wish to make any definite arrangements until I had visited Nacimiento, and see what might there be done.

On the road we passed over the site of the town of Colhué, destroyed by the Indians and never rebuilt. The line of streets and the foundations of the houses, though overgrown with grass and weeds, could be plainly traced.

These were the first proud monuments I had seen of the prowess of the Araucanians. The rude hut of the Indian stood near, while his cattle grazed peacefully among the ruined habitations of his once lordly oppressors.

By three o'clock we came in sight of the hill of Negrete; so named in honor of Egidius Negrete, who here defeated the Araucanians in a most sanguinary battle, thereby saving the town of Nacimiento, which was threatened with destruction. In this neighborhood live many scattered Chilenos.

The plain is here a waste of fine volcanic sand, such as we had before met near the "Rio Claro;" and as the sun was broiling hot, while the air was filled with clouds of impalpable dust, our ride for the next two hours was exceedingly disagreeable.

Just beyond the hill of Negrete runs the river Vergara, upon the western bank of which, on a high, commanding position, stands the town of Nacimiento. The most prominent object is the large fort overhanging the bank of the stream. The place, as seen from a distance, presents a striking appearance.

The river here is crossed in barges, and, as before, my supposed official capacity secured me a free passage.

The town afforded no accommodations for strangers; but no sooner had I presented the letters given me by the Governor at Concepcion, than I was kindly received and comfortably lodged by the military commandant, Don Bartolomé Sepulvedà.

It was found, on inquiry, that a party of traders had started only a few days before for Valdivia; but there were no others bound in that direction, and I should be obliged either to start out by myself, at considerable expense for servants and guides, or wait, it was impossible to tell how long, for company.

The commandant highly approved the plan proposed by Sanchez, and advised me by all means to adopt it: of Sanchez himself he spoke in the highest terms, assuring me that of all the government interpreters he was the best-informed, and the most trustworthy. It was therefore settled that an application should be sent as soon as possible to the Governor at Concepcion, who alone could grant to the interpreter the necessary leave of absence.

A barge that was going down the river to Concepcion offered the speediest means of communication, and by it a letter was sent.

More than a week elapsed before an answer arrived, but though impatient of delay, through the kindness of my entertainers I was enabled to spend the time agreeably.

The days were passed in reading, strolling about the town, and bathing in the Vergara. This pure, limpid stream, flowing calmly along, forms a striking contrast with the head waters of the Bio-Bio, into which it flows a short distance below the town. Unlike most of the rivers in Chili, it flows from south to north instead of from east to west, and not being a mountain stream, the current is not rapid, nor is the bottom strewn with rolling stones. This stream, with its grassy banks and untroubled waters, offered the only opportunity I had yet seen in the country for the enjoyment of a good fresh-water bath. At all hours of the day numbers were to be seen refreshing themselves in the cool waters; the men in a state of entire nudity, the women without much superfluous clothing, and the proximity into which the two sexes were thrown was something rather unusual.

The town of Nacimiento is about as large as Los Angelos, and quite as well built; it boasts two quite creditable churches, with high wooden steeples. One of the churches, however, having fallen into disuse, and consequent decay, had been turned into a storehouse for the garrison. But the fort is the great lion of the town. Built under the old Spanish government it is, like all the public works undertaken at that time, solid and well-constructed, without regard to expense; it, too, has been allowed to go to decay.

The garrison is small, consisting of only one battalion, and that far from full; but it is kept in constant practice, and I noticed, even when not on duty, the men amused themselves in sham-battles and games calculated to perfect their military skill. It is to these frontier posts that Chili owes most of her good soldiers; they are the schools to which newly-levied troops are always sent. The liability to be called into action at any moment to quell disturbances among the Indians, renders constant vigilance necessary, and fosters a better discipline than is elsewhere found.

The evenings were usually spent in visiting, and I was quite favorably impressed by the refinement of this last outpost of civilization. Wherever we went, a guitar was never wanting, nor some person to play it, and with dancing and music a few hours could always be pleasantly passed.

In these little out-of-the-way places society has one charm for the stranger which the larger towns are less apt to present: it is that of originality, or, rather, nationality.

In the capital, and in the sea-port towns, where there is an influx of foreigners, the higher circles of society have taken a foreign tone, and adopted a European model. In Valparaiso the standard is rather English—in Santiago it is decidedly French.

This spirit of imitation is natural and praiseworthy, but it produces a cloying sameness; it is a leveler, destructive alike of national and personal individuality, and the traveler, tired of seeing continually reproduced the manners, customs, dress, and even ideas with which he has always been familiar, will tarry with pleasure in those spots presenting the freshness of originality. Such spots only exist where a continual jostling with the exterior world has not abraded the salient angles of the national character.

Commerce, the great civilizer, is also a great equalizer—a destroyer of all that is romantic or picturesque, and he who would study the inner life of a people, must seek his pleasure and information far away from the busy marts of trade.

During my stay here I made the acquaintance of an old lady who afforded me no little amusement; like many others, she had an overweening opinion of the greatness of her own country, and but very indefinite ideas of any other. That her geography should be at fault was nothing surprising, for the same might happen to nearly all of the old school, and many even of the new; but her opinion of foreigners in general, though probably not confined to herself, was entertaining, and such as strangers do not generally hear.

She had many questions to ask, and was surprised to learn that the *Franceses* (for under that comprehensive title she embraced all not Chilenos or Spaniards) were more or less like her own countrymen. She had met many foreigners, and could not but admit their general integrity and industry. "But," she would always add, "it is a great pity that they are not Christians!"

In vain I endeavored to expostulate, explaining that though differing on some points of religion from herself, they were still Christians.

"How can that be, Sir; are they not Moors?"

"No; they are Protestants."

"Well, they are heretics, which is all the same!" and from that position she could not be driven.

During these conversations the old lady sat, Turkish fashion, upon a rug spread on the floor, smoking her cigarito and sucking unnumbered "matés."

A copper-colored little rascal, to whom she applied the affectionate epithets of "indio" and "chino," serving as her Ganymede, sat near at hand, ready to bring the kettle from the coals when needed. For his especial benefit she kept a species of cat-o'-nine-tails, and whenever he nodded, which he was apt to do as the conversation became prosy, the lash would descend upon his shoulders, accompanied by an outcry such as you would make to a dog caught in the act of stealing meat. He would start up, look round, rub his belabored back, and in another moment nod, much to the exasperation of his mistress.

Knowing that foreigners, generally, do not take "maté," she did not offer it at first, but at length she began persuading me to *try one*, at the same time enjoining great care not to burn my mouth.

Wishing to surprise her, I took the maté as though unused to it, and having finished the contents, handed it back. Encouraged by this, she pressed me to take another, which I did; a third followed, and a fourth, and so on, until I had taken eight or nine, when handing back the calabash to be again replenished, the old lady looked at me in blank astonishment, and snatching the "maté" from my hand, she tossed it into the corner, followed by the sugar-box and spoon, exclaiming,

"Caramba! you drink more maté than I myself!"

I protested that I had merely done so to oblige her,

but in my subsequent visits she never allowed me to exceed the third "maté."

One night, during my stay at Nacimiento, as I was about to retire, my attention was called to something black moving upon the wall. On inspection, my visitor proved to be nothing more nor less than an ugly scorpion. A smart rap with the heel of a boot effectually stopped his crawling, but it was not without a cold shudder that I saw his hooked tail writhing about in his death-agony.

When I mentioned the circumstance to the family, they laughed heartily at my alarm, assuring me that scorpions, though common about old houses, were perfectly harmless — seldom stinging, and causing but trifling inconvenience. There is, in fact, no venomous reptile of any kind known in Chili, except the small black spider before spoken of, which is rarely met with.

CHAPTER X.

Return to Los Angelos.—The Siesta.—Table Etiquette.—Night at San Carlos.—Doña Pablita.—The Pillow.—Hair Shirts.—Introductory remark to a History of the Araucanians.

When the Governor's reply at last arrived, it became necessary for me to return to Los Angelos, to which station Sanchez was attached.

The route by which we returned was different from that by which we had come, and much shorter. Following the banks of the Vergara for a short distance, we came to its junction with the Bio-Bio, where we crossed in barges; our road then struck off across the plain, and after a ride of some four hours we reached Los Angelos.

As the Intendente had left town, I went with the Governor's letter to the house of the military Commandante, who kindly invited me to lodge at his quarters, and sent orders for Sanchez to be in readiness to accompany me within twenty-four hours.

As it was desirable to reduce every thing to as small a compass as possible, I left behind my mattress and almofrez, carrying for bedding only a couple of blankets and some sheets, in accordance with the advice of the guide, who assured me that sheep-skins in abundance would never be wanting with which to make a comfortable bed. He laughed at the idea of carrying any cooking apparatus, declaring that the squaws would feed me better than I ever had been fed in any other part of Chili. He even counseled me to leave my pistol, which he considered a useless encumbrance; but on that point I demurred, preferring to carry it along as a pleasant traveling companion.

The poncho which I usually wore was heavy, and I determined to buy another more convenient for warm weather. With some difficulty I found one to my taste; but as it required binding to prevent the edges from raveling out, I left it with the shopkeeper's wife (the real *business man* as it seemed), who told me to call for it at a certain hour. The time arrived, but the poncho had not been finished, and another hour was named.

Punctual to the appointment, I again called. The shop-keeper sat dozing behind his little counter. When I asked for my purchase he started up, rubbed his eyes, and pointing mysteriously to a carefully closed door behind him, ejaculated, "*Esta dormiendo, Señor!*" ("She is asleep, Sir!")

"But I want my poncho," said I, supposing he misunderstood me.

"My wife is asleep, Sir!" he again answered, pointing to the door, as though it closed upon a sanctum he dared not enter.

"Very well, then, give it to me yourself!"

He only shook his head—he could not interfere in his wife's affairs.

"Then why don't you wake her up?" I cried impatiently.

"*Interomper la en la siesta, Señor!*" ("Impossible—disturb her in her siesta!") he answered, his eyes dilating in amazement, "Impossible, Sir!"

I urged the appointment of the hour, my hurry, etc., but to no purpose. I must wait "*un ratito*" (which might mean five minutes or an hour), until the lady finished her nap—for she could not be disturbed.

After another half hour I found the lady awake and much refreshed by her nap. She made no apologies for having kept me waiting, for she did not consider time of any value.

Disturb an alderman, if you will, at dinner, a philosopher in a brown study, a preacher during the writing of a sermon, but respect the sacredness of the Spaniard's siesta!

In Valparaiso the impulse of commerce and the example of foreigners have almost entirely abolished the time-honored siesta; in Santiago, among the more active classes of the community it has gone into disuse, though ladies and people of leisure still cling to their noonday or after-dinner nap; but in the country and interior towns it is universal, and it is affirmed that many of the old school undress and turn into bed for the siesta with as much formality as if retiring for the night.

Leaving all my extras with the Commandante, who promised to take charge of them until my return, we started, and about sunset reached San Carlos. As we hoped at this place to procure a servant for the journey, we determined to remain over night at the house of one of Sanchez's numerous "compadres."*

* "Compadre and "comadre"—sponsors, male and female, for a child at its baptism; also bride's-maids and groom's-men in marriages.

The house at which we stopped was, like most of the others in the village, without paint, whitewash, flooring, or much pretensions to furniture, but our reception was cordial.

My projects seemed to surprise the good people, who could not understand why a *caballero* should wish to expose himself to hardships and even perils; but they satisfied themselves with the pithy remark—"*Pero ve Vd. que los forasteros no son como nosotros!*" ("Surely these foreigners are very different from us!")

While this interesting conversation was going on, I overheard a female voice whispering, "*Que lastima!*" ("What a pity!")—and turning in the direction from which the noise proceeded, I saw a tall, handsome girl looking at me with an expression such as any woman might wear if gazing at an innocent lamb led to the altar. What the pity was, I did not ask; but it evidently related in some way to myself; for the moment our eyes met, her long silken lashes fell upon her cheek, and with a blush she turned away.

Supper came, served by our fair friend of the silken lashes. The seat of honor was assigned to me, and the others were monopolized by the men. This arrangement was not to my taste, and I protested against such an exclusion of the ladies—especially the one who had taken the trouble to serve up the meal.

The young lady seated herself at the table with ap-

Throughout all Spanish countries these words are much used as terms of endearment; and one of the most ordinary salutations of the lower classes on meeting is, "Como le va compai're?"—"Ay vamo' comai're!"

parent reluctance; but all my efforts at conversation were unavailing. An opportunity however soon occurred of breaking the ice; for raking up from the depths of the casuela a chicken liver, she harpooned it with her fork and passed it over, fork and all, for my acceptance, adding, of course, the usual "*Dispensa Vd. la mano*" ("Excuse the hand from which it comes.") This delicate attention was immediately reciprocated by a gizzard from my own plate!

After the interchange of such civilities, reserve quickly disappeared, and we were soon as intimate as old friends. This custom, like that of passing the same glass from lip to lip, is probably of Oriental origin, descending to the Chilenos, through the Spaniards, from the Moors. Like all the purely national customs it is fast going out of use, except in the country or among the lower classes; in the higher circles of the cities it is unheard of. True, on one occasion, I received such an attention from a lady at a party in the capital; but as it came in the questionable shape of a head of garlic from the turkey dressing, I never could fairly make up my mind whether it was intended as a mark of special favor or as a practical joke.

Such manners may not indicate the highest refinement, but they evince a cordiality of feeling, and have an appearance of good-will, for the absence of which no amount of mere form can compensate.

The Sandwich Islander, with his forefinger, dabs the luscious "poé-poé" into your open mouth; the Arab tears off a tit-bit of meat, and passes it to you in his hand; the Chilena offers you a dainty morsel upon her fork; the American asks you to drink, and stands treat; the Englishman requests the pleasure of a glass of wine with you, and expects you to help yourself from your own bottle. The one extreme may be worse than the other, but the truth lies, as usual, about in the middle.

Supper over, I retired to one corner to enjoy a smoke; no sooner had I taken out my cigarito, than my fair friend rose, and taking it from my hand, lit it at the candle, taking a few puffs, by the way, so that it should not go out. I offered her one, but she would not accept it—"she never could smoke"—at the same time making a wry face to convince me; but there was something scientific in the wreathing of the smoke, as it curled from her lips, that made me doubt her words. Of course she was merely showing me an ordinary civility, not dreaming that it would lead to conversation; but, before our chat was ended, the candle had burnt low in its socket, and I was convinced that, despite her artless looks, this village beauty was a sad coquette.

My bed was brought in and made up on a raised platform, some six inches high, running along one side of the room and serving as a species of divan.

Trusting to my saddle, I had thought it unnecessary to carry any pillow; the quick eye of Doña Pablita (for such was her name), immediately detected the want, and running off she brought her own for my use, nor would she admit a refusal. It was very soft, immaculately clean, and withal a pretty pillow—for pillows in Chili always are pretty—it was not of silk, nor of satin, covered with costly lace; but the pink muslin shone with a warm glow through the fine linen, and the delicate edgings, I knew, were worked by the fair hands of the owner. Under such auspices I retired, and laid my cheek upon the soft down in anticipation of pleasant dreams.

Have you never lain awake through the long hours of the night, your mind reveling in delicious fancies, your eyes unwilling to close upon the pleasing sights that seemed to dance before them? I often have; and I now lay for many a half hour unable to sleep; but alas for sentiment, I was kept awake, not so much by thoughts of the gentle Pablita, as by the swarms of fleas that poured in upon me from all directions.

When we started on the morrow our hosts bade us a kindly farewell, and promised to pray for our safe return; especially Doña Pablita, who promised to intercede with St. Joseph for our especial protection: in return for which good offices, I engaged to bring her a present of a "ternerito negro" (a little black steer).

This young lady had a great deal of a certain kind of piety, the common property of her countrywomen, and it was painful to see that she wore a "hair shirt." On twitting her upon the enormity of the crime which must have dictated so great a penance, she told me that her father having joined the army during the late civil war, she had made a vow to Our Lady of Something, to wear a hair shirt for the term of one year, in case of his safe return; a vow she was religiously fulfilling.

Weeds are much worn in Chili, in compliance with vows, yet as there are various colors, according to the saint invoked, the ladies generally display considerable taste and coquetry in making their penance as becoming as possible; but hair shirts and flagellations are not so much in vogue.

At the ferry I was both surprised and gratified to meet a young officer whom I had known in Santiago; he was in command of the garrison, and seeing my name in the passport, had come down to see me and have a chat about old times. He seemed rejoiced to meet some one who could give him news from many of the friends he had left behind. He counted the weary months he had passed since leaving his native Santiago, and yearned to return; for the love of home is strong in the breast of every Chileno, and in none more so than in that of the Santiaguino.

Once on the southern bank of the river I considered myself fairly started, and gladly bade a short farewell to civilization.

We stopped as before at Budeo, where the family of my guide was still staying.

In order that the reader may understand the peculiar interest attaching to the tribe of Indians whose territory we were about to enter, he should be somewhat acquainted with their history, and it will be well to drop our narrative for the present, and devote a few chapters to those events which have given lustre to the Araucanian name.

The earliest authentic notices we possess of the aborigines of Chili, have descended to us from the Peruvians, who, though unacquainted with the art of writing, carefully preserved and transmitted, from generation to generation, the traditions of their race. After the subjugation of Peru by the Spaniards, these traditions were collected and rescued from oblivion by Garcilazo de la Vega, a converted Peruvian, and a lineal descendant from the Incas.

The letters and narratives of the Spaniards themselves furnish us with the details of events subsequent to the conquest.

The only history of the Araucanians with which I am acquainted, is contained in the Abbé Molina's work* on Chili, from which the following abstract of their wars with the Spaniards has been principally drawn.

It is, however, but fair to state that a great part of Molina's history seems to have been taken from the "Araucana" of Ercilla, who, though himself an eyewitness to many of the scenes depicted in his poem, so mixes up fact and fancy that it is often difficult to distinguished between the two. It shall be my endeavor to present to the reader an account of those events only of historic importance, which are undoubtedly true, throwing out all the fine speeches and marvelous adventures, which, though chronicled by the poet, seem unworthy of record on the page of history.

* The "Saggio della Storia de Chili" originally published in Italian, 1782, and subsequently translated into English by R. Alsop. The learned Abbé's history contains a disquisition on the manners and customs of the Araucanians, which I have found extremely useful, not only as confirming my own observations, but also as furnishing many facts with which my guide seems to have been unacquainted.

The History (Natural and Political) of Chili compiled by M. Claudius Gay, and recently published in Paris by order of the Chilian government, may contain much valuable additional information, but I have not had the opportunity of consulting it.

CHAPTER XI.

The Aborigines of Chili.—Conquest of Northern Chili by the Incas.—First Expedition of the Spaniards under Almagro.

THE aborigines of Chili, and of a portion of the present Argentine Republic, were of one race, spoke but one language, and were characterized by the same manners and customs, slightly modified by the influences of climate, soil, and geographical position.

They designated themselves by the comprehensive name of "Alapu-ché," or "Children of the Land."

According to general geographical divisions they were distinguished as "Pehuenché," or People of the East; "Moraché," People of the West; and "Huilliché," Far-off People, living to the South.

These general divisions were divided into provinces, as, for instance, that of the Purumancians, which were in turn subdivided into particular districts.

Without stopping here to examine into their polity, it will be sufficient to state, that from the earliest period of their history of which we have any knowledge, the people of these provinces lived as separate tribes, under district governments.

Of these various tribes the most important was that of the so-called "Araucanians," an appellation

F*

which, though improperly given by the Spaniards, has become world-renowned, and can not now be changed. To their achievements the reader's attention will be principally called, but it will also be necessary to dwell incidentally upon the history of the other Chilian tribes.

In the year 1450 the Peruvian Inca, Yupanqui, desirous of extending his dominions toward the south, stationed himself with a powerful army at Atacama. Thence he dispatched a force of ten thousand men to Chili, under the command of Chinchiruca, who, overcoming almost incredible obstacles, marched through a sandy desert as far as Copiapo, a distance of eighty leagues.

The Copiapins flew to arms, and prepared to resist this invasion. But Chinchiruca, true to the policy which the Incas always observed, stood upon the defensive, trusting to persuasion rather than to force for the accomplishment of his designs. He declared to the people that he had come as a friend, not as an enemy—not to destroy, but to promote their happiness, by giving them laws and a religion superior to their own. Yet, while he proffered peace, he warned them of the consequences of resisting the "Children of the Sun."

Such representations were well calculated to produce a powerful effect upon the minds of a rude, imaginative race, and the Copiapins for a long time wavered between an unwillingness to surrender their cherished liberties and the fear of offending those whom they deemed more than mortal.

While perplexed by these conflicting doubts, the

arrival of the second Peruvian army induced them to lay down their arms.

The Inca, pleased with so easy a conquest where he had anticipated the most obstinate resistance, sent a third army with instructions to push onward to the south. The adjoining province of Coquimbo was easily subjugated, and steadily advancing, the Peruvians, some six years after their first entering the country, firmly established themselves in the valley of Chili, at a distance of more than two hundred leagues from the frontier of Atacama.

The "Children of the Sun" had met thus far with little resistance, and, encouraged by success, they marched their victorious armies against the Purumancians, a warlike people living beyond the river Rapel. But these "free dancers," though of the same blood, and speaking the same language as the more northern tribes, were imbued with a far different spirit.

To the summons of the Inca they returned a haughty and indignant answer. Several days were allowed to pass, and again they were called upon to yield; but they deigned no other reply than that of drawing up their forces in battle array within sight of the enemy. A third time were they warned of the danger of resisting.

"Go back!" they said to the messenger, "Go back and tell your general that we have come not to parley, but to fight!"

A desperate battle followed, in which the superior discipline of the Peruvians was met by the reckless bravery of the Purumancians, who sought, by sudden attacks and overwhelming numbers, to break through the solid ranks of their adversaries. For three days the conflict raged with little cessation. Great numbers were killed, and as neither army remained in a condition to renew the combat, both retired. The Peruvians recrossed the river, and the Purumancians returned to their homes, proud of their successful resistance to a power hitherto deemed irresistible.

Learning the result of this battle the Inca Yupanqui influenced by motives of humanity, ordered his generals to relinquish the idea of further conquests, and seek by the introduction of wise laws, and by instructing the people in agriculture and the arts, to establish themselves more firmly in the territory already acquired.

To what extent the Peruvians were successful in the endeavor to ingraft their civilization, religion, and customs upon the Chilians, it is at this distant day impossible to determine, since the earliest historians differ widely on the subject. Certain it is, that on the arrival of the Spaniards the Incas, at least nominally, ruled the country, and received an annual tribute of gold from the people.

In the year 1535, after the death of the unfortunate Inca Atahuallpa, Diego Almagro, fired by the love of glory and the thirst for gold, yielded to the solicitations of Francisco Pizarro, the conqueror of Peru, and set out for the subjection of Chili, which, as yet, had not been visited by any European.

His army consisted of five hundred and seventy Spaniards, well equipped, and fifteen thousand Peruvian auxiliaries.

Regardless of difficulties and dangers, this impetuous soldier selected the near route that lay along the summits of the Andes, in preference to the more circuitous road passing through the desert of Atacama. Upon the horrors of this march, of which so thrilling an account is given by Prescott in his "Conquest of Peru," it is unnecessary for us to dwell; suffice it to state, that on reaching Copiapo no less than one-fourth of his Spanish troops, and two-thirds of his Indian auxiliaries, had perished from the effects of cold, fatigue, and starvation.

One of the Incas who accompanied the expedition, wishing to revive the drooping spirits of the Spaniards, and impress them with the importance of their conquest, obliged the people of Copiapó to deliver up all the gold in their possession, amounting to about one million of dollars.

This gold he presented to Almagro, who, thinking it but the precursor of untold wealth, ostentatiously distributed the whole sum among his followers.

Every where the Spaniards met with a friendly reception from the natives, who regarded them as a superior race of beings, and the after conquest of the country would probably have been attended with no difficulty had a conciliatory policy been adopted; but this naturally inoffensive people, aroused by acts of the most barbarous cruelty, soon flew to arms.

Despite the opposition of the natives, who were now rising in every direction to oppose his march, Almagro kept on, overcoming every obstacle, until he reached the river Cachapoal, the northern boundary of the Purumancian territory. Here the Peruvian allies would have persuaded him to pause, representing to him the desperate valor of that people; but such considerations only increased the ardor of a man accustomed to conquest, and he determined to advance.

No sooner did the Purumancians find their territory invaded, than they assembled in vast numbers to repel the aggressor.

At the first sight of the brilliant European arms and gayly-caparisoned horses, they were filled with a terror that was augmented by the loud report of the musketry; but soon regaining their wonted courage, they charged boldly upon the enemy, using their clubs and lances with great efficiency.

With a degree of skill not to have been expected in so rude a people, they formed in regular battalions, falling upon the Spanish lines with such well-directed attacks, that even the veterans of Peru with difficulty maintained their ground.

When night at length separated the combatants, the Purumancians withdrew and encamped near the field, eager to renew the contest on the morrow.

Almagro immediately called a council of his principal followers. They were disappointed and chagrined; they had found but little gold; and where they had anticipated an easy conquest, they had met with a determined resistance, gaining a victory that only in name was not a defeat. Unanimously they proclaimed in favor of abandoning the expedition; and recrossing the Cachapoal, they commenced their return to Peru.

Almagro, subsequently having failed in an attempt

to overthrow the Pizarros, was captured and beheaded; his followers, driven to desperation by the ridicule which their poverty and ill-success every where excited, became notorious, as the "men of Chili," for their reckless character.

CHAPTER XII.

Valdivia's Expedition.—Santiago built.—Reinforcements demanded. —Treaty with Purumancians.—Foundation of Concepcion.—Opposition of the Araucanians.—Defeat and Death of Valdivia.

PIZARRO, ever desirous of conquering Chili, in 1540 dispatched Pedro Valdivia for that purpose, with some two hundred Spanish soldiers, and a large body of Peruvians.

This general took the same route that had been followed by Almagro; but, more prudent than he, selected for the journey a season of the year when the Cordilleras, but little obstructed by snows, were easily passable. He reached Chili without having sustained any loss, but his reception was far different from that of his predecessors. The Copiapins, who had welcomed Almagro with presents of fruit and gold, received Valdivia in hostile array; but the rude valor of a people who had become enervated and unaccustomed to war under the mild sway of the Incas, could offer no effectual resistance to the advance of the Spaniards, who pushed steadily on until they reached the river Mapoclio, and encamped upon the site of the present capital of Chili.

Valdivia finding the location pleasant, and the surrounding plain fertile, here founded a city on the 24th February, 1541. To this first European settlement in Chili he gave the name of Santiago, in honor of the patron saint of Spain. He laid out the town in Spanish style; and as a place of refuge in case of attack, erected a fort upon a steep rocky hill, rising some two hundred feet above the plain.

The Mapochins, awaking too late to a sense of the danger that awaited them, should these strangers become firmly established in their midst, took advantage of the temporary absence of the Spanish leader with a portion of his troops, to fall unexpectedly upon the infant settlement. So sudden was this onslaught that the terrified people with difficulty escaped, and sought refuge in the fort.

Having reduced the town to ashes, the Mapochins scaled the rocky sides of the hill, and attacked the fortress on every side, leaping the moat, and climbing the very walls.

Dreadful was the carnage made in their ranks by the artillery; but, unterrified, they advanced in so great numbers, and with such resolution, that the place must soon have fallen had not Valdivia—apprised of the danger—returned in haste. Cutting his way through the surging mass of naked savages, who in vain hurled stones against his mail-clad warriors, or strove to drag them from their saddles, he reached the gates of the fortress in time to rescue the besieged from their perilous situation.

The Indians, despairing of success after the arrival of this reinforcement, retired from the contest.

But though foiled in their first attempt to throw off the Spanish yoke, the Mapochins did not relinquish the hope of regaining their freedom. They besieged the city with unremitting vigilance, cutting off every avenue for supplies: again and again they destroyed the ripening grain of their enemies, who, even beneath the very guns of the fort, were able to raise barely enough for a scanty subsistence. In the hope of reducing by famine a foe whom they could not conquer by force, they even laid waste their own fertile fields, and retiring to the mountains, desolated the beautiful plain that they had proudly named "The land of many people."

He who examines the history of this period will be at loss whether more to admire the heroic bravery and self-sacrificing patriotism of the Indian, or the chivalrous daring and patient endurance of the Spaniard.

The admirable traits of Valdivia's character were displayed in a remarkable degree. By his own example he inspired all; he encouraged the faint-hearted; he reconciled the discontented by his prudence; and by firmness he held in check the turbulent: his untiring exertions alone prevented the colonists from giving up an undertaking with which they had become heartily disgusted, and abandoning the country forever.

Convinced that without additional force further conquest would be impossible, he dispatched to Peru two officers, Monroy and Miranda, with six companions, and an escort of thirty horse, to report to Pizarro the straitened condition of the Chilian expedition, and to beg reinforcements.

They proceeded without difficulty as far as Copiapo, where they were attacked by the chief of the district and completely routed. Of the whole party only Monroy and Miranda escaped. They too would have perished, for they were sentenced to death, and had actually been bound to the stake, when they were rescued by the interposition of their conqueror's wife, who begged that they might be spared, unbound them with her own hands, and tenderly dressed their wounds. This kindness was repaid by an act of the blackest ingratitude.

While riding out one day in company with the son of their benefactress, Monroy fell suddenly upon the young chieftain, mortally wounding him with a poniard, while Miranda, turning upon the officer in command of the guard, wrenched from his hand the lance which he bore, and breaking through the ranks of the terrified escort, they fled. Favored by fleet horses, they made good their escape, and taking their way through the trackless desert, they succeeded in reaching Peru.

The enormity of this treachery was augmented by the fact that it was unnecessary; for, being never closely watched, an escape would at any time have been easy without having recourse to violence.

Such crimes only tended to embitter the hatred which the Spaniards had every where incurred by their cruelty and rapacity.

On the arrival of a second army from Peru, Valdivia, whose ambition had always been to conquer the southern provinces of Chili, advanced into the country of the Purumancians.

Here history is probably defective, as we have no account of any battles fought with these brave people, who so successfully withstood the encroachments of the Incas, and repelled the invasion of Almagro. We simply learn that the Spanish leader eventually gained their good-will, and established with them an alliance both offensive and defensive—a wise measure, without which the Spaniards might never have been able to subject the country, for these formidable enemies became, in after wars, most efficient auxiliaries against the indomitable Araucanians.

In the following year (1546) the Spanish forces crossed the river Maulé, the southern boundary of the Purumancians, and advanced toward the Itata.

While encamped near the latter river, they were attacked at the dead of night by a body of Araucanians. So unexpected was the approach of this new enemy, that many of the horses were captured, and the army with difficulty escaped total destruction.

After this terrible defeat, Valdivia finding himself unable to proceed, returned to Santiago. Soon after he went to Peru in hope of there being able to collect an army adequate to the subjugation of the Araucaians. But that unhappy country was distracted by civil wars, and it was not until the restoration of order, some two years subsequently, that he was enabled to raise a large band of followers, with whom he returned to Chili.

Considering the Spanish power well established in Northern Chili, after nine years of possession, he divided the lands and inhabitants among his principal adherents, and again marched to the South.

Reaching the bay of Talcahuano without having met with any opposition, on the 5th of October, 1550, he founded the city of Concepcion on a site at present known as Penco.

The new settlement was not long allowed to remain unmolested, for the Araucanians gathering to the number of four thousand men, under Aillavalu, crossed the Bio-Bio and advanced as far as the Andalien, where they were met by the Spaniards, who, confident of victory, had marched out into the open plain to receive them. Unappalled by the discharges of the musketry, they moved rapidly both upon the front and flanks of the invaders, who were drawn up in solid squares, supported by the cavalry. The battle raged furiously for many hours: the slaughter was great on both sides; and more than once the Spanish ranks were broken and thrown into a confusion from which they with difficulty recovered. Valdivia's horse was killed, and he himself barely escaped with life. Though he had served in many battles in both hemispheres, he afterward declared that never before had he been exposed to so great peril.

The victory seemed doubtful, when Aillavalu, advancing rashly before his troops, was slain; and the Indians, finding themselves without a leader, retreated slowly and in good order. The Spaniards felt no desire to pursue, feeling amply satisfied with the maintenance of their position and the semblance of a victory.

Withdrawing to their own territory, the Araucaians called a council of the nation for the election of a new *Toqui*. The choice fell upon Lincoyan, a chief who had gained great reputation both for discretion and valor.

But Lincoyan was little to be feared; he was an excellent subordinate, but utterly unfitted to command; though not wanting in personal valor, he was devoid of moral courage; he dared assume no responsibility, and too much dreaded defeat ever to be victorious.

Collecting a large army, he crossed the Bio-Bio, and marched upon the town.

So great was the consternation inspired by his approach that the inhabitants fled to the fort, and the soldiers prepared themselves for the battle by confession and communion. But after much delay, and some ineffectual skirmishing, he suddenly withdrew beyond the Bio-Bio.

The Indians themselves were unable to comprehend the object of such a movement; but the Spaniards, never at loss for a miracle, attributed their delivery to the intervention of the saints; and there were not wanting those who gravely asserted that they had seen St. James upon his white steed charging on the ranks of the infidel barbarians.

For two years the new city remained unmolested, and Valdivia, supposing that the spirit of the Araucanians had been broken, determined to invade their territory.

In 1552 he crossed the Bio-Bio and marched through Encol and Puren as far as the river Cantin, upon whose banks, at its confluence with the Damas, he founded a city, naming it "El Imperial," in honor of Charles the Fifth, or, as some assert, on account of having there discovered certain rudely-carved figures, bearing some resemblance to the double-headed eagle of Austria. Passing beyond the limits of the Araucanian territory, he founded a town, to which he gave his own family name, "Valdivia." He also dispatched an officer with sixty men to establish a post on the shore of a lake lying near a volcano; from the great wealth of the surrounding district, this settlement afterward became known as *La Villa Rica*, "The Rich City."

Throughout this march the Spaniards met with but little opposition, for though the timid Lincoyan, with a large army, hung continually about their skirts, ever waiting for an opportunity to strike, he never dared to give the blow. So easy was the conquest, and so favorable were the prospects of peace, that Valdivia magnanimously divided the country among his followers and returned to Santiago.

In 1553 Valdivia again repaired to the south, and established posts at Puren, Tucapel, and Arauco; still later he founded his seventh and last city, to which he gave the name of Las Fronteras.

For a long time dissatisfied with the supineness of Lincoyan, the Araucanians finally convened the national council, and chose, in his stead, as commander of their armies, a chief renowned for his prowess and great bodily strength.

Caupolican, the newly-elected Toqui, signalized the commencement of his rule by a well-directed attack upon the Spanish post at Arauco.

Failing to reduce the fort both by stratagem and assault, he determined upon a blockade, and invested the place so closely that the besieged were soon glad to escape under cover of the night. Destroying the fortifications, he moved rapidly upon the fort at Tucapel, which he attacked so resolutely, and with such perseverance that the exhausted and famishing garrison determined to abandon the place. Caupolican wisely allowed them to depart without molestation, and setting fire to the deserted buildings, he calmly awaited the appearance of the forces that he foresaw would soon march to attack him.

Nor was he long obliged to wait, for no sooner did the news of these disasters reach Concepcion, than Valdivia, hastily assembling an army and neglecting the prudent counsels of his officers, marched in search of the enemy. When near Tucapel a few horsemen were sent forward to reconnoitre, but they did not return; and advancing, the Spaniards were filled with horror as they beheld the gory heads of their murdered companions hanging from the topmost branches of the trees. A short distance further on the army of Caupolican was seen drawn up with admirable order in battle array; while beyond, the smoke was rising from the blackened ruins of the fort.

During the battle which ensued the Araucanians exhibited great coolness, those in the rear marching in regular squadrons to the relief of those in the front ranks, who in turn retired to re-form and hold themselves in readiness to assist their comrades; but after several hours of hard fighting, unable longer to withstand the terrible effects of the musketry, they began to fly, and were hotly pursued by the Spaniards, who, thirsting for revenge, pressed forward in confusion. At this critical moment, a young Araucanian captive, named Lautaro, who had been reared in Valdivia's family, rushed among his discomfited countrymen, exhorting them to pause and turn upon their enemies, who were but a handful of weakened and dispirited men, whose only strength consisted in that superior order which they had now forgotten.

By eloquent entreaties he succeeded in inspiring the fugitives with fresh courage, and rallying, they fell upon their pursuers, who, borne on by the ardor of the chase, had become dispersed in all directions. The scattered horsemen were every where overwhelmed by numbers, dragged from their saddles, and trampled under foot.

The Spaniards, in turn, were struck with panic; the carnage was dreadful; and of the whole army, only two persons survived to bear to Concepcion the tidings of their defeat.

The unfortunate Valdivia was captured; and though he sued for life, promising, if released, to abandon the country forever with all his followers, he was put to death. This happened on the 23d December, 1553. There are many and conflicting accounts of this event, and at this day it is impossible to determine the truth; but the story which seems most deserving of credit, is that Lautaro wished to save the life of his former master, when an aged chief, seizing an ax, dashed out the brains of the captive general, reproaching his countrymen for their folly in trusting to the promises of so perfidious an enemy.

Valdivia was one of the most remarkable men that figured in the conquest of the Spaniards in South America. He was a brave soldier and a prudent general. Though deeply imbued with the romantic spirit of the times, he was far in advance of his age; for we do not learn that his triumphs were sullied by any of those deeds of cruelty and bigotry which have left so foul a blot upon the otherwise fair fame of too many of his countrymen. He does not seem to have been avaricious, the love of glory being to him a greater incentive than the love of gold.

The great and fatal mistake of his life was that of holding too lightly the prowess of the Araucanians, and scattering his forces throughout their territory in such small numbers and at such distances that they could be easily attacked and defeated in detail, before assistance could reach them from abroad.

CHAPTER XIII.

Battle of Marigueno.—Destruction of Concepcion.—Concepcion rebuilt and again destroyed.—Expedition of Lautaro against Santiago.—His Defeat and Death.

IMMEDIATELY after the destruction of Valdivia's army, Caupolican led forth the youthful Lautaro, and presenting him to the assembled multitude as the saviour of his country, by whose exertions alone the enemy had been vanquished, elected him Vice-Toqui, and gave him command of one half the forces. The people by acclamation assented to this wise choice, and none more readily than those whose rank would have justified them in claiming that honor for themselves.

A discussion followed upon the proper manner of prosecuting the war so favorably begun. Many of the younger chiefs proposed to march forth and attack the enemy in his strongholds; some wished even to advance upon Santiago itself; but the more aged prudently advised their countrymen to be content with securing the victory at home by driving out the Spaniards from the posts they still held south of the Bio-Bio.

Caupolican wisely adopted the counsels of the aged chiefs, determining to attack the remaining Spanish towns, and leave his youthful lieutenant, with a large force, to guard the frontiers of the north.

When the defeat and death of Valdivia became known to the Spaniards, the people of Puren and Frontera fled for safety to Imperial, while those of Villa Rica sought refuge in the fort at Valdivia.

In Concepcion the news created the greatest dismay; but Francisco De Villa Gran, who had been left in command of the town, was a bold, energetic soldier, and collecting a large body of Spaniards and Purumancians, he pressed forward to meet the victorious Caupolican.

Lautaro foreseeing the approach of the enemy, stationed his own army upon the lofty hill of Marigueno—a rugged mass of rock lying directly on the road to Arauco. The summit of this hill being flat and covered with trees offered a fine encampment, while the ruggedness of the sides, in some places flanked by the waves of the sea, in others by almost impenetrable thickets, rendered it easily defensible. In this position he awaited the Spanish general.

In a narrow defile, through which ran the road, a strong body of Araucanians were advantageously posted as an advance-guard. With them the battle commenced. For several hours they defended the pass; but finally giving way, they retreated slowly, fighting as they went, toward the summit, where the Indian army lay encamped.

The Spaniards were surprised, at the very moment when they thought the battle ended, to find a second army drawn up to oppose them. Yet confident of victory, they pushed resolutely on. But they were met by a spirit equal to their own; for the fierce warriors of Arauco, urged on by the voice of their youthful leader, displayed more than their accustomed valor, and made a most efficient use of the horses and European arms which were the proud trophies of their recent triumph over Valdivia. The fire of six field-pieces, however, told with terrible effect upon their ranks, and they soon began to waver.

Lautaro seeing the impossibility of maintaining his position in the face of the Spanish cannon, determined to capture them. For this purpose he selected one of his bravest officers, to whom he assigned a body of picked men, while he himself, to divert attention from the real purpose, fell furiously upon Villa Gran's flank.

So bold and sudden was the attack, and so unexpected the design, that the artillerymen were thrown into confusion and driven from their guns, which were borne off in triumph by the exulting savages.

Disheartened by so irreparable a loss, the Spaniards in turn began to give way, and Villa Gran, having first dispatched an officer to secure the narrow pass in which the battle began, reluctantly ordered a retreat. All was now confusion: the fugitives strained every nerve, but the Indians pursued so hotly that Villa Gran himself was saved from capture only by the heroic exertions of a few of his followers. On reaching the defile, they found it already occupied by a band of the bravest Araucanians, whom the far-seeing Lautaro, confident of the victory, had dispatched for the purpose early in the action. The road, too, had been obstructed with the trunks of fallen trees, over which the horses could with difficulty advance.

The slaughter here was dreadful, and the Spaniards

must have been annihilated but for the desperate courage of their leader, who, placing himself at the head of his few remaining troops, charged furiously upon the enemy, and succeeded in breaking through the pass and escaping with a handful of men to Concepcion.

Great was the consternation of the people of Concepcion. With the small surviving force it was impossible to defend the fort, and it became necessary to abandon their homes before the arrival of Lautaro, who was momentarily expected.

The women, the children, the aged, and the infirm were hastily placed aboard the ships, to be conveyed to Imperial and Valparaiso, while the more hardy portion of the inhabitants took up their long and weary march for Santiago, which place they reached in safety, after great sufferings and privations.

Scarcely had the flying citizens found shelter in the woods when the haughty Araucanians were exulting over the smoking ruins of the deserted town.

The amount of booty that the savages bore back to their homes was great; for such was the precipitation of the fugitives that they took away only the most necessary articles, leaving all their treasures as spoils for the victors.

Imperial and Villa Rica having received the reinforcements which were sent by Villa Gran at the earliest opportunity, were enabled to withstand protracted sieges.

The year following orders were received from the Royal Audience at Lima to rebuild Concepcion.

Though convinced of the futility of the attempt, Villa Gran, unwilling to disobey his instructions, dispatched a body of troops and a number of colonists to re-establish the devoted city.

Lautaro, apprised of their design, immediately crossed the Bio-Bio. The Spanish soldiers, most of whom had but recently arrived from Peru, and little understood the character of the Chilian Indians, marched confidently out into the open field to await the attack. Again were they defeated, and fled to the fort in precipitation; but so closely were they pursued, that they were unable to close the gates upon the enemy, and the Araucanians entering, slew many of the Spaniards within their own intrenchments.

The terrified colonists rushed, some to their ships, and others to the neighboring woods, while the ill-fated city was a second time given up to the flames by the victorious Lautaro.

Emboldened by repeated success the young Araucanian hero now determined upon an enterprise more grand than any he had yet undertaken. Undismayed by the length of the march, and the difficulties to be overcome, with an army of only six hundred chosen men he set out for the north, intending to attack the city of Santiago itself—the great stronghold of the Spaniards in Chili.

He soon reached the Maulé, which was crossed without opposition. Here an opportunity was offered for Lautaro to conciliate the Purumancians, who terrified by his approach, and disheartened by the numerous defeats of the Spaniards whom they had hitherto deemed invincible, might easily have been induced to break their unnatural alliance, and make with the Araucanians a common cause against the common enemy. But the impetuous young chief, forgetful of all policy in his desire to be revenged upon these traitors to their race, mercilessly laid waste their territory, burned their houses and destroyed their crops, and subsequently fortified himself in their midst upon the banks of the Rio Claro.

The object of this latter step it is difficult to conceive. Had he pushed on, the city of Santiago might have fallen; but the delay was fatal.

The Spaniards, on learning the approach of the enemy, were astonished by his boldness. They could scarcely believe that an untutored barbarian had conceived a design of such magnitude. But the Governor, who was none other than that Villa Gran who suffered so terrible a defeat at the hands of the stripling Lautaro, on the hill of Marigueno, well knew the character of the foeman against whom he would have to contend, and without loss of time he set to work to guard every avenue of approach, to fortify the city, and enable it to withstand a protracted siege.

Day after day passed, yet the enemy did not make his appearance, and the Santiaguinos, emboldened by this delay, sent forward a company of horse to reconnoitre, which was attacked near the Araucanian camp, and driven back with much loss.

A second expedition met with no better fate, for, deceived by a pretended flight, the Spaniards allowed themselves to be drawn within the Indian intrenchments, where they were cut to pieces by their cunning foe, the horse only being enabled to escape by leaping the palisades.

A third army was dispatched, under command of

the Governor's son, who stationed his forces within a short distance of the enemy. Three times did he march to the attack, and as often was he driven back with serious loss, until despairing of victory, he broke up his camp and returned to Santiago.

It has been asserted that the cause of this precipitate retreat was the discovery of a design entertained by Lautaro, of turning the course of the river Mataquito in such a manner as to inundate the Spanish camp. But this story, probably, has no higher authority than Ercilla, who often deals in the marvelous. That the Spaniards may have heard some such rumor, and been influenced by it, is possible. That the Araucanian leader should have conceived such an idea is highly improbable; but the project itself, to one acquainted with the mechanical skill of the Indians, and the nature of the country, seems simply ridiculous.

Learning the ill success of his son, the Governor, though still suffering from the effects of illness, determined to conduct the war in person, for he longed to wipe out, by victory, the remembrance of his former disgraceful defeat.

Collecting a force of two hundred Spaniards and a thousand allies, he set out. Marching with great rapidity, yet with the utmost secrecy and caution, by unfrequented paths, he succeeded, under the guidance of an Indian spy, in approaching the Araucanian camp without detection. At early dawn the signal for the attack was sounded. The surprise was complete. The enemy, who had observed the most unceasing vigilance during the night, growing careless on the approach of day, had incautiously retired to rest. Lautaro, wearied by constant watching, was sleeping. At the first alarm, springing from his couch, he hastened to rally his followers for the fight. But it was too late; the assault had been as overwhelming as unexpected, and all was confusion. As he rushed forth to the foremost ranks, a dart from the hand of one of those very Purumancians whose fields he had so ruthlessly devastated, pierced his heart, and he fell expiring to the ground.

The Araucanians crowded around the lifeless body of their chief, fighting with all the reckless energy of despair.

In vain did Villa Gran again and again offer quarter, and entreat them to submit. His proffered mercy was met with scoffing and execrations. Scornfully did they refuse to survive the loss of their cherished leader. Though hemmed in upon all sides, with every avenue for escape closed, they obstinately courted death in whatsoever shape, and when wounded and exhausted threw themselves in impotent rage upon the leveled lances of the Spanish soldiery.

Of this whole devoted band of some six hundred heroic men, not one remained alive to bear back to his afflicted countrymen the sad tidings of Lautaro's fall.

Thus ended the career of one who stands unequaled in the annals of Indian wars. Though but nineteen years of age at the time of his death, he had displayed a military skill, and a fertility of resources not unworthy of an experienced general. Opposed by veteran leaders, and by the best soldiers of Europe, he achieved, in the short space of two years, a series of brilliant victories which threatened the Spanish settlements in Chili with annihilation, and gave an undying lustre to his country's name.

The very enemy vied with his friends in doing honor to his memory, and there were not wanting Spanish writers who, in their generous enthusiasm, held him up to the world as unsurpassed even by the noblest heroes of antiquity.

CHAPTER XIV.

Mendoza rebuilds Concepcion.—Cruelty to Prisoners.—Attempted Surprise of Imperial.—Death of Caupolican.—Progress of Hostilities.—Janaqueo.—Martin Loyola.—Destruction of the Cities of the Plain.—Conclusion.

In 1557 Don Garcia de Mendoza set sail from Peru, and reaching Concepcion in the month of April, disembarked his forces upon the island of Quiriquina, which lies at the mouth of Talcapuano Bay, the harbor of Concepcion.

Immediately he dispatched a messenger to the Araucanians, inviting them to send a deputation to his camp for the purpose of hearing proposals for the establishment of a permanent peace.

The crafty savages joyfully accepted his invitation, sending several of their shrewdest chiefs, to whom Mendoza displayed his entire armament, taking them through every part of his camp, hoping thereby to impress them with his power, and convince them of the folly of continuing the war. They minutely examined every thing, and listened attentively to the proposals of peace, but returned only to exhort their countrymen to increased exertions in preparation for the coming campaign. Their love of liberty was but inflamed by the knowledge of the formidable force to be brought against them, and they burned for an opportunity to revenge the death of their cherished Lautaro.

In August, Mendoza passed over to Penco, and erected a strong fort, preparatory to rebuilding the city of Concepcion.

Scarcely three days were allowed to pass before Caupolican crossed the Bio-Bio, determined for the third time to crush this ill-fated settlement. The fort was attacked with great fury: some of the Indians dragged up the steep hill branches and trunks of trees with which to fill the fosse; others leaped the ditch, and tried to scale the walls; many gained the very ramparts, and threw themselves among the garrison; but they were driven back, and their dead bodies, falling into the ditch beneath, soon formed a bridge for the transit of their companions. Caupolican himself several times gained the ramparts, and again leaped back among his followers, each time bearing as trophies the arms of some conquered foe.

The Spaniards possessed the advantage both of position and of weapons; but the Araucanians were so overpowering in number that the ultimate capture of the fort appeared inevitable.

Meantime the troops remaining aboard the ships and on the island having watched the combat for several hours, and seeing the danger that menaced their companions, manned the boats, and went to the rescue. Landing, they fell vigorously upon the rear of the Araucanians who, thus exposed between two heavy fires, were finally obliged to abandon the attack, and retreated with heavy loss.

The Spaniards, soon after this battle, received a considerable reinforcement from Peru; and Caupolican, despairing of ever being able to drive them from

Concepcion, retired from the frontier, immeasurably chagrined at the idea of having been twice defeated where his young lieutenant had been as often victorious.

The Araucanians were, in turn, now called upon to stand on the defensive; for Mendoza, crossing the Bio-Bio with an army larger than any that had yet been brought into the field by the Spaniards, carried the war into the heart of the Indian territory. Actuated by a mistaken policy he laid waste the country, destroying every thing that came within his reach, and mutilated the prisoners that fell into his hands, hoping, by means of intimidation, to break the spirit of a people whom arms could not subdue; but, as might have been expected, the effect of such acts of barbarity upon a free and haughty race was only to increase the bitter hatred they already felt for their cruel enemies, and nerve them to greater exertions. The mutilated victims who, deprived of their noses and ears, with their tongues cut out, or with their hands lopped off, had been sent back to strike terror into the breasts of their countrymen, went from house to house in every direction, by the sight of their maimed limbs and disfigured countenances inflaming the minds of the people against the brutal invaders, who could use such fiendish cruelty toward helpless captives, whose only crime had been that of loving their country and their liberties too well.

The Spaniards were continually harassed upon their march, and many sanguinary battles occurred, but the vast superiority of the European armament more than compensated for disparity of numbers; and keeping on toward Tucupel, Mendoza founded, upon the scene of Valdivia's defeat, a city which he called Cañete—from his own title, he being the Marquis of Cañete. He then marched to Imperial, which place still successfully maintained itself against the Araucanians.

Caupolican failing in an endeavor to take the town of Imperial by assault, sought to capture it by stratagem. For the accomplishment of this end, a shrewd officer, by the name of Pran, was selected, who, in the disguise of a Purumancian, easily obtained admission to the town, and became acquainted with many of the captives and allies about the camp.

By conversing with all he discovered the feeling of each toward the Spaniards, and was not long in fixing upon one—Andressillo by name—who apparently entertained sentiments of the bitterest hostility toward his imperious masters, and seemed well fitted to aid in any attempt for their overthrow. To him Pran cautiously divulged his real character, and the nature of his designs.

The cunning Andressillo pretended to enter warmly into the plans suggested, promising a hearty co-operation, and advised that, in order to insure success, the Araucanians should hold themselves in readiness to surprise the place on the morrow at noon-day—at which time, he said, the Spaniards were accustomed to retire for the *siesta*, leaving the gates closed but unguarded.

The two conspirators parted joyfully: the one to communicate his success to Caupolican; the other to reveal to Mendoza every thing that had transpired. Both parties took measures accordingly.

The Araucanians marching toward the town with the greatest secrecy, concealed themselves in the neighboring thickets, impatiently awaiting the arrival of noon. At the time agreed upon they neared the walls. All was still; no sentinel appeared upon the ramparts, and the gates were closed. Presently Andressillo opened the gates, and beckoned them to come on. They advanced in breathless silence, and with noiseless tread entered the town.

The Spaniards lay scattered around, apparently in deep slumber; but no sooner were a certain number of the Indians within, than the gates were closed behind them, and a murderous fire of musketry commenced from hidden foes in every direction, while the soldiers springing up, charged furiously upon the entrapped and bewildered savages. At the same time the cannons poured volleys upon those without the walls, and the cavalry charging out from a side gate, completed the discomfiture of the whole army.

Of those who had been decoyed within the walls not one escaped, and the few that were taken alive were treated with the most inhuman barbarity; some were even tied to the cannon's mouth, and blown into the air; the heads of many were severed from their bodies, and placed upon poles planted around the ramparts.

Fortunately the Araucanian general and his officers of higher rank, deeming a victory to be obtained by stratagem unworthy of warriors, did not accompany the army, and thus escaped destruction.

Caupolican, unsubdued by repeated misfortunes, fled from place to place, striving by every means to rally his countrymen; but he was taken, not long after, by treachery, and delivered into the hands of Don Alonzo Reynoso, governor of Cañete.

If we may believe the romantic account of Ercilla, the wife of the unfortunate chieftain, on learning his capture, hastened to upbraid him with cowardice in allowing himself to be taken alive; and scornfully threw to him her infant child, exclaiming:

———"No quiero titulo de madre
Del hijo infame, del infame padre!"

("I do not wish to be called the mother of the infamous son of an infamous father.")

With a refinement of barbarity, this noble warrior was doomed to death by the horrible punishment of impalement—an inhuman sentence, that was enforced upon the vanquished hero after he had been duly instructed, converted, and baptized in the religion of his executioners.

He heard the announcement of his fate with composure, and marched with a firm step to the place of execution; but, on mounting the scaffold and beholding the horrid instrument of torture and the hideous negro who approached to enforce the decree of death, he, for the first time, comprehended the nature of the indignity he was about to suffer. With one kick of his manacled foot he sent the black monster reeling to the ground, and, turning upon the assembled multitude, he bitterly complained of the inhumanity of the punishment, demanding, as a warrior and in the name of justice, that some worthier instrument, some nobler hand might be found to terminate his existence; but, overpowered by numbers, he was forced upon the stake. Not an exclamation of agony escaped his lips; not a muscle of his frame quivered; and he bore the agonies of torture with unflinching fortitude, until a flight of friendly arrows pierced his bosom and he expired.

Caupolican was succeeded in the Toquiship by his own son, who, with various success, prosecuted the war—greatly harassing the Spaniards—until, in the year following (1559), he met with an overwhelming defeat at the hands of Mendoza. Fearing to suffer his father's fate if taken, he slew himself when on the point of being captured.

In this battle the overthrow of the Araucanians was so complete that Mendoza, deeming it decisive, immediately commenced rebuilding the various towns and forts that had been destroyed by the Indians—especially Arauco, Tucapel, and Villa Rica.

The Council of the nation, convening after the death of Caupolican the younger, elected Antihueno—a man renowned for courage and determination—to take command of the army.

The new Toqui was unremitting in his exertions to collect an army. Gathering the scattered bands of his countrymen, he practiced them, by continually skirmishing with the enemy, until feeling himself able to make a decided stand, he encamped on the hill of Marigueno, which, aside from the impregnable nature of its position, abounded with associations that served to arouse the enthusiasm of the Araucanian warriors. Here he was attacked by a son of the very Villa Gran who, on this same spot, had been defeated by Lautaro.

The son was more unfortunate than even the father had been: his army was almost annihilated, and he himself perished in the midst of the battle.

Flushed with this victory, Antihueno advanced upon Concepcion; but finding the town too strongly garrisoned to be attacked, and capable of withstanding a protracted siege, he returned across the Bio-Bio, and advanced upon Cañete, which was deserted by the Spaniards on his approach.

Having burned Cañete he proceeded to invest Arauco, which place, after a protracted siege, was also abandoned by the garrison.

Antihueno afterward led an army to the attack of Nacimiento, in 1564; but he was slain in the battle, which ended in a terrible massacre of his army.

The death of Antihueno was followed by thirty years of uninterrupted war, in which only two considerable battles were fought—both of which took place upon the famous hill of Marigueno. In the former the Araucanians, as before, triumphed; but in the latter the Spaniards, under Alonzo Sotomayor, gained a complete victory.

This period was also signalized by the exploits of the Araucanian heroine Janaqueo, the wife of a chief who was defeated and slain by the Spaniards.

Learning the death of her husband, she put herself at the head of a band of Puelches and hung round the camp, and along the route of her enemies—harassing them continually, and even defeating some of their most experienced leaders. Frequenting the most inaccessible fastnesses of mountain and forest, and moving from place to place with rapidity, she was always at hand to take any advantage which occasion might offer for sudden attack, yet never to be encountered when sought.

This Amazon was finally conquered, not by the valor of her foes, but by the power of love—laying down her arms to save a brother, who, captive among the Spaniards and under sentence of death, was promised both life and liberty on condition of persuading his sister to abandon her unnatural profession and retire to her home.

In the year 1594 Martin Loyola, a nephew of the celebrated St. Ignatius, founder of the order of Jesuits, was appointed Governor of Concepcion. One of his first official acts was an attempt to establish friendly relations with the Araucanians.

Though really desirous of ending the war in which they had been so long engaged, these unconquerable freemen insisted upon the abandonment by the Spaniards of all posts south of the Bio-Bio, as the first step toward the establishment of peace; but to such terms the Governor would not listen, and hostilities were renewed.

Loyola, like most of his predecessors, was actuated by the ambition of founding cities, and accordingly marched into the Araucanian territory, and established a colony at a place which he named "Coya," in honor of his wife, a Peruvian princess of the Inca blood.

The Toqui Paillamachu for a long time strove to reduce this settlement, as well as that of Puren and several others; but he could accomplish little against the cautious Loyola, who carefully fortified all the Spanish posts, and for four years baffled every attack.

Yet the Araucanian chief did not despair; he was ever on the alert, watching for some favorable moment to strike a decisive blow: that moment at length arrived. On the 22d of November, 1598, the Spanish governor, who was returning from the Indian country, having reached a position where he thought no further danger was to be apprehended, encamped for the night without observing the usual precautions against surprise. But Paillamachu had been secretly following his march, and no sooner were the Spaniards wrapt in sleep than the Indians fell suddenly upon them. Loyola and his whole retinue perished.

This bold stroke must have been long meditated, and its effect calculated; for no sooner had the Spanish general been slain, than a huge bonfire was kindled upon the nearest hill: from hill-top to hill-top answering flames shot high in air; lofty summits upon the far horizon soon blazed responsively; and from province to province the fiery telegraph ran along the mountain ranges—its ruddy glare every where calling the expectant people to arms. Every Spaniard found without the walls of the towns was massacred, and within forty-eight hours Osorno and Villa Rica, Valdivia and Imperial, Cañete, Angol, Coya, and Arauco were all closely invested by bands of exulting savages.

Without delay Paillamachu marched upon Concepcion, which he easily captured and burned. Chillan suffered the same fate; and laying waste the surrounding country, he returned, laden with an immense booty, to lay siege to the yet remaining Spanish towns.

When the news of the death of Loyola and of the destruction of the frontier towns reached Santiago,

Pedro Viscara, a veteran soldier, took up his march with a strong force, and passing the Bio-Bio relieved both Coya and Angol, whose inhabitants were drawn off in safety, and settled in Chillan and Concepcion, both of which were rebuilt. But all efforts to succor the other towns were unavailing: one by one, after sieges of various duration, they were taken and destroyed. The inhabitants were spared; the men were reserved as slaves, and the women became the concubines of their captors.

In 1602, about three years from the first insurrection, of the numerous Spanish forts and settlements south of the Bio-Bio, Nacimiento and Arauco only had not fallen. Valdivia and Osorno were afterward rebuilt. About the same time a fort was erected at Boroa. This fort was soon after abandoned. Valdivia, Osorno, Nacimiento, and Arauco still remain. But of all the "cities of the plain" lying within the boundaries of the haughty Araucanians, not one ever arose from its ashes; their names exist only in history; and the sites where they once flourished are now marked by ill-defined and grass-grown ruins.

From the period of their fall dates the independence of the Araucanian nation; for though a hundred years more were wasted in the vain attempt to reconquer the heroic people who had thus thrown off the galling yoke of oppression, the Spaniards, weary of constant war, and disheartened by the loss of so much blood and treasure, were finally compelled to sue for peace; and in 1724 a treaty was ratified, acknowledging their freedom, and establishing the limits of their territory.

CHAPTER XV.

Plans for the Journey.—Delay at Budeo.—Our Stock in Trade.—Close Quarters.—Indian Graves.—Burial Feasts.—Funeral Rites.—"Alhué Mapu," the "Land of the Dead."—State of the Soul after Death.

DURING the few days that we remained at Budeo (at which place, the reader will remember, our narrative was dropped), Sanchez and myself had many discussions as to the proper course to be pursued on our intended journey.

I wished to proceed without concealment, and inform the Indians of the true object of my visit, telling them that I had come among them actuated by the desire of becoming acquainted with the manners and customs of a people who had so successfully defended their liberties against the power of Spain, extorting praise from their enemies, and making the name of "Araucano" renowned in the history of heroic deeds. Such a course seemed to me the best calculated to win their confidence and good-will, to say nothing of the doubtful morality of an attempt to deceive them. But Sanchez was of another way of thinking. My ideas, he said, though no doubt very fine, would be far above the comprehension of the Indians, who would view me with suspicion, and probably nip all my fancies in the bud by turning me out of the country on the first intimation of a desire to pry into their mode of life.

As to the impropriety of deceiving them, that he could not see; for being habitual liars themselves, he thought it but fair to fight them with their own weapons.

I was loth to give up the old-fashioned idea that honesty is the best policy; but the "Capitan" cared little for abstract principles; he had spent the greater part of his life among the Indians, knew them by heart, had always been accustomed to make them believe whatever he pleased, and could guarantee the success of his own plans; but mine he would not father. Under the circumstances it was necessary to give him a *carte blanche*, with the understanding that he should do all the lying, and shoulder the responsibility, to which he readily agreed. His plan was the following:

We were to form a trading expedition; but he, instead of myself, was to be the "patron;" for he had determined not to carry me in that capacity, on reflection that "caballeros" never go on such trips themselves, but always make use of interpreters and half-breeds to buy cattle and transact their business for them. For me he had hit upon something better.

During the war of the Chilian independence, among other royalists who sought protection in the midst of the Indians, and with them fought against the republicans, was a subordinate named Vega. While thus engaged he had lived in the family of Mañin (who is now the most influential of the Araucanian chiefs); but the war coming to an end, he returned to Concepcion, where he married and settled down.

More than thirty years had elapsed since then; but the mind of the Indian still reverted with pleasure to his friendship with the Spaniard, and he frequently questioned Sanchez about Vega, expressing a great desire to see him or some of his children.

The old chief's wishes were at last to be gratified, for Sanchez had determined to present me as one of the sons, under the sounding title of Don Eduardo de la Vega; assuring him that I had come expressly to make him a visit in my father's name.

Having secured the good wishes of Mañin, no one would dare to question further, and there would probably be no difficulty in obtaining permission for me to go wherever I chose.

In order to quiet any suspicion that might arise from my language or appearance, that I was other than a Chileno, it was to be represented that my father had sent me, when a child, to Europe for my education, and that I had but lately returned to Chili.

Having agreed upon all the details, and studied the part assigned me, it next became necessary to arrange all my traps in small packages convenient for use, cutting the handkerchiefs, etc., intended for presents, so as to have every thing easily attainable. The stock which I had laid in at Concepcion and Los Angelos consisted of the following articles:

Some six yards of red flannel cloth.

As many more of blue flannel.

Six dozen cotton handkerchiefs of all colors and sizes.

One gross of brass thimbles.

Two dozen harmonicons.

Three dozen German Jew's harps.

One dozen sleigh bells.

Five pounds of glass beads, assorted colors,

And two pounds of indigo, besides an old pair of epaulets intended to adorn the shoulders of the great Mañin.

Sanchez had his stock, which, being intended for trade, was composed of more valuable articles, such as silver spurs and belts. He also carried a good deal of money in silver dollars, halves, and quarters, and as I did not wish to be troubled with the care of it, I also lent him my purse for the journey.

When all was in readiness for a start, we were delayed by bad weather, which continued for several days, and for a great part of the time we were confined to the house. As the cooking had to be done within doors, what with the smoke, crowd, and damp, we were far from comfortable. During the day this could be endured, but at night it became insufferable.

The house, if such it might be called, was a mere basket, letting in rain in every direction, and measuring scarcely twelve feet by ten. It contained three rude bedsteads, for the accommodation of two married couples and a pair of grown up girls, while upon the ground were huddled some sixteen young men and children, packed away on bull hides like herrings in a box. In the midst of this motley throng I lay in state, with a whole hide to myself.

As long as we were awake the dogs were not allowed to enter the door; but the moment we closed our eyes the whole dripping pack came sneaking in.

Soon I was roused by a weight upon my feet, and found a lean and hungry animal lying across my legs, while another was snugly stowed away at my side. A few kicks drove them away, but they soon returned. A little pommeling brought a temporary relief, but only to be followed by more determined encroachments, until I was obliged to rise and grope round for a stick, which, once found, I laid about me lustily.

There was a tremendous yelping and howling of the fugitives, and many muttered imprecations of sleepers, disturbed by the operation; and laying the stick under my pillow, *i. e.*, saddle, I went to sleep. But in the morning I found that the dirty curs had monopolized my blanket entirely, while the vivid sense of something crawling round me, was satisfactory proof that fleas prefer a dry man to a wet dog: a preference which certainly does no discredit to their taste.

Not far from Sanchez's house we saw an Indian burial-place, but we did not visit it; for the Mapuchés, unlike the North American tribes, avoid the resting-places of their dead, always passing them in silence, and with averted faces, and dislike to see strangers, especially whites, approach them. As there were many Indians scattered about in the neighborhood, we did not wish to excite their suspicions.

There were said to be many buried here, but no monuments, or other indications of graves were to be seen, except in one instance over the resting-place of a celebrated chief named Cari-Coyam (The Green

INDIAN GRAVE.

Oak). At both the head and the foot of this grave was an upright, forked stick, supporting a transverse pole, over which was hung the skin of the chieftain's favorite horse, while a long bamboo lance, planted in the ground, with a little white pennant fluttering in the wind, denoted the rank of the deceased.

The steel head of the lance, we noticed, had been replaced by a nicely whittled wooden barb, quite as useful, no doubt, as any other in the spirit-land. On the same principle, though the ordinary arms and horse trappings are buried with the dead, in case of articles of value, such as silver spurs, bits, and head-stalls, wooden proxies are substituted. He would probably get even a wooden horse to ride, were it not for the predilection for horse-flesh of his bereaved relatives, who, though they kill the horse, always eat the flesh, and allow the spirit to content himself with the skin and soul.

It is, however, only on the demise of important chiefs, or men of wealth, that the friends are treated to a feast, for the ghosts of the commoner sort are not supposed to ride; on ordinary occasions, therefore, the funeral rites are few and simple.

The corpse is exposed on an open bier for several days, during which time the friends and neighbors assemble to condole with the bereaved family. It is then borne to the grave by the principal relatives, preceded by a company of young men, who ride forward at full speed, as though to prepare the way for the deceased. In the rear follow the women wailing, rending the air with their cries, and making every demonstration of the profoundest grief, while another walks behind the procession scattering ashes along the way, to prevent the departed from returning to his former abode.

The body is placed in the grave in a sitting posture, with the face turned toward the West, the direction of the spirit-land. The saddle and arms of the dead are placed by his side; some provisions are added for the journey, together with a few beads, or a small sum of money, necessary to pay the Mapuché Charon. The friends then wish the deceased a pleasant voyage, bid him good-by, cover up the grave, and retire.

In the case of a woman the ceremonies are the same, with the exception that instead of a saddle and arms, a distaff, or some culinary utensils, are placed in the grave.

It has been asserted, that when a distinguished chief dies, one of his wives is killed and interred with him; but Sanchez assured me that no such custom exists, though possibly some few cases of the kind may have happened.

The Indians can not tell the exact whereabouts of their Styx, though they generally suppose it is the ocean. Nor can they give the location of their Elysium, which they call "Alhué-Mapu" (The Land of Spirits). "How can we tell," they say, "when we have never been there?" Much less do they know of the occupations of the soul after death. In fact, it is a subject about which they seldom bother their brains, for though they have some ill-defined notions that there is another life after this, a change of place, perhaps, rather than of state, when questioned, they seldom fail to answer, "*Chum péchy nai?*" (Who knows?) with the same air of perfect blankness which accompanies the Chileno's "*Quien sabe!*"

I could not learn that they believe in any reward or punishment after death for the actions of this world, though they attribute much of the good or evil fortune of life to the pleasure or wrath of the Great Spirit. Some few there are that have a confused notion of heaven and of hell, but such ideas have undoubtedly been acquired by occasional intercourse with Christian missionaries.

According to Molina, the Mapuchés believe the dead to watch over and protect the living, and join them in battle against the enemies of their country; when the thunder cloud lowers over the distant Cordilleras, they imagine their departed warriors to be riding upon the storm, chasing away some invisible foe, and frequently they encourage the aerial combatants by exclaiming, "Well done! well done! good friends!"

CHAPTER XVI.

Leave Budeo.—Pincheira and his Followers.—The Silversmith.—The Missionary.—Antichéo.—Mapuché Eloquence.—Dignity and Wives.—Our Supper.—Calbucoi.—Trading.—Levying Tribute.

LEAVING Budeo we journeyed in a southeasterly direction, striking off into the heart of the Araucanian territory.

Rising from the narrow valley through which runs the Budeo river, we came upon rolling ground. Though still in the great central plain of Chili, the surface of the country is here undulating, and in other respects also it is much more beautiful than the unvarying dead level to the northward. The rains, which at the south are heavy and frequent, give to every thing a freshness and verdure, and collecting in small streams, wear for themselves channels which give a pleasing diversity to the otherwise monotonous landscape. Upon the summits of the higher hills, and in all the moist nooks, grow fine old oaks, and other stately trees, which become more numerous as you advance.

Our party numbered four, there being, besides Sanchez and myself, two "mozas," one of whom, my squire, José by name, was a tall, athletic dare-devil, rather fond of a vagabond life, but too lazy to be adventurous: the other was short, well-knit, and active, always on the alert, and for his spirit a great favorite with all who knew him. He was an adopted member of Sanchez's family, and rejoiced in the name of Juan de Dios (John of God), though commonly known by the familiar and somewhat equivocal sobriquet of "Guacho" (a foundling, or child of doubtful origin).

Sanchez, or, as he was generally called, Don Panta (the Indian contraction for Pantaleon, his Christian name), improved on acquaintance. He was a large, well-formed man, between forty-five and fifty years of age, with a fine eye, Roman nose, heavy chin, and a missive head covered with curling black hair sprinkled with gray. Though without much education, except such as he had been able to pick up, he was intelligent, inquiring, and communicative—proud, though without reserve, and highly imbued with a certain kind of honor, which the nature of his former life had rather tended to foster than to destroy, for in his younger days he had been, if not a freebooter, the next thing to it.

His father, at the breaking out of the Chilian revolution, held a commission in the royal army, and when the cause of the crown became desperate, with many others fled across the mountains and joined Pincheira, a Spaniard who had collected a band of royalists and Indians for the purpose of harassing the republicans, in hopes that the revolution might finally be quelled.

The original object of Pincheira and his followers was honorable, and their conduct, during the continuance of the war, to a certain extent justifiable; but he was weak-minded, and unable to control the lawless men who flocked around his standard. On the declaration of peace, fearing treachery, or perhaps hoping that, by protracting the struggle, the royal cause might be revived, he refused to lay down his arms, and was declared an outlaw.

His camp immediately became the rendezvous of all the desperate characters who, on the establishment of order, were obliged to fly from the punishment due for crimes committed during the troubled times of war. These desperadoes, acknowledging no authority, and obeying no law except their own unbridled passions, were for many years the scourge of the Chilian frontier. Without the hope of quarter, they gave none: like the Ishmaelites, their hand was against every man and every man's hand against them; like the winds they moved about, with their flying tents, homeless and untraceable.

Sweeping through the gorges of the Cordilleras, in the silence of the night they would pour down upon defenseless hamlets, sparing neither age nor sex, unless to carry off some tender child to slavery, in hope of future ransom, or to consign some helpless female to a fate more horrible than slavery or death. Before the tardy troops could be gathered to repel their attack, laden with spoil, they would regain the fastnesses of the mountains or the trackless expanse of the pampas.

So great was the terror inspired by these sudden incursions among the people living near the mountain passes, that to the present day, though every trace of the formidable band has disappeared, many a Chilian mother hushes her crying babe with the dreaded name of Pincheira!

The father of Pantaleon, while serving under Pincheira, learned the language of the Indians, and gained such an unbounded power over them, that he became generally known upon the frontiers as "El Rey Sanchez" (King Sanchez). He was finally captured, and summarily put to death by Coronel Godoi. Many others were taken and executed upon the spot; and not long after the band was entirely broken up, principally through the influence of Pantaleon Sanchez, who succeeded in obtaining favorable terms for most of those implicated. He himself, in consideration for this service, was taken into the employment of the government as interpreter. Having spent fifteen years of his youth among the Indians, and been in constant communication with them ever since, he spoke their language as fluently as his own, and was in every way conversant with their manners and customs.

The pastures along our road were black and charred, having been recently burnt over, in large tracts, by the Indians, in order to produce a fresh growth of herbage on the fields dried up by the summer heats. Owing to the late rain the new grass was sprouting vigorously, and the ground was gayly sprinkled with little tulip-shaped flowers of a blood-red hue; we also saw great quantities of a coarse prickly plant, which is regarded as excellent fodder for horned cattle.

In passing a little trickling rill, I noticed a bed, some six inches thick, of scoriaceous lava, much resembling the recent deposits at Antuco. Near the same spot was also a small hillock, composed apparently of the same material: in each case the overlying covering of soil was but a few inches thick. Further to the south we subsequently noticed similar strata in passing many of the small brooks. As there were no volcanic vents nearer than the main chain of the Andes, these deposits struck me as being interesting. They are probably very common, but it is only where the soil has been washed away by action of the streams that they are exposed to view.

Near a small stream called Chumalco, we stopped at the house of a silversmith—a rude tinker, who manufactured spurs and other articles for the Indians and traders. His workshop was a small shanty, and all his tools were of the rudest description. His wares, though rough and uncouth, boasted a sort of barbaric magnificence, and were suited to the taste of his customers; for the Indians not only are suspicious of all bright and polished work, but they also have their own ideas of fashion, which occasionally varies; and in buying a pair of spurs, they are as fastidious about the *mode* as any French belle in the purchase of a bonnet. At the same time they have a supreme contempt for any thing that is not what it pretends to be, and the poorest "hueñi," with an iron spur on his heel, or with none at all, would not accept a plated or German silver pair; he would feel himself insulted by the offer.

Besides bits, spurs, stirrups, head-stalls, and saddle ornaments of silver, the Indians use a great many

INDIAN SPUR.

ear-rings, breast-pins, and other trinkets of the same metal: indeed, it is the only metal which they use for ornamental purposes. Gold is never seen in their possession. There exists a common opinion that they make no use of gold, because they regard it as the cause of all their wars with the Spaniards, and wish to conceal its existence in their country; but Sanchez thought the reasons which influence them to be very different, namely, the difficulty of procuring it in any part of their territory without great labor, and their inability either to work it into the desired forms or test its purity. If manufactured abroad, they would be unwilling to purchase it; for they will not buy articles of silver even, unless made by some Indian smith, or by one who lives in their midst.

The amount of silver consumed in the manufacture of trinkets for the Indian trade is large; and as it is drawn entirely from the currency of the country, there results a great scarcity of small coin in all the frontier provinces. If we suppose two or three thousand people to be engaged in trading with the Indians, and estimate that each trader disposes annually of twenty or thirty dollars, it will be readily seen that the abstraction of such an amount in hard dollars, halves, and quarters from districts neither populous nor rich, is calculated to produce considerable inconvenience.

A league farther on, we came to another brook called Malven, near which live a number of scattered "Christianos" (*i.e.* Chilenos). Here, also, there resided at the time an aged Dominican friar, who for several years had been attempting to convert the Indians. Though much reverenced, as priests always are, for his sacred character, and respected as a benefactor—for by some knowledge of medicine, he had made himself extremely useful—he probably could not boast a single convert, and was even regarded with suspicion.

In vain he had endeavored to gain permission for the introduction of a mission, and the establishment of a convent of his brethren. The answer he received from the Indians was characteristic, and proved that former experience had not been entirely forgotten:

"Father," they said, "whenever you wish to come among us, you shall be welcome to food and shelter; but if your brothers come, they will need land upon which to build a house; they must eat, and we shall be obliged to give them cattle; they will then need more land for their cattle; other Christians will come to live with your brethren; they, too, will need houses, cattle, and lands; thus you will become rich, and we shall become poor, and be driven out!"

Beyond Malven the Indians became more numerous, and we met many upon the road. They expressed considerable surprise at my appearance; but they were all acquainted with "Panta," as they called Sanchez, and readily credited the account he gave of me. There was but one exception, a boy about twelve or thirteen years old, who had lived among the Chilenos sufficiently to learn something of their language and customs; he insisted, from the fact of my wearing a broad-brimmed felt hat, that I must be a friar in disguise, and made a number of remarks about the "pichi patíru" (little priest), that caused a great deal of merriment. This boy had just captured, in a neighboring stream, a "buillin," a species of castor, from which he was about stripping the skin, which he readily bartered for a Jew's-harp, and promised to have dried and dressed for me on our return.

On the road we met a party of squaws, the first whom I had fairly seen. Their long hair was dripping, for they had just been enjoying a bath; and over their backs, slung by a band passing over the forehead, they bore large earthenware jars filled with cool water, and covered with branches of fragrant mint. Most of them led little round-bellied children by the hand, and one or two had papooses strung over their backs. They were decked out in all their finery, with a profusion of silver ornaments and beads of all colors, and really presented a picturesque appearance, though little could be said of their beauty.

The Indians (especially the women) residing near rivers are much addicted to bathing—a redeeming feature in their otherwise filthy habits.

In the evening we stopped at the house of an old chief named Antichéo (The Albatross of the Sun). Drawing up at a respectful distance before the cross bar, which is set up in front of every house as a barrier, we waited for several minutes until the chief came out and saluted us, one after the other. He then invited us to dismount, but we declined, and after a short conversation made our way to a neighboring clump of apple-trees, under whose branches we proposed spending the night, in preference to exposing ourselves to the vermin in the house.

No sooner had we encamped than we were besieged by a crowd of men and boys, drawn together by curiosity, and possibly by the hope of some present or the chance of pilfering. They were mostly dressed in the "chiripa," a garment not unlike the poncho in shape, which is wound round the person from the breast to the feet, and is confined at the waist by a belt. Some wore ponchos also, and a few had on shirts, generally the worse for wear and dirt. One brawny fellow, though shirtless, had got himself into a very small vest, while he sported an old, greasy cap, adorned with a tarnished silver band, in lieu of the cotton hankerchief, or more national red or blue fillet, which is generally worn to confine the hair.

They exhibited none of that moroseness and stoical indifference which we are apt to attribute to all Indians; but, on the contrary, they were lively, talkative, and inquisitive in the extreme. They left nothing unexamined, scrutinizing closely even my hat, pantaloons, and boots, which they felt, handled, and pulled about, with exclamations of surprise accompanied by laughter and jokes.

Soon the old chief joined the party and entered into conversation. He had much to ask in regard to the feelings and intentions of the government toward the Indians, and he seemed to have many misgivings about the proposed visit of President Montt to the southern provinces· he was fearful that it boded no good, and was apparently much relieved by the explanations which Sanchez gave. The amount of deference shown him did not seem to be great; and I was rather surprised by the apparent want of respect for superiors observable, especially among the boys, who were under no restraint, joining in the conversation, and expressing their opinions in a manner which would have done credit to that precocious youth "Young America" himself.

During our talk a courier was announced as coming from Mañin, in regard to some robberies that had lately taken place.

The messenger, without leaving the saddle, delivered his errand in a monotonous sing-song tone, accompanied by occasional grunts and the frequent repetition of such words as, "piu," "pi," "pioe" ("I say," "said I," "said he"): he was listened to by the chief, standing, while all the rest observed a respectful silence. The answer was returned in the same monotonous manner, without any gesticulations or inflections of the voice—very much as school-boys repeat lessons which they have learned by rote.

But though the speakers appeared to me to go through their parts in a very humdrum style, Sanchez said that they both had the reputation of being orators, and were much admired for the purity of their diction.

The Mapuchés have their own ideas of eloquence, which is much cultivated as the surest road to distinction; for any young man, whatever his rank, if possessing fluency of speech and a retentive memory, may aspire to a high position. The chiefs always select, as their immediate attendants and messengers, those youths who are capable not only of clearly expressing their own views, but of reporting exactly the words of others, which is highly important in the transmission of oral communications. These messengers, by associating with the chief men and speaking in the national assemblies, gain great influence, and often supersede those who by birth are their superiors.

There have not been wanting Spanish writers who have highly eulogized the eloquence of the Araucanians; but, tried by classical models, they do not deserve the exaggerated praise they have received, and fall far short of our North American Indians both in the matter and delivery of their speeches. Could the truth be known, we should probably discover that both the Araucanians and the Mohawks owe much of their oratorical fame to a certain tendency to "highfalluting," which all interpreters seem to have.

A timely hint that we had not yet dined, was responded to by our host, who ordered a sheep to be killed for our use. The animal was tied up by the hind legs to a bough, and his throat was cut; a woman stood by with a wooden bowl to catch the blood, into which she threw a handful of salt to hasten coagulation; another brought a basket, in which she received the entrails and carried them off to the house—for both the blood and the entrails are eaten by these people, the former raw or stewed, the latter made up into tripe. The skin was stripped off, the sheep divided along the spine from tail to head, and one-half, spitted upon a sharp stick, was soon roasting over the blazing fire.

The chief then rose, bidding us good night—an example that was followed by the rest, with the exception of a few loafers who hung round in expectation of sharing our meal.

The green sod was our only table-cloth, and circling round the steaming meat, we hacked it to pieces with our jack-knives, handing a rib to each of the hangers-on, who sat by in silence expecting their portion.

To our feast was added a jug of something called "mudai"—a kind of fermented liquor, rather muddy but not unpleasant to the taste. As I was lifting it to my lips Sanchez cried out, jestingly,

"Take care, Señor! you know not what you are drinking!"

But contenting myself with the thought, that "where ignorance is bliss 'tis folly to be wise," I took a long pull at the jug and passed it on. Had I seen, as I afterward did, the process of manufacturing this beverage, it probably would never have reached my lips, much less my stomach.

So soon as our visitors withdrew—which they did when nothing remained to eat—we made our beds of saddles and ponchos, under the apple-trees, and retired, after stowing away every thing as securely as possible; "for," said our guide, "these fellows will steal the tongue out of your head if you sleep with your mouth open!"

Early in the morning we were favored with more visitors. Among others came an old man who spoke Spanish tolerably well. He said that he had known my father Vega, and had a great many questions to ask about him, some of which it puzzled me no little to answer, as I had never seen the old gentleman whose name I bore. He then inquired about the President, his character, and designs in regard to the Indians. Being tolerably well satisfied on these points, he went on to ask if His Excellency was powerful and wealthy; and, as a still further test of importance, wished to know the number of his wives.

"He has but one," I answered.

"Hué!" cried the astonished savage, "only one?" holding up a single finger, that there might be no mistake.

"Yes; only one."

"He must be very poor, is he not?"

"Why so?" I asked.

"Because even I, who am poor, have two; many of our 'ghelmenes' (gentlemen) have five; and the President, who is a great 'cazique' (chief), ought to have at least ten;" and he counted on his fingers "Quiñé, epu, quéchu, mari" (1, 2, 5, 10), as if to determine more fully the relative degrees of importance.

It seemed that he could hardly reconcile himself to the idea that he was not doubly as important a personage as the President.

The explanation that Christians have but one wife apiece did not satisfy him. He could see no harm in having more; for his people had always lived happily with their numerous wives, and he argued that such would not be the case if the practice were sinful and displeasing to the Great Spirit. When I recalled the polygamic tendencies of the wise men of old, I could not but think that my friend argued well, "according to his light."

This has ever been the great stumbling-block with the missionaries (who may be said to have accomplished nothing with the Mapuchés), for they have always commenced by an onslaught upon the national polygamy—the most deeply rooted and cherished of their social evils. Such a course is honest, but its policy may be questioned; for were they to leave this reform as the last, instead of endeavoring to make it the first, and not attack the stronghold until they have acquired sufficient influence to destroy minor evils in detail, much more might be accomplished in the end; for such an institution can only be gradually abolished.

After a hearty breakfast we rode up to the chief's house, made some presents of indigo and beads to his wives, distributed a few handkerchiefs and Jew's-harps among his children, and taking a formal leave, departed, accompanied by one of his nephews, a rather handsome and intelligent young man, who, from motives of friendship for "Panta," agreed to make one of our party.

Crossing the Rénayco, a small stream, we called at the house of Calbucoi, one of the most powerful chiefs in this neighborhood, but he was not at home. Passing on, we met him in the fields trading with some half breeds. He was a corpulent, thick-set old gentleman, with a big head and a pleasant, good-natured face. His nephew, one Railému, accompanied him—an unprepossessing young man whom we did not wish to meet, since his knowledge of Spanish, which he spoke fluently, might have enabled him to detect that I was a foreigner.

The whole party were collected round a poncho spread upon the ground, on which piles of dollars and silver spurs were glistening as a tempting lure for the owner of many herds. But the old chief was wary and incredulous. Carefully he tried each article, smelled of it, tasted it, rung it, to test the purity of the metal; and lastly, pulling out from his girdle a balance, with a beam some six inches long of bamboo, and scales of leather, he proceeded to weigh each one separately, using some silver dollars which he carried about his person as standards. The nephew was no less cautious, and both seemed well posted up in the tricks of the trade.

Sanchez did not wish to purchase any cattle here, and rejoiced that the "powers that be" were so much engrossed with the important matter of buying a pair of spurs as to take no notice of our movements. We gave the potent Calbucoi a flaming red cotton handkerchief, glorious with yellow flowers, as a kind of tribute for the privilege of traveling through his dominions, and hurried on.

TRADING WITH THE INDIANS.

This system of levying tribute is universal among the petty chiefs, but fortunately their demands are so very moderate as to make the principle hardly worth quarreling about. An English gentleman of my acquaintance, long resident in Chili, related an amusing adventure growing out of this custom.

While traveling he had occasion to pass through the district of a native chief, and was surprised at being stopped on the road with a demand for tribute. Falling back upon his rights as an Englishman, he refused compliance with so unjust a demand, declaring that being merely a traveler, not a trader, such a molestation was contrary to the comity of nations. His guide counseled compliance, the chief insisted; but he absolutely refused, and was turning to pursue his journey when a young hotspur sprang into a cabin, seized a horn, and applying it to his lips, blew a blast, terrible as ever was blown upon a ram's horn: instantly the hills around echoed with responsive blasts from sympathizing rams' horns. The alarm was sounded in every cabin: in a moment there was an arming in hot haste, and a thick gathering of wild horsemen rushing from every direction, brandishing their long lances for the fight.

When John Bull's back is fairly up, he is not to be bullied, and there was an immediate cocking of pistols, when the guide, running up in an agony of despair, exclaimed,

"For God's sake, Señor, what are you about? Give them something, *if it is only a pocket handkerchief!*"

The absurdity of his position struck the Englishman immediately; and laughing at his own hastiness, he gave the enraged chieftain a jack-knife.

Peace was restored on the spot—the Cazique was delighted, swore eternal friendship for the munificent stranger, apologized for the detention, and insisted that some of the bravest warriors of the tribe should escort him, as a guard of honor, for several miles upon his way.

CHAPTER XVII.

Mapuché Etiquette.—The formal Introduction.—The Itch.—Horsemanship.—Indian Manners.—Commercial Honesty.—Trees.—Burning the Grass.—The "Island of Heaven."—Domestic Arrangement.—Dogs and their Privileges.

OUR next stoppage was at the house of another chief named Kilal.

As before, we drew up ceremoniously before the cross-bar and waited until the master of the house came out and saluted us with the usual greeting—"*Mari, mari, peñi!*" (literally "a hundred, brother!"—probably a contraction of "a hundred welcomes!" or some other primitive salutation). He then called to his wives, two of whom, after saluting us with "*Emy é?*" ("Is that you?") the usual female greeting, proceeded to sweep the inclosure, which was shaded by a rude shed of canes, and spread sheep-skins upon the ground for our accommodation. This being done, we were invited to dismount.

Entering the inclosure we squatted cross-legged upon the sheep-skins, while our Indian traveling companion began the formal discourse which forms one of the most striking features of the Mapuché etiquette. It is but the interchange of set compliments; but the omission of it, except between near neighbors or intimate friends, would be deemed unpardonable.

If the guest is a stranger, the host begins by addressing him with "I don't know you, brother!" or, "I have never seen you before!" Thereupon the stranger mentions his own name and residence, and goes on to ask the host about himself, his health, and that of his father, mother, wives, and children; about his lands, crops, cattle, and flocks; the chief of the district, the neighbors, their wives, children, crops, etc., are next inquired about: have there been any disturbances, diseases, deaths, or accidents? If the responses given are favorable, the questioner goes on to express his happiness, and moralizes to the effect that health, wealth, and friendship are great blessings, for which God should be thanked. If, on the contrary, the answers should convey bad news, he condoles with the afflicted, and philosophizes that misfortunes should be borne with equanimity, since man can not always avoid evil.

The guest having finished, the host commences, in turn, to ask all the same questions, making such comments as the answers received may demand.

This formality occupies ten or fifteen minutes. The questions and answers are recited (by rote) in a low, monotonous voice, with a sing-song tone not unlike the saying of the rosary, or the chanting of friars. At the end of each sentence, if the last word ends in a vowel, the voice is raised to a shout; but should the final letter be a consonant, it is rounded off with a nasal grunt. The listener expresses his satisfaction, occasionally, by a sound between a grunt and a groan, or indicates surprise by a long-drawn "*Hué!*" With these exceptions, he never interrupts until the speaker gives notice by a peculiar cadence of the voice that he has said his say. During this palaver the speakers often do not look at each other, and frequently even sit with their backs turned to one another.

These compliments once gone through with, all formality is dropped, and conversation commences in an easy and natural manner.

The remains of this custom may still be traced among the Chilenos of the lower classes in the interminable and unvarying questions and answers always heard when they visit or meet casually. Again the same thing may be noticed in the formal "recado" which a servant always delivers when sent on an errand; as, "Muy buenos dies, Señor! como esta su merced! Manda decir mi Señorita Doña Marequita, que como esta la sulded de su merced? que se alegra mucho que no tenga su merced novedad ninguna," etc. When this introduction is ended, but not till then, he goes on and delivers his message; and if interrupted, he will, as like as not, start and go over it all anew.

Such customs are apt to throw an Anglo-Saxon into a fidget; but, springing as they do originally from kind-heartedness, and indicating a friendly disposition, they should command indulgence, if not admiration.

Seeing that we were tired of sitting in one position, the chief ordered for our use some stools that were covered with sheep-skins, and placed them for us to rest our elbows upon. At the same time one of the women appeared, and placed before each of us a dish of mutton broth. The broth was very rich and excellent; but eating in a reclining position I found rather awkward; and though the bowl was well enough, the wooden spoon baffled me completely, for its form was such that I could not accommodate my mouth to it.

My clumsiness created a good deal of mirth; and after greasing my whole face and filling my mustache with broth, I was obliged to give up the wooden spoon and resort to my own, which, with knife and fork, I always carried in my saddle-bags.

It added nothing to my appetite to see several naked children playing about, with blotches all over their bodies, which they were continually scratching; the effect, as I learned, of the itch. Had I known the general prevalence of this disgusting disease among the famed sons of Arauco, it might have deterred me from my journey; but the garrulous Ercilla had forgotten to describe this "peculiar institution;" and though I had heard it spoken of by the Chilenos, I did not realize that, as I afterward became convinced, there is in the whole nation scarcely a man, woman, or child, entirely unscathed by this revolting affliction.

Among other medicines I carried a specific for this unpleasant companion; but I depended principally upon a free use of soap and water, and the continual wearing of thick gloves to protect the hands, which are most exposed to the contagion: with these precautions, though several times badly frightened, I escaped.

The itch is national with these people, and must have existed among them from time immemorial, as a natural consequence of their mode of life. It is said that, long before the true nature of the disease was known in Europe, the Mapuchés had a method of picking out from the skin the minute animalculæ by which the irritation is caused.

There are certain little inconveniences and drawbacks connected with what poets and philosophers are pleased to call a state of nature, which only they can appreciate who have seen man when farthest removed from the amenities of civilized life. Doubtless we should lose much of our respect and admiration for the patriarchs of old, were we more intimately acquainted with their domestic life.

After the siesta, Kilal accompanied us across the Nininco, a small stream, to the boundless fields where his herds of cattle were roaming unrestrained. Half a dozen "hueñis" were in attendance, well mounted, and the chase soon became exciting. Nothing could be more picturesque than these young savages scouring over the plain, their long hair floating in the wind, and their lassos whirring through the air as they dashed after the startled animals.

These Indians are fine horsemen, seeming, as they course along, almost to form part of the animals they bestride. Their dexterity with the lasso is admirable; and it is wonderful to see the apparent ease with which they select any particular animal of the herd, separate him from his companions, and capture him; but sometimes a fleet horse, grown wary by experience, may be seen baffling all their manœuvres, and leading them a long chase far over the plains.

The Mapuché saddle is extremely simple, being formed of a rude wooden tree, under which a few skins are placed, and over it is thrown a saddle-cloth of thick leather. The stirrup, when not of silver, is generally a piece of cane bent into a triangle, just large enough to admit the great toe; the bit, like that used by the Chilenos, is very heavy and powerful; the reins are made of raw hide firmly twisted, or of horse-skin ingeniously braided, and sometimes interwoven with threads of silver.

MAPUCHE SADDLE-TREE, SADDLE-CLOTH, AND STIRRUPS.

Contrary to the general practice of the Chilenos, the Indians leave the saddle-girths very loose, depending entirely upon skillfully balancing the person for maintaining the seat. This is rendered necessary by the fact that, when away from home, they never unsaddle on dismounting, nor take the bit from the horse's mouth, even though they should be several hours afoot, for, like all savages, they are suspicious; and, fearing treachery, they are continually on the alert, ready to mount and fly at a moment's warning. The horse's wind and strength are thus saved, as his lungs are unrestrained.

I was again struck by the forwardness and impertinence of the boys, who gathered round, fingered my dress, saddle, and stirrups, and laughed immoderately at my expense, keeping up a running fire of comments, very amusing to every one except the one most concerned, who, fortunately, did not understand the many flattering compliments paid him.

This sauciness, which among other nations would entitle a youngster to a sound cuffing, is rather encouraged among the Mapuchés, who think that such license fosters a spirit of independence; and never punish their male children, considering chastisement degrading, and calculated to render the future man pusillanimous and unfit for the duties of a warrior. Yet, despite their impertinence, the Indian boys are really good-natured; and, though rough jokers, there is no malice in their tricks, nor any deliberate intention to injure their victim.

With such an education, or rather want of education, in youth, it may appear singular that, as a people, the Mapuchés are far from rude in their social intercourse.

They have their peculiar etiquette, in the observance of which they are unusually scrupulous. They always salute on meeting, though perfect strangers; in conversation they never interrupt each other; they never pass directly before a person, or between two that are conversing, without apologizing for so doing; and in many other respects they display a degree of good-breeding worthy of more civilized nations.

After considerable chaffering—to which the Indians are very much addicted—several animals were agreed upon, for which Sanchez was to call on his return.

To my surprise he paid for them on the spot; but he said that, though given to stealing, the Mapuchés are, in all fair business transactions, far more trustworthy than the "Christianos."

"In my own countrymen I have not the same confidence," he added; "for were I to pay a Chileno for a horse in advance, he would be sure to cheat me if he could."

For several miles we rode over a beautiful rolling plain, interspersed at intervals with fine trees, until we came to the small river Kaillim, that runs through a deep gorge, the hills on either side of which rise very abruptly, and on the north are heavily wooded.

Houses were to be seen scattered along the stream at short distances, the population being here concentrated, as near the water-courses it generally is.

To the south of the stream, after climbing the hills, we came upon a beautiful undulating plain, covered with luxuriant grass, and scattered with large oaks at such short intervals that, as we rode along, we were one-half of the time in the shade. These oaks were noble, wide-spreading trees, and gave to the whole country, unencumbered by brush or undergrowth, the appearance of a well-tended English park; but an occasional huge trunk, charred by fire and ready to fall, or already prostrate, told the melancholy tale that these sylvan monarchs are passing away.

The custom of annually burning the grass—which is practiced here as by the North American Indians—is rapidly destroying the forests of Southern Chili; gradually giving to the plain the same appearance that it wears farther to the north; and though it has been denied by those whose opinions are entitled to great weight, I could not escape the conviction forced upon my mind, that the plains of Central Chili were probably once covered with groves which have disappeared in the same manner—leaving the fields, deprived of protection, parched and desolate, causing the rivers to dry up, and the springs to sink back into the earth.

In such a climate, it has been urged, for want of rain and moisture in the atmosphere, trees could never have extensively prevailed; but the effect has, perhaps, been mistaken for the cause, and this very scarcity of rain may be owing, in great measure, to the destruction of woods which once existed. The influence upon climate of the clearing of extensive tracts is well understood in the United States; and, what is more to the point, the opinion prevails among many of the most intelligent people of Santiago, that rains are becoming perceptibly of greater frequency in that region as the neighboring plains are brought more and more under cultivation.

The sun had already set when we drew rein in front of a house belonging to an Indian named Chancay-Hueno ("The Island of Heaven"), a particular friend of Don Panta's. The master of the house happened not to be at home; but his wife—for in this case there was but one—welcomed us cordially, and invited us to dismount. She had a pleasant smiling face, and a low, soft, musical voice, which had a tone of sadness in it that attracted my attention, and invested her with a sort of melancholy interest.

Chancay did not arrive until it was quite dark. On entering he at first took no notice of us; but turning to his wife, said:

"Put more wood upon the fire, that I may have light to see the face of my friends."

The order was obeyed by throwing fresh canes upon the embers; and so soon as he could distinguish our features by the bright, resinous blaze, he saluted us severally, and entered into conversation with Sanchez. Having expressed his satisfaction at our visit, and talked for some time in a friendly manner, he turned to our Indian companion, who was a stranger to him, and said:

"Your face is new to me, my brother!"

The usual fifteen minutes of complimentary shouting and grunting here ensued, during which the rest were silent; and, drawing a little to one side, I had an opportunity of examining somewhat the domestic arrangements of the "Island of Heaven."

The house, which was built of cane and thatch, was rectangular, some thirty feet long by fifteen broad, and much resembled the ordinary ranchos in common use among the poorer classes throughout Chili. In the middle of the roof was a hole, which served as a chimney to the fire built directly beneath it on the bare ground. This hole, and the low door, were the only apertures for the admission of light and air.

In two of the corners were rude frames of cane covered with hides, serving as bedsteads, and in a third stood a kind of bin, formed by a neatly-made partition of cane-work: this was the granary for stowing away wheat. The rest of the room was littered with earthenware pots, wooden dishes, spoons, and other domestic utensils scattered about in admirable confusion; while from the black, cobweb-covered rafters above, hung ears of Indian corn, joints of meat, pumpkins, strings of red peppers, and a grass net filled with potatoes. In the midst of these symbols of peace and plenty were suspended, ready for immediate use, two long lances, with their iron points directed toward the door. But they had grown rusty during long years of peace, although their tips were protected by bits of fat meat.

One of the posts supporting the roof was somewhat inclined from the perpendicular, and notched so as to form a ladder by which to reach a sort of loft up in the region of soot and smoke, where sacks of beans and other luxuries were carefully stored. Over the beds dangled spurs, bits, and stirrups of silver, with breast-pins, ear-rings, strings of beads, and numerous incomprehensible nick-nacks, evidently intended in some way to increase the charms of the fair lady of the house.

Squatting among the ashes and almost over the fire, leaning forward upon her gaunt, withered arm, was a wrinkled, blear-eyed old woman, looking more like a dried monkey than any thing human, unless it be a mummy revived. She was peering intently through the smoke, looking at me as though unable to make up her mind what I might be, and occasionally intimating her feelings by a long-drawn "Hué!" or by a guttural grunt of surprise. Judging from her appearance, she must have been very old. Near her sat our hostess, her daughter, who was stirring round in a large pot over the fire—an operation that she varied occasionally by pulling a thong attached to a hanging cradle, in which a little black-eyed, bullet-headed baby lay staring round at the company. At times, as she raised her hand to shield her eyes from the ruddy glare and the heat of the fire, I could see that she, too, was furtively engaged in studying me out.

As soon as the formal compliments came to an end, the caldron was tipped over, and we were liberally supplied with meat and broth. The supper was excellent, and I should have enjoyed it highly had I not been pestered by the attentions of a dog, that insisted on sticking his nose into my dish every time I put it down. A good kick would easily have rid me of this troublesome companion, had Mapuché etiquette allowed me to bestow one on the offender; but on the old principle of "love me, love my dog," any indignity offered to this "custos fidus et audax," would have been considered an insult to our host.

We made up our beds in the open air, using for matresses a pile of soft skins, which our kind hostess offered for the purpose. "For," said she, laughing, "our 'pichi huenthu' (little man) must not sleep upon the hard ground."

CHAPTER XVIII.

Female Dress, Paint, Beads, etc.—The borrowed Children.—Swathing Infants.—Mapuché Marriages.—Value of a Wife.—Infidelity.—A Case in Point.—Female Virtue.

At Chancay's we remained several days, and as Sanchez was here upon very familiar terms, I had an excellent opportunity of studying the peculiarities of the Araucanians.

Our hostess, out of respect for her guests, or actuated possibly by a pardonable female vanity, appeared, the morning after our arrival, in a fresh coat of paint, and with all her finery on.

The colors used for painting are red and black: two species of earth, which are mixed with grease to prevent their being easily washed off when once applied. The red is put on in a broad belt from ear to ear, over the cheek, eyelids, and nose. The black is used to give effect to the eyebrows, which are pulled out so as to leave only a fine line; with it, too, the eyelids and eyelashes are tipped in the same manner, and for the same purpose, that the "henna" is used by the women of the East. The lower edge of the red belt upon the cheek and across the tip of the nose is also frequently lined or scolloped with black.

The fancy of individuals will sometimes vary the "mode" by the addition of black tears rolling down the cheek; but the established fashion is generally rigidly observed, though subject, I believe, to periodical modifications. The effect produced by the colors is peculiar. The black, undoubtedly, imparts to the eyes an unusual brilliancy; but the red gives them an unearthly glare and a blood-shot appearance that is far from agreeable.

The female head-dress, composed entirely of beads of various colors, so arranged as to form figures, struck me as being very pretty. It fell quite low upon the forehead, and descended behind over the shoulders and back, fringed at the bottom by a row of brass thimbles, strung together so as to jingle like bells.

The hair was divided into two queues, wound round with bright blue beads, and connected at the ends by another string of brass thimbles. On ordinary occasions this head-dress is not worn, but the queues, wound with beads, are twisted round the head like two snakes, the ends falling down over the face, or sticking out in front like horns. At other times a simple fillet, ornamented with beads, is worn to confine the hair.

The neck is incased with a leathern collar, studded with silver. A great profusion of beads, in strings of various colors, are worn hanging upon the breast, with the addition of silver dollars, thimbles, etc., according to the wearer's means. Upon the wrist and ankle, bracelets and anklets, also of beads, are worn; but anklets are not worn by the women alone, for woolen ones of various colors are worn by the "ghelmenes" as a distinction of rank.

The dress of an Indian belle is composed of two

MORUCHE WOMEN.

garments, not unlike the "chiripa" of the male in form and texture, though differently worn. One is wrapped round the person just under the arms, and pinned up over the shoulders (so as to leave the arm bare), while a broad leathern belt, with silver buckles, confines the garment at the waist. The other is thrown over the shoulders like a cloak, and pinned in front with a silver pin, the head of which is sometimes globular, but more frequently it is flat, and about the shape and size of a small dinner plate. These garments are for the most part of home manufacture, of a black or deep indigo hue; but sometimes they are made of red European flannel.

With the addition of massive silver ear-drops the picture is complete.

Though the love of paint and finery is generally considered distinctive of the milder sex, it is not exclusively so, for the young bucks sometimes endeavor to make themselves more killing by the same means, and though generally content with a few dabs and streaks upon the cheek, there are not wanting those who paint elaborately all around the eye, and even color their lips red.

Our hostess, despite her paint, had a pleasing face; not that her features were fine, for, like those of her countrywomen generally, they were too purely animal, but owing to a subdued expression of melancholy that she habitually wore. She was lively and talkative; she seemed gentle and affectionate; yet some secret grief was evidently preying upon her happiness. I mentioned my impressions to Sanchez, who confirmed them, and gave a very simple explanation: Though for several years married she was childless, the little children in her charge being *borrowed* from a sister-in-law more abundantly blessed.

There is inherent in the female breast a yearning for some object upon which to pour out its love, that makes sterility always a misfortune; but among the Mapuchés, as, in fact, with all primitive people, it is a reproach. The case is infinitely aggravated when the husband is under no restraint, but may at any moment take another wife upon whom to bestow those affections due to her toward whom he has grown indifferent, for want of that most sacred and indissoluble of all ties, a smiling offspring.

The children were two, a little boy and a girl. The former, a bright, intelligent youngster, about seven years old, rejoiced in the name of "Panta," having been so called in honor of Sanchez. The little girl was younger, and bore the poetical cognomen of "Elyapé," a contraction of "Elya-pewé-coyam," signifying "The Oak that Buds in the Spring." She was a pretty, sprightly child, but in vain I endeavored to make her acquaintance, for having once seen me take off my hat—an operation that frightened her as much as though I had pulled off my head—she avoided me in horror ever after, and would scream at the slightest motion of my hand toward my hat.

Besides these two, there was a *papoose* that I used to see occasionally hanging from a peg, or leaning up against the side of the house; it was closely bandaged, and tied so immovably to its bamboo frame, that the motion of its eyes alone gave any indication of life. One would suppose such continual restraint irksome to a child; but the little thing never showed any uneasiness, and subsequent observation convinced me that, in all babydom, there is nothing more quiet and contented than a papoose.

PAPOOSE AND CRADLE.

Molina, who is usually very accurate, says that the Araucanians never swathe their infants; but I found the custom universal, and though the same practice prevails, to some extent, among the lower classes of the Chilenos, it is not to be supposed that the Indians have borrowed it from the Spaniards. Such a mistake, however, is not remarkable in one who never visited the people whom he describes, but depended upon others for his information.

The real mother of the borrowed children was a fat, good-natured creature, that had picked up a few words of Spanish; and with my few words of Indian, and the aid of a Mapuché dictionary, we managed to carry on considerable conversation. She was frequently accompanied by a younger and handsomer woman than herself, whom she pointed out, with evident satisfaction, as her "other self"—that is, her husband's wife number two, a recent addition to the family. Far from being dissatisfied, or entertaining any jealousy toward the new-comer, she said that she wished her husband would marry again; for she considered it a great relief to have some one to assist her in her household duties, and in the maintenance of her husband.

This feeling was not, perhaps, an unnatural one, as among the Mapuchés the females do all the labor, from plowing and cooking to the saddling and unsaddling of a horse; for the "lord and master" does little but eat, sleep, and ride about, justifying himself in such a course by the reflection that, as his wives cost him a high price, it is but fair that they should work enough to make up the outlay.

It is true that an Araucanian girl is not regularly put up for sale and bartered for, like the Oriental houris; but she is none the less an article of merchandise, to be paid for by him who would aspire to her hand. She has no more freedom in the choice of her husband than has the Circassian slave.

As every where else, mutual attachments do sometimes spring up; and though the young people have but little opportunity of communicating freely, they will occasionally resort to amatory songs, tender glances, and other innumerable little tricks, which lovers only understand. Matrimony may follow; but such a preliminary courtship is by no means considered necessary, nor is the lady's consent deemed of any importance.

Generally, when a young man makes up his mind to marry, he first goes to his various friends for assistance in carrying out his project. If he be poor, each one of them, according to his means, offers to make a contribution toward the expenses: one gives a fat ox; another a horse; a third, a pair of silver spurs. A moonless night is selected, and a rendezvous named. At the appointed time the lover and his friends, all well mounted, congregate as agreed. Cautiously and in silence they approach and surround the residence of the bride.

Half a dozen of the most smooth-spoken in the company enter and seek out the girl's father, to whom they explain the object of their coming; set forth the merits of the aspirant; the convenience of the match, etc., and ask his consent, which is usually granted with readiness; for, perhaps, he considers his daughter somewhat of an encumbrance, and calculates upon what she will bring. Meanwhile the bridegroom has sought out the resting-place of his fair one; and she, as in duty bound, screams for protection.

Immediately a tremendous row commences. The women spring up *en masse*, and arming themselves with clubs, stones, and missiles of all kinds, rush to the defense of the distressed maiden. The friends interpose to give the lover fair play, with soothings and gentle violence endeavoring to disarm the fierce viragoes; but they are not to be appeased, and happy the man that escapes without a broken pate, or some other bleeding memento of the flight.

It is a point of honor with the bride to resist and struggle, however willing she may be, until the impatient bridegroom, brooking no delay, seizes her by the hair, or by the heel, as may be most convenient, and drags her along the ground toward the open door. Once fairly outside, he springs to the saddle, still firmly grasping his screaming captive, whom he pulls up over the horse's back, and yelling forth a whoop of triumph, he starts off at full gallop. The friends sally out, still pursued by the wrathful imprecations of the outraged matrons, and follow fast in the track of the fugitives.

Gaining the woods, the lover dashes into the tangled thickets, while the friends considerately pause upon the outskirts until the screams of the bride have died away, and they are satisfied that no one is in pursuit, when they quietly disperse.

It is to be supposed that the lady finally yields to the strong arm and ardent entreaties of her gentle wooer; for, without further marriage ceremonies, the happy couple emerge, a day or two after, from the depths of the forest as man and wife.

Sometimes the parents of the girl are really opposed to the match. In which case the neighbors are immediately summoned by blowing the horn, and chase is given; but if the fugitive once succeed in gaining the thicket in safety, the marriage can not afterward be annulled.

A few days are allowed to pass, and then the friends call upon the happy bridegroom. Each one brings his promised contribution; and driving the cattle before them, the whole bridal party set off to the former residence of the bride. The presents are formally handed over to the father, who, if he considers that he has received the full value of his daughter, manifests extreme pleasure at the marriage, and mutual congratulations are exchanged.

The girl's mother alone does not enter into the general joy; for she is supposed to feel highly outraged by the robbery of her child, and expresses her indignation by refusing to speak to, or even look at her son-in-law. But at the same time, good breeding requires that she should show some civilities to her guests; and, accordingly, seating herself beside the bride (with her back turned upon the bridegroom), she says, "My daughter, ask your husband if he is not hungry." The question is put, and by the intervention of this *medium* a conversation is carried on, and the party are finally regaled with a meal, in the preparation of which the old lady exhausts her culinary art.

The point of honor is, in some instances, carried so far, that for years after the marriage the mother never addresses her son-in-law face to face; though with her back turned, or with the interposition of a fence or a partition, she will converse with him freely.

Such is the usual process of getting a wife; but sometimes a man meets a girl in the fields, alone, and far away from her home; a sudden desire to better his solitary condition seizes him, and without further ado, he rides up, lays violent hands upon the damsel, and carries her off. Again at their feasts and merry-makings (in which the women are kept somewhat aloof from the men), a young man may be smitten with a sudden passion, or be emboldened, by wine, to express a long slumbering preference for some dusky maid;

his sighs and amorous glances will perhaps be returned, and rushing among the unsuspecting females, he will bear away the object of his choice while yet she is in the melting mood.

When such an attempt is foreseen, the unmarried girls form a ring around their companion, and endeavor to shield her; but the lover and his friends, by well-directed attacks, at length succeed in breaking through the magic circle, and drag away the damsel in triumph; perhaps, in the excitement of the game, some of her defenders too may share her fate.

In all such cases the usual equivalent is afterward paid to the girl's father.

The various amounts contributed by friends toward paying for a wife, are considered debts of honor, to be repaid whenever the benefactors themselves may be in need of similar assistance, or at the latest, to be refunded on the first marriage of a daughter who is the fruit of the union.

Marriage is not considered indissoluble, but the husband may, even after a term of years, allow his wife to return to her father's house, if she be so disposed, with the freedom of marrying whomsoever she may please; though in such a case the first husband may claim from the second the full price which she originally cost.

A widow by the death of her husband becomes her own mistress, unless he may have left grown up sons by another wife, in which case she becomes their common concubine, being regarded as a chattel naturally belonging to the heirs to the estate. A custom so revolting seems hardly credible, but my guide assured me that there could be no doubt of its existence.

Infidelity (in the female) is a crime always punished by death, and the guilty paramour, if taken in the act, is apt to share the fate of the false wife; but should he escape for the moment, he may subsequently be made to pay, to the injured husband, the original cost of the wife.

An instance of this kind came under my notice while at Nacimiento.

A trader of that town had entered the Indian country, accompanied by his son. The young man, being fair and comely to look upon, found favor with a frail dame, who, allured by his gallant bearing, and possibly by a few strings of beads, forgot that she was the wife of a potent chieftain, and being detected in certain peccadillos, suffered death at the hands of her infuriated lord. The young man, favored by a fleet horse and by the shortness of the distance, made his escape, and reached Nacimiento in safety.

In a few days he was followed by a deputation, sent by the Cazique of the district, to lay the merits of the case before the Intendente. They represented that though it was in their power to have seized upon the property of the trader, rather than do any thing calculated to disturb their amicable relations with the whites, they preferred to leave the case to the Chilian authorities, trusting that the laws would compel the offender to make the proper restitution, especially as the woman had cost a large sum, and was a particular favorite with her husband.

The Intendente, after due deliberation, induced the

young trader to compromise the matter with trinkets and clothes supposed to be an equivalent for four or five fat oxen, the value of the deceased—the Indians agreeing, on their part, that in any trading operations for the future he should be unmolested, and be received upon the same footing as though nothing had happened.

The virtue of the Indian women has often been highly extolled, but Sanchez, I thought, rather ridiculed the idea. Fraility, he said, in an unmarried female, though something of a disqualification for matrimony, was not looked upon as very disgraceful. Any passably good-looking young man, with beads and trinkets at command, and a not over-delicate taste, would, he imagined, meet with quite as much favor among these dusky maidens of the forest as among the fairer daughters of civilization—possibly with rather more.

Man, when left to his animal nature, without religion, or a high code of morals to govern his actions, is not apt to put much restraint upon his passions, nor to have any very exalted notions of abstract virtue. The children of Arauco, famed though they be for the valor of their arms, are no exception to this rule.

CHAPTER XIX.

Superstitious dread of Writing, etc.—Hatred of the English, and its Origin.—Use of Iron.—Mapuché Graves.—Return of Captives.—The Evil Eye.—Raising of Sheep.—Introduction of Carts by Traders.—Tactics of Chilian Officials.

In order to see what effect would be produced, I showed my drawing materials and sketches, and offered some of my paints to the women; but though they admired the colors, especially the vermillion, they would not accept them, evidently fearing that they might produce some mysterious effect upon the wearer. It was only after painting my squire José all the colors of the rainbow, to convince them that there was nothing to be dreaded, that they would allow me to paint the faces of the children. The little things required a great deal of scrubbing before the water-colors could be induced to stick to their greasy skins; but when painted, their mothers were perfectly delighted, and they afterward complained very much because the colors came off when the children were bathed; yet though they brought back the children to be repainted, they themselves could not be persuaded to use the bright pigments which they so much admired.

The paper and pencils surprised them, and they were much amused when I made some rough sketches of dogs, chickens, and other familiar objects, which they easily recognized. A woman was setting near, of whom I drew a rude outline, painting the head-dress, beads, etc., of appropriate colors. The men laughed heartily at the sight, and even she was rather pleased; still they evidently entertained some suspicions, and though Sanchez attempted to explain every thing to their satisfaction, none of the rest would consent to be drawn.

Sanchez also showed and explained to them the likeness of my father (*i.e.* a sketch taken from an old man at Budeo, who was said to resemble Vega), and told them that I intended showing it to Mañin. I added, that as my father was anxious to see his old friend once more, I wished to take a portrait of the great chief himself; but they all shook their heads, and one remarked,

"Mañin has a temper like a mad bull; beware that you do nothing to give him offense!"

This unwillingness to have one's portrait taken is universal among these people; for, being superstitious and great believers in magic, they fear lest the one having the painting in his possession may, by machinations, injure or destroy the one represented.

The same superstitious dread applies in the case of names also, and few Indians will ever tell you their names, being in possession of which, they fear that you may acquire some supernatural power over themselves. Asking our Indian companion his name one day, he replied,

"I have none."

Thinking that he had mistaken my meaning, I again asked, and was told,

"I don't know."

I, of course, thought that my "Indian-talk" had been unintelligible to him; but Sanchez afterward told me that my question had been properly worded, and explained the cause of my receiving such unintelligible answers to so simple a question.

Writing being far above their comprehension, is regarded by them as a species of magic. They were especially amazed when they saw the dictionary (written by a Jesuit missionary), and learned that by consulting it I could find out words in their own language. All attempt to explain this mystery was vain, for they were fairly stupefied, and could scarcely credit their senses.

One of those present having pointed to some object and asked its Indian name, I referred to the dictionary and immediately answered him. He was incredulous, and leaning over, he peered into the book as if to see if he could recognize any resemblance between the thing itself and the printed word. I pointed out the word; but, not satisfied with looking, he laid his hand upon the page to feel the letters. A passing breeze at that moment rustled the leaves. He jerked back his hand in an instant. Had that mysterious book whispered to him in an unknown tongue? It was upon his left hand, too, and therefore of ill-omen! He withdrew; and wrapping his poncho about his head, sat for several hours in moody silence.

It was not considered safe to write when any of the Indians were present, for fear of exciting suspicion; and it was only by stealth that I could occasionally take notes of what I saw. For this purpose I availed myself of a neighboring thicket, to which I could repair and be hidden from view. Even then I was likely to be questioned if long absent from the house. But the fact of my traveling in company with Sanchez, who was universally esteemed, taken in connection with the ostensible motive of my visit, quieted all doubts, and no one for a moment questioned my being what I professed to be.

Chancay's brother—who had traveled in trading expeditions over the pampas as far as Buenos, and had thus been thrown in contact with foreigners—perhaps suspected from my appearance that I was no Chileno; for he used occasionally to call me *pichi Ingles* (little Englishman). Whether he really thought me such or was merely joking, I never could determine. But Sanchez stoutly denied that I was either an Englishman or a Frenchman; and declared that I could not speak a word of French or English. If I differed in any thing from the Chilenos, he said, it was owing entirely to my having been educated in Spain.

Though an Englishman in their midst would be as great a curiosity as an Araucanian in the streets of London, these Indians have an antipathy to the very name of "Ingles." This feeling at first seems unaccountable; but it was probably implanted by the agents of the old Spanish Government, and more recently has, perhaps, been fostered by the Chilenos as a safeguard against the attempts of any foreign nation to gain a foothold in Southern Chili; for, in the early history of the country, two efforts were made to dispossess the Spaniards of the provinces lying south of the Bio-Bio—the one by the English, who, in 1586, landed at Quintero, under Sir Thomas Cavendish, and endeavored to establish friendly relations with the Indians, but were repulsed by the Spaniards—the other by the Dutch, who, in 1600, took and plundered Chiloe, putting the garrison to the sword. They also wished to form an alliance with the neighboring tribes, whom they had intended to supply with arms, to be used against the Spaniards; but their designs were frustrated by a sudden attack of the Araucanians, who, regarding all Europeans as enemies, made an unexpected descent upon the island, and drove the Dutch back to their ships with great loss.

The prejudices of the Mapuchés may possibly have been fortified by the missionaries, as the most effectual obstacle to the success of rival missions; for though the Indians make no pretension to Christianity, they have a most holy horror of "moros," "hereges," and "infieles," terms which throughout Chili are indiscriminately applied to all without the pale of the True Church.

I was frequently interrogated about the "Ingleses." Were they not a very bad people, and exceedingly anxious to gain possession of the Mapuché country, etc. I vindicated their character, and assigned reasons why they would not desire such a conquest; but it was not prudent to say too much in their favor, since, by so doing, I might bring myself into bad repute.

Chancay had somewhere picked up an idea of a locomotive, which he described as a fiery monster, much fleeter and stronger than the horse. He had been told that the "moros" made use of such infernal inventions, and wished to know if, in my travels, I had seen one. He was surprised to learn that such things were about to be introduced into Chili, and asked if they did not bode evil to the Indians. I tried to explain somewhat the construction and object of railroads, but as Mr. Llanque-Hueno, who acted as interpreter, did not understand Spanish very perfectly, it is doubtful whether the audience were much the wiser for my explanation, although they seemed satisfied on the main point, that nothing was to be dreaded, and that steam-engines were promotive of peace rather than of war.

In the neighborhood of Chancay's house, I noticed that many of the large trees were girdled, for the purpose of destroying them, as is commonly practiced in the thickly wooded parts of our own country. This is the only means the Indians have of getting rid of trees, for the ax is utterly unknown to them; the nearest approach which I met to any thing of the kind, was a small instrument for chopping, that looked somewhat like an adze; but it was rudely constructed, and utterly worthless except for the most trivial purposes.

Whether this instrument was entirely of their own workmanship, I did not think to inquire, supposing the Mapuchés to be unacquainted with the manufacture of iron implements. But Molina contends that they were well acquainted with that metal before the conquest of the country by the Spaniards—an opinion which he fortifies by adducing the specific Indian name for iron, "panilhué."

The learned Abbé may be correct in his surmises,

but if so, the Indians certainly profited but little by their knowledge, for in their early wars they made no use of iron arms, and subsequently they have depended entirely upon the Spaniards for bits, knives, spear-heads, and the few other articles of the kind which they require.

There was a marked difference between the burial-places hereabouts and those more to the north, although it may have been merely an accidental one, growing out of the greater abundance of wood in this vicinity. Instead of the simple uprights and cross-pole, described at Budeo, nearly all the graves were surrounded by rough-hewn boards, forming a rude fence, from the midst of which rose the long, quivering lance.

MAPUCHE GRAVES.

In one of our jaunts we stopped to see an Indian woman, who in her infancy was captured, and had been brought up among Christians.

Though the government of Chili many years since commanded all Indian captives to be restored to their friends, numbers were unwilling to return to a state of barbarism, which they had been taught by their captors to regard with horror. This woman long refused to go back to her home, but yielded, at length, to the tears and entreaties of an aged mother. She seemed overjoyed to meet some fellow-Christians, and paid us much attention. She dressed like a Chilena, eschewing entirely the Indian costume; spoke Spanish like any Penquista, and was in no way distinguishable from the lower classes of the population throughout Chili.

She expressed strong hopes of being able to convert some of her family to Christianity; and though her own religion was probably not of the highest order, much might be accomplished by the persevering efforts of persons in like situations. But, as a general rule, those who, after living among the whites, return to their parents, so far from exerting a marked influence over the Indians, are prone to relapse very soon into heathenism. This is especially true of women; for being highly prized for wives on account of their superior accomplishments, they are soon carried off by some amorous chieftain, and in the cares of a family they soon forget whatever of Christianity they may have learned.

The subject of captives is the one in relation to which the Indians are said to feel themselves most aggrieved by the Chilian government.

A mutual agreement having been made that all captives of either nation should be given up to their relations when demanded, the Indians faithfully complied with their part of the obligation, even forcing those to return who were unwilling; for as many had been captured in their childhood and grown up habituated to an uncivilized life, they were loth to begin a different mode of existence among those whom they considered not as brothers, but as strangers. But the authorities of Chili, actuated by motives of humanity, refused to make use of coercion for the return of Indian captives, leaving them at liberty to go back to their homes, or remain with their masters, as they might see fit; and it is probable that much individual influence, perhaps even intimidation, was used to prevent their return, for fear of their relapsing from Christianity.

The number of Indian captives among the Chilenos is probably much greater than is generally supposed; for, being scattered about in menial capacities, they are seldom brought to notice. There are, the Indians contend, several hundreds, whose parents yearn for them incessantly—complaining bitterly that their children, torn away by violence, are living in bondage amidst a strange people.

Returning to the house of our host, we found the women and children weeping bitterly for the loss of a sheep that had gone astray. Though they would willingly sacrifice a sheep at any time for the sake of entertaining a friend, the loss of one was regarded as a sad calamity, not on account of the value of the animal lost, but as an indication of bad luck—a forewarning, perhaps, of greater evils in store.

Chancay himself seemed no less distressed than the women and children, and his dread of some baneful influence at work upon his flocks reminded us of the verse:

> "Nescio quis teneros oculus mihi fascinat agnos;"

for the Mapuché of to-day is no less a believer in the "Evil eye" than was the old Roman two thousand years ago.

There is no country better adapted to the raising of sheep than that possessed by the Araucanians. The mutton—which forms an important article of their diet—is of excellent quality, far superior to that raised on the arid plains of Central Chili. The fleeces also are fine, and if properly washed would command a high price.

Heretofore the wool produced has been consumed by the Indians themselves; but within two or three years it has become an article of trade with the Chilenos. As nearly every family has its flock, the quantity of wool which might be exported is considerable, and probably will be much increased as the demand becomes greater.

One of the greatest drawbacks to traders was the necessity of transporting the wool upon pack-animals, at an expense which greatly curtailed the profits which they would otherwise have enjoyed. But this has of late been obviated by the use of ox-carts.

The first introduction of carts by the traders gave alarm to the Indians, who feared some sinister design—thinking that perhaps the government had adopted this mode of testing the practicability of invading their country with artillery. Every means short of actual violence was used to obstruct their way. Trees were felled along the accustomed routes, and other impediments were so placed as to render not only the advance, but the return of any wheeled vehicle extremely difficult. Not content with these measures, they determined to send a deputation of inquiry to Sepulveda (the Commandante of Nacimiento), in whom they placed great confidence, to learn the meaning of the late innovations.

The Commandante pretended to be surprised, and indignantly declared that the audacity of the traders should be severely punished. Having thus gained their confidence, he inquired of the complainants the object of the traders, and what they carried on their carts.

"Nothing but wool," was the answer.

"Is it possible!" said he, on receiving this reply. And then, as if struck by a sudden idea, he exclaimed:

"Who knows? Perhaps the poor fellows had not horses and mules enough to transport their wool, and were obliged to use oxen instead!"

The thought was a novel one to the Indians; and after due consideration, they admitted the force of the explanation, and concluded:

"Well! let the poor devils use their carts until they are rich enough to buy horses and mules?"

This is but a fair specimen of the tactics pursued by the government agents in treating with the Indians. The Mapuché is impatient of contradiction, and brooks no command. It is impossible to accomplish any thing by combating his prejudices; but by appearing to coincide with his views, and gradually turning his thoughts in another direction, he is easily convinced, and may, for the time at least, be influenced to adopt any desired course—though, when left to himself, he soon returns to his own prejudices, or allows himself to be reasoned into some still different course by the next comer.

CHAPTER XX.

The sick Woman.—The Cautery.—Skill of the Mapuchés in Medicine.—Machi, or Doctors.—Their Cures and Incantations.—Divinations.—The Machi of Boroa.—Remedies.

In one of my rambles with Sanchez, we entered a house, and were surprised to find the whole family in tears—especially the father, who wept like a child over his sick wife who lay groaning upon the ground. She was troubled with a large tumor upon the breast, caused, it was said, by falling from her horse.

My advice was solicited, but I had none to give; and finally, for want of something better, the husband turned her over and applied a cautery to her back. This was done by pressing firmly down upon the skin a small ball of pith, which was lighted and allowed to burn until entirely consumed. The poor woman writhed in agony as the burning pith sank into the quivering flesh, and her tormentor seemed to feel her every pang as he stood brushing away the tears that rolled down his dusky cheeks. And yet this man had the reputation of a brave soldier, and would have borne with unflinching stoicism any torture at the hands of an enemy: nor was he an exception to his race; for the valiant warriors of Arauco, the descendents of the Caupolicans and the Lautaros of history, in the bosom of their families are as tender-hearted as women.

I could not exactly see the philosophy of applying a cautery to the back to remove a tumor in the breast, but judging from the numerous small scars upon the woman's person, the remedy must have been her husband's panacea.

The Mapuchés have their medicine-men, who really possess considerable skill in the treatment of disease, and are well acquainted with the proper use of emetics, cathartics, and sudorifics—they all blister, and frequently bleed. The latter operation is performed with a small piece of flint or obsidian. For the purpose of injection, they make use of a bladder, as is still commonly practiced among the Chilenos. Their remedies are principally, if not entirely, vegetable, though they administer many disgusting compounds of animal matter, which they pretend are endowed with miraculous powers. Many of their medicines are among the most efficient of the *materia medica;* as, for instance, sarsaparilla, and that excellent febrifuge, now so well known to Europeans—the *canchalagua.**

By frequent amputations the Mapuché doctors have acquired a knowledge of anatomy extraordinary in a barbarous people; but being without a written language, they advance but little from generation to generation. Advancement is farther checked by the system of imposture they adopt, shrouding every thing with mystery, and attributing all success to supernatural agency, rather than to the natural effects of physical causes.

* This word, which has been changed from the Spanish *cachaulagua* to *canchalagua*, is a corruption of the Mapuché *cachaulahuen.*

Though invested with no sacerdotal character, they pretend to be diviners and magicians, and possess much skill in the performance of sleight-of-hand tricks, which enter largely into the working of their cures.

The doctors, as far as I could learn, are generally known as *machis*, and the performance of their cures is called *machitun*. The Abbé Molina enumerates besides the machis, two other kinds of doctors—the *ampives* and the *vileus*. The former are empirics who confine themselves to botanical medicines; the latter are practitioners who believe all diseases to proceed from insects. But the Jesuit Febres, whose opportunities for studying the peculiarities of the Mapuchés were unequaled, makes no distinction in his dictionary between the three terms, which he seems to consider synonymous.

These medicine-men are but few in number, and as they demand exorbitant remuneration for their services, they are seldom appealed to, except in cases of dangerous illness.

When the doctor is called upon to administer to a sick person, he comes in the evening, which is the time most favorable for his proceedings, and having first stripped and made himself as horrible as possible with paint, he commences his *machitun*.

The patient is laid upon his back in the middle of the hut, and all the family are turned out of doors, or made to sit with their faces toward the wall. Having examined the symptoms of the disease, the machi begins a long incantation, which consists of a monotonous song, accompanied by the beating of a small drum, formed by straining a sheep-skin tightly over a wooden bowl. With contortions and violent gestures the singer becomes more and more excited, until, working himself up to the proper pitch, he falls backward upon the ground, with rolling eyes, foaming mouth, and spasmodic convulsions, and remains for some time in an apparent trance.

At this signal the young men, naked and hideously painted, mounting their horses, bare-backed, rush frantically around the house, screaming, shouting, waving torches over their heads, and brandishing their long lances to frighten away the evil spirits that are supposed to hover round, seeking to injure the sick man.

Recovering from his trance, the medicine man declares the nature and seat of the malady, and proceeds to dose the patient, whom he also manipulates about the part afflicted until he succeeds in extracting the cause of the sickness, which he exhibits in triumph. This is generally a spider, a toad, or some other reptile which he has had carefully concealed about his person. The medicines are then left to do their work; and if the sick man recovers, the cure is considered miraculous; if he dies, his death is deemed in accordance with the will of God, or else it is attributed to the machinations of some secret enemy.

After death the services of the machi are again required, especially if the deceased be a person of distinction. The body is dissected and examined. If the liver be found in a healthy state, the death is attributed to natural causes; but if the liver prove to be inflamed, it is supposed to indicate the machinations of some evil-intentioned persons, and it rests with the medicine-man to discover the conspirator.

This is accomplished by much the same means that were used to find out the nature of the disease. The gall is extracted, put in the magic drum, and after various incantations taken out and placed over the fire, in a pot carefully covered: if, after subjecting the gall to a certain amount of roasting, a stone is found in the bottom of the pot, it is declared to be the means by which death was produced.

These stones, as well as the frogs, spiders, arrows, or whatever else may be extracted from the sick man, are called *Huecuvu*—the "Evil One." By aid of the *Huecuvu*, the machi throws himself into a trance, in which state he discovers and announces the person guilty of the death, and describes the manner in which it was produced.

The most implicit credence is yielded to these divinations; and frequently the person accused is pursued by the relatives of the deceased, and put to death. Some of the most sanguinary broils that ever disturbed the tranquillity of the nation arose from this cause. Instances sometimes occur in which the friends of the deceased make a formal application to the Cazique of the district for the delivery of the supposed offender, to be executed after having first been tortured for the sake of extracting a confession of guilt. Such demands at times are acceded to, and the pain of torture does not always fail to extort an admission of the imputed crime.

By such means the machis obtain a terrible influence, which they but too well know how to use for the gratification of private revenge.

To discover the perpetrators of murders and other

crimes, the medicine-men are also consulted; and their declarations are considered at least strong presumptive evidence against the accused. A case of this kind came subsequently under my own observation. The year before an Indian had been secretly assassinated in an unfrequented spot. All investigation had been baffled, until, at last, the friends of the murdered man determined to consult the famous machi (a woman, as it happened) of Boroa. The decision given was, that the murder had been committed by an Indian and a Christian conjointly; and on examination, it proved that both the men indicated were, at the time named, at or near the place of the occurrence.

The Indian was living at Budeo; and the Christian, after a trading expedition, had returned to his home. While we were staying at the house of a chief on our return, I noticed a long and earnest conversation going on in an undertone between Sanchez and the Cazique: this consultation, I afterward learned, referred to the murder and the revelations of the machi. The friends of the deceased had determined to capture the Indian supposed to be guilty, and wished Sanchez to exert his influence with the authorities at Los Angelos, that the Chileno might be arrested and brought to trial.

The office of medicine-man, though generally usurped by males, does not appertain to them exclusively; and at the time of our visit the one most extensively known was a black (or *meztizo*) woman, who had acquired the most unbounded influence by shrewdness, joined to a hideous personal appearance, and a certain mystery with which she was invested; for, though her general outline was that of a woman, she wore the male dress, spoke in a coarse, harsh voice, and sought in various ways to render her true sex doubtful. But such instances are rare; for the right of women to take a share in the learned professions is a doctrine belonging to a much higher state of civilization than that to which the Mapuchés have attained.

Besides the regular practitioners, every old woman here, as all the world over, has her own infallible remedies for ordinary complaints; and generally the more absurd and disgusting their composition, the greater the faith accorded to them.

The belief in nauseous and ridiculous nostrums, so common among the lower classes in Chili, is probably of Indian rather than of Spanish origin; and I doubt whether the Guasos, as a mass, are much better off than their Mapuché brethren. As, however, the greater part of their complaints arise from repletion, any thing calculated to induce vomiting can not but be beneficial, and to that end most of their medicines are admirably adapted.

CHAPTER XXI.

Form of Government of the Araucanians.—Council of Peace.—National Assemblies.—Council of War.—The Colyico.—Peculiarities in the Mapuché Head and Foot.—The Jew's-harp.—Primeval Forest.—Ketredeguin.

After several days spent with Chancay, Sanchez and myself determined to set out, unaccompanied by the rest of the party, to pay our formal court to the great Mañin. But before proceeding farther, it may not be amiss to acquaint the reader with the nature of the Araucanian government, in order that he may fully understand the importance of this lordly savage, to whom all the minor chiefs yield a ready submission.

Araucania is divided into four parallel provinces known as, *Lauquen-Mapu*, the Sea-Country, including the districts of Arauco, Tucapel, Illicura, and Boroa; *Lebun-Mapu*, the Country of the Plain, which includes Encol, Puren, Repoura, Maquegua, and Mariquina; *Inapiré-Mapu*, the country lying at the foot of the Cordilleras, comprising Malven, Colhue, Chacaico, Quecherigua, and Guanague; and *Piré-Mapu*, the valleys of the Andes. These districts are subdivided by small streams into minor divisions, which are possessed by clans having hereditary chiefs, who exercise a species of patriarchial authority, and may be regarded as the heads of families.

The obligations of the clansmen to their chief are of a general and trifling nature. He is the arbiter of all disputes, and the dispenser of justice, from whom there is no appeal; but he raises no tribute, and requires no personal service except in war, or for the transaction of public business. Though the land, wherever unoccupied, is considered the common property of those who belong to the clan, the chief alone can dispose of it by sale or otherwise to persons who do not. But even he is unable to sell it to any but Indians; for, as a means of preserving their territorial integrity and national independence, it was long since decreed by the Araucanians, that any person guilty of selling lands to the whites should be put to death. Yet there are not wanting those who have succeeded, first by intoxication, and afterward by threats of exposure, in wheedling the natives out of large tracts of land, which the purchasers occupy as tenants until an opportunity may arrive of openly asserting their claims.

These chiefs (properly called *Apo-Ghelmenes*, though usually known among the Chilenos as *Caziques*) are independent of each other, and politically equal, though in each district there is always some one to whom, on account of distinguished family, great courage, or superior abilities, a certain authority is conceded by the rest. The office of Cazique, though descending to the eldest son, may be otherwise disposed of by the dying incumbent, who frequently sets aside the natural heir to favor a younger son, and sometimes even selects as successor a person not of his own family. Should a Cazique die, leaving neither male issue, brothers, nor a chosen successor, the power of election reverts to the people, who generally create a new Cazique from among the *Ghelmenes*, a class of hereditary nobles occupying an intermediate position between the chiefs and the common herd.

From among the chiefs of the various districts one is selected as *Toqui*, or head of the province. The various Toquis form what is termed the Council of Peace; to which, under ordinary circumstances, is intrusted the general supervision of the nation. This council is in turn presided over by one of its own members, who might be termed the President of the Peace Council. This *Grand Toqui* is the highest officer in the state: to him it belongs to watch over the common weal; to give notice to his colleagues of whatever may occur of general importance; to adopt for the public good such measures as may be rendered necessary by particular emergencies; and when momentous questions arise, to call together a general assembly of the nation.

In these general assemblages, though the discussion of public topics is mostly left to experienced and prominent chiefs, the right of every one to a hearing is admitted, and suggestions, even from sources least entitled to respect, are fully considered, if deemed of importance.

These national councils, which are but seldom convened, are the occasions of much ostentation, as each one strives to outdo his neighbor in rich apparel, costly ornaments, and fine horses; they are also accompanied by much feasting, drunkenness, and revelry. The consultations of the day are usually followed by a feast, succeeded by bacchanalian orgies, continuing through the night, and often during the following day, until headaches and satiety induce the drunken legislators to resume their labors.

Some have discovered in this weakness a deep design, assuring us that the Araucanians argue topics of importance when *thirsty*, ponder upon them when *drunk*, and decide when *sober*, in order to avoid rash and hasty conclusions. But the explanation, though ingenious, is gratuitous. The Indian gets tipsy for the love of the thing, rather than for the sake of deriving any wisdom from intoxication, and revels after his patriotic labors just as many a Congressman, after a hard day's work, indulges in a spree by way of relaxation.

Laws the Araucanians can scarcely be said to have, though there are many ancient usages which they hold sacred and strictly observe. Nor does their mode of life offer those inducements to ceaseless litigation that are found where the diversity of interests is greater. Blood is avenged by blood at the hands of the relatives of the slain, and thefts are satisfied by restoration of the property stolen, or a greater amount, as may be decided by the Cazique, to whom such matters are referred.

In time of war the Araucanian government is much more efficient. No sooner are hostilities resolved upon than the Council of Peace becomes powerless, and is superseded by a Council of War, presided over by a Toqui, who, during the continuance of the war, has an unlimited power, except over life. He appoints his officers, determines upon the number of men requisite for the army, and informs the Toqui of each *Uthal-Mapu* what contingents will be required from his province. Men, horses, and provisions, are all subject to his control, and though he may be deposed by the popular vote, he is, during his continuance in office, irresponsible for his actions.

When the war is ended the Council of Peace once more becomes supreme, and the Toqui of Peace is again recognized as the head of the government.

Mañin, whom we were about to visit, has held this office of Toqui of Peace for more than twenty years, and great is the respect paid to his authority, not only on account of his station and family, but still more for his superior wisdom, for he has done more than any other person could have accomplished to heal the domestic dissensions of his countrymen, and avoid collisions from abroad.

We were accompanied for some distance upon our road by a Chileno who worked for a neighboring Indian, receiving for his labor in cultivating the land a certain percentage of the produce. There are many such scattered around the country, mostly fugitives from justice, picking up a livelihood by doing odd jobs. Frequently they marry native women, and rapidly fall to a level with the Indians, with whom they readily assimilate, preserving no distinction except the name of Christianity.

Our road lay to the eastward until we rounded a hill, when we again turned to the south.

Near this hill we stopped to barter for a horse, and I was much struck by the appearance of the stragglers drawn together by our arrival. They belonged to the warlike tribe of Colyico, and were physically the finest specimens I had yet seen of the Mapuchés, being taller and more robust than the generality of their countrymen. In this respect the Araucanians disappointed me, for they by no means came up to my conceptions of the "gente indomitable," as described by Ercilla. They are generally of about the middle height, broad-chested, thick set, inclined with age to corpulency, and, as a race, far inferior in appearance to the North American aborigines. The calves of their legs and their ankles are large and fleshy, and the foot, though very short, is broad and high, rising abruptly from the big-toe to the ankle with very little curve. The head, too, of the Mapuché is of a peculiar shape; it is narrow and low in front, broad and high behind, and forms almost a straight line with the back of the neck, which is massive and short.

This marked type of head and foot is found universally among the lower classes of the Chilenos, and to a certain extent (according as the old Spanish blood has been more or less corrupted) among the highest classes also. So much is this the case, that most foreigners in Santiago experience difficulty in procuring shoes, which are always found to be too broad, and too high in the instep, to fit the European foot. The shape of the head, as noticed more especially among the females, who wear no bonnets, seldom fails to attract the stranger's attention.

These facts clearly indicate that great preponderance of Indian blood in the people, which a knowledge of Chilian history would naturally lead us to expect, for the "peons" are but the descendants of subjugated Indian tribes, and we know that the Spanish conquerors, being military adventurers, with few exceptions, brought no families with them, but on settling down in the country, intermarried with the native women.

The Chilenos themselves are apt to ignore these truths, and the epithet "Indio" is resented as a most insulting term of abuse. On one occasion Lieutenant Gilliss having sent to the statistical office to inquire the relative proportion of pure and mixed races in the country, was answered, rather indignantly, that there was scarcely one Chileno in ten with a drop of Indian blood in his veins! Had the answer been that there was scarcely one in a hundred of unmixed Spanish origin, it would have been much nearer the truth.

Several of the Indians that we saw at Colyico were painted with red and black, and, owing perhaps to the streaks about their eyes, looked unpleasantly scowling. Though their manner was friendly and respectful, I could not help thinking that I was too hasty in packing away my revolver in the valise, as a useless encumbrance; but this feeling soon wore off. Sanchez, as well as the rest of the party, carried no arms except the "machete," a long knife which every "Guaso" considers indispensable for all the manifold purposes of cooking, eating, and horse-doctoring. At the outset he had advised me to carry no arms, assuring me that I would travel more safely than in any other part of Chili, and for aught we saw to the contrary, he was right.

On resuming our journey we distributed among the by-standers a few handkerchiefs and Jew's-harps, with which, especially with the latter, they seemed much pleased.

This instrument has become national with the Mapuchés, as much so as the guitar with the Spaniards, and no young gallant is considered fully equipped and provisioned to lay siege to a lady's heart if unprovided with a Jew's-harp. As the troubadours of old wore their lutes suspended from the neck by silken cords, so the Mapuché lover carries always with him his amatory Jew's-harp, hanging upon his breast, dangling from a string of many-colored beads, and carefully tied upon a little block of wood.

The Indians play this simple instrument very well, and almost entirely by inhaling instead of exhaling. They have ways of expressing various emotions by different modes of playing, all of which the Araucanian damsels seem fully to appreciate, although I must confess that I could not.

The lover usually seats himself at a distance from the object of his passion, and gives vent to his feelings in doleful sounds, indicating the maiden of his choice by slyly gesturing, winking, and rolling his eyes toward her. This style of courtship is certainly sentimental, and might be recommended to some more civilized lovers, who always lose the use of their tongues at the very time they are most needed.

With the dulcet strains of half a dozen German Jew's-harps still echoing in our ears, we plunged into a dense thicket, entering one of those primeval forests that skirt the first ranges of the Cordilleras; standing, as they have stood for centuries, undisturbed in their solemn majesty, and never resounding to the stroke of the woodman's ax. The silence was imposing: there was no sound of bird nor other living thing, and though we kept a bright look out for the diminutive deer that are said to abound, we saw nothing to indicate their presence.

Many of the trees were of species entirely new to me, rising frequently with immense trunks to great heights, without branches, and leafless except at their summits; but twined and festooned with innumerable creeping vines, prominent among which was the graceful "copigue," gorgeous with its crimson blossoms. Underneath there was but little bush, except where the "coligué," growing in dense brakes, lifted its taper points, twisting and intertwining high in air, almost like creeping vines.

But there was little time to stop and admire, for the tortuous path wound among rocks, between thick trees, over stumps and fallen trunks, keeping us continually on the alert to avoid barking our shins, or twisting our feet; while at intervals we were obliged to lie forward over the horses' necks, in passing beneath the matted coligués arching overhead. Sometimes we would plunge down steep gullies, floundering about in deep quagmires, faced by slippery banks. The path, by frequent travel, was deeply worn, and altogether it seemed to me rather the worst specimen of a road I had ever seen.

As we picked our way cautiously, in single file, we were overtaken by an Indian, whose approach was first announced by a loud salutation, "*Mari-mari epu!*" ("Good day both of you!") breaking the stillness of the forest. Riding up, he began speechifying at

Sanchez, droning over the usual compliments in the most approved style of polite monotony. This was carried on for nearly an hour, and was evidently intended to relieve the tedium of the journey; but upon me it had an opposite effect, and I should have fallen asleep in the saddle, if not aroused by an occasional bump against the trees.

Leaving the woods, we came out upon a fine plain, studded with clumps of trees, and saw, for the first time, the summit of Ketredeguin, directly to the eastward. This prominent peak is a truncated cone, presenting every appearance of a volcano, not only from its form and color, but from the fact that while the base is covered with snow, the top is perfectly bare. No smoke was visible; nor could I learn of any former eruptions, though a half breed, familiar with the mountain districts, asserted that he had seen smoke issuing from a vent hole upon the eastern declivity, and others, who had visited the neighborhood, informed me that around the base there are large beds of scoria.

As most of the Chilian volcanoes are slumbering, exhibiting, only at long intervals, slight signs of activity, it is probable that Ketredeguin is one of these dormant volcanoes, the number of which, in the Andes of Chili, I have reasons for believing much greater than is generally supposed.

CHAPTER XXII.

Visit to Mañin.—Origin and Traditions of the Mapuchés.—Distribution of Presents.—Munchausen Stories.—Adoption.—Namcu-Lauquen.—Names.

THE regal palace of Mañin is situated in a pretty, open nook, backed by wood-crowned hills, at whose feet winds a crystal brook, dancing merrily over its pebbly bed. With its green meadows, pure waters, and lofty trees, this seemed one of the loveliest spots in what is undoubtedly the finest portion of Chili. Sanchez extolled the fertility of the soil.

"If these barbarians could only be expelled," he said, "we Christians would soon get rid of the trees!"

"Better," I answered, "that the barbarians remain, and that the trees be allowed to stand."

"What are they good for?" was the reply.

We found the house in no way differing from the ordinary Indian houses, except that it was larger than usual, being about eighty feet long by thirty broad. The "ramada" (or shed, serving as a protection from the sun), was very large, of the same length as the house, before which it stood, and about sixty feet wide. It was supported by some five rows of posts, twelve or fifteen feet high, and was capable of holding a large number of persons. It had doubtless been built with a view to accommodate the congress of chiefs that occasionally assembles here for consultations. Along one of the sides was a rude divan, raised two or three feet from the ground, and about four feet wide, constructed of rough-hewn planks supported on logs. The back of this sofa was formed by the huge trunk of some former monarch of the grove—the whole was spread with sheep-skins covered with ponchos. Upon this seat of honor reclined Mañin as we approached.

"I bring you the son of your old friend Vega," said Sanchez.

"Vega!" exclaimed the old man rising, with an air of surprise; and seizing my hand, he pressed it to his heart. This token of affection I reciprocated, not without some compunctions of conscience at the manner in which I had insinuated myself into the confidence of the noble savage, accompanied by the pleasant reflection that, if detected in my villany, not only that confidence but my ears also might be forfeited.

After an interchange of very hyperbolical compliments, we were told to be seated on the divan, and leaving pleasure to follow business, the Toqui began sounding Sanchez as to the movements and intentions of the Chilian government. He seemed ill at ease about the intended visit of the President, fearing that it boded no good to the Indians, and his conscience was evidently troubled by the reflection that, in the late civil war, he had taken an unnecessarily prominent part in favor of the unsuccessful revolutionists, a crime which he could hardly hope had been forgotten.

During this *big-talk* I amused myself by examining the appearance of the old chief and his domestic arrangements.

"Mañin-Hueno" (The Grass of Heaven), or, as he is generally called by the Chilenos, "Mañin-Bueno (*i. e.*, The Good), is very old, his age being variously estimated at from ninety to a hundred, and even more; but in his appearance there is little to indicate so advanced an age. Erect, though not vigorous, with a bright piercing eye, and his long black hair, but sparsely scattered with gray, he might be taken for a person of sixty. His nose is slightly aquiline, his cheek deeply furrowed, his chin massive, and his whole air is that of one of strong will and accustomed to command. His voice is deep, but not harsh, and he speaks deliberately, as though weighing well the import of his words; he also listens attentively, as becomes one chosen for his superior wisdom to preside over the welfare of the nation.

The dress of the Grand Toqui was not, it must be confessed, such at might have been expected, considering his exalted rank. He wore a shirt that probably had been used for several months without washing, a ragged military vest, and a poncho, tied round the waist and falling to the feet like a petticoat; a red and yellow handkerchief surmounted his head and completed his costume. I noticed, however, hanging overhead a bridle, bit, headstall, and reins, covered with massive silver ornaments; and though the powerful Mañin is generally considered a poor chief, two hundred hard dollars would scarcely have furnished the silver lavished upon his various horse trappings.

Near us hung several joints of suspicious-looking meat, the remains of a cow that had been found dead and cut up for use. Under the circumstances we did not regret that no meat was set before us, though we were regaled with toasted wheat and "mudai." The dishes and spoons were wooden, nor did we either upon this or upon any other occasion catch a glimpse of those massive silver plates which the Araucanian chiefs are often represented as setting before their guests. The Mapuchés are very extravagant in ornamenting their horses and wives, but in no other respect do they display much barbaric magnificence, and they care more about the quantity of their food than about the style in which it is served up.

So soon as the affairs of the nation had been fully discussed, Mañin turned to me and made many inquiries about my father and friends. Though it puzzled me to give the exact number of my brothers and sisters, and to tell whether my mother was living or dead, my story was plausible enough, and seemed to be satisfactory.

Next followed questions about Spain, Buenos Ayres, and Lima, marked by shrewdness, and displaying more geographical knowledge than I expected; particular inquiries were made about the Spanish government, and the probability of its ever reconquering the Chilenos; for, strange to say, these people cherish a strong love for the Spaniards (in contradistinction to the Chilenos). They long for the return of those days of vice-regal power, when the behests of the king were communicated through "parlamentos," at which the chiefs were received with trumpets, banners, presents, and other marks of respect calculated to conciliate and flatter. Under the republic an opposite system is pursued; the Indians are generally treated with ill-disguised contempt, and they do not fail to perceive the difference.

The fact that the present Spanish sovereign is a queen, caused much surprise; the old savage was unable to comprehend that a woman could occupy any other than a subordinate position in any well-regulated community.

I tried to discover whether the Indians retain any traditions of times anterior to the Spanish conquests, especially of the encroachments of the Peruvian Incas; but I was surprised to find that their historical recollections extend scarcely farther back than the wars of the South American independence. In regard to the Spanish conquests they have but the most vague and confused ideas. The ruins of the "cities of the plain" are scattered in their midst; ditches, orchards, and other traces of a superior cultivation still mark the site of the once flourishing establishments of the Jesuits. But the Indian passes by all these in silence. He has an indistinct remembrance that the white man once flourished here—he recalls the mysterious influence exerted over his people by the children of Loyola—perhaps he has heard the old men recount the terrors of a conflict long since past; but the deeds, the very names of those who restored their country to freedom are forgotten. Some of the questions which I wished to ask respecting the wars with the Spaniards, Sanchez thought it better not to interpret, assuring me that the Indians were entirely ignorant on the subject, and he thought it well that they should remain so.

As far as I could learn, the Mapuchés have no idea whatsoever of their origin, but assert that they always lived in the same place and manner as at present; nor have they any traditions respecting the deluge.*

* Molina says that they assert at times that their ancestors came from the East, and at others that they came across the sea from the West. Again he says:

"The Chilians call their first progenitors Peñi Epatun, which signifies the brothers Epatun; but of these patriarchs nothing but the name is given. They also call them 'Glyce,' primitive men, or men from the beginning, and in their assemblies invoke them, together with their deities, crying out with a loud voice 'Pom, pum, pum, mari, mari, Epunamum Aninxalguen Peñi Epatun!' The signification of the first three words is uncertain, and they might be considered as interjections, did not the word 'pum,' by which the Chinese call the first created man, or the one saved from the waters, induce a suspicion, from its similarity, that these have a similar signification. The 'Lamas,' or priests of Thibet, from the accounts of natives of Hindostan, are accustomed to repeat on their rosaries the syllables hom, ha, hum, or om, am, um, which, in some measure, corresponds with what we have mentioned of the Chilenos." (Mol. Hist. Chil., Vol. ii. Chap. i., Eng. Trans.)

According to Hooker in his "Himalayan Journals," lately published, the universal Buddhist formula is "Om mani padmi om" (*i.e.* "Hail to him of the lotus flower and the jewel!"). These are evidently the words of a prayer referred to by Molina, but when their meaning is understood, they seem to have no relationship to the Mapuché words given.

Molina also informs us that these Indians have a tradition about a deluge; but from the details given he thinks it must refer to some volcanic eruption, accompanied by a flood and earthquakes.

The old chief, learning that I had been somewhat of a traveler, was anxious to gain information about countries of which he had heard much: as, for instance, the land of pigmies, that of the giants, and that in which the people carry their heads under their arms: all these regions had been described to him by the traders who had often visited them in the pursuits of commerce; but I was forced to acknowledge that I had never visited either Lilliput, or Brogdignag. He did not know that he had been, all his life, in close proximity to the most renowned giants of the world, and was surprised to learn the fabulous reputation of his neighbors, the Patagonians. Both he and Sanchez had roamed over the plains of Patagonia, where they had met many nomadic tribes, mostly Mapuchés; but though those Araucanians who live among the mountains, and are larger and more athletic than those dwelling in the plains, frequently wander as far as the Strait of Magellan, he had never met any of them that equaled the gigantic proportions of the people described by the early navigators.

So far we had been unmolested by women, children, and the usual hangers-on, who kept at a respectful distance, only venturing to approach when summoned by Mañin; but the moment the baggage was opened, and it was understood that there was to be a distribution of presents, they began to appear in every direc-

This explanation is plausible, and the event referred to was probably an earthquake like those that destroyed Concepcion and Valparaiso, when the sea, after retiring from the shore, rushed back and overwhelmed the ruined cities.

tion, though still hanging back until called by name. First came the wives, eight in number, to each of whom was given an ounce of indigo, a string of beads, and a dozen brass thimbles. One of the wives, named Juana, laid claim to an extra string of beads on the score of being a Christian. She was rather pretty, and had once been white, though burnt by exposure to near the Indian complexion. When a child she was captured from the whites; and on the conclusion of peace, having become habituated to the Indian mode of life, she preferred remaining as the favorite wife of a powerful chief to returning to her parents, who were of humble position. She had several pretty children and one grown-up daughter, who was absent at the time.

After the women, the children came trooping in, some twenty in number. And I was surprised, considering the advanced age of Mañin, to see among them two or three still at the breast, brought by their mothers to receive a share of the spoils. Each one received a bright cotton handkerchief and a Jew's-harp, or a string of beads; and two or three of the young men, the oldest of whom was about twenty, received a double share, out of consideration for their years.

The air was immediately vocal with the sound of sweet music made by a score of youngsters capering about with red and yellow handkerchiefs on their heads, and, attracted by the dulcet harmony, a dozen men and women, old and young, came shuffling in from as many different directions. Each one was introduced as some near relation of the chief, and as such, of course, was entitled to something.

But the climax was capped by the presentation to Mañin himself of a pair of gold epaulets. (As they had belonged to an officer long since dead, and of a rank now abolished in the Chilian army, I *got them cheap*). These were the admiration of all beholders, and were accompanied by a very complimentary speech, to the effect that "they had been selected not for their value, but as emblems of authority worthy of one who, both in peace and in war, had been preeminent among his countrymen," etc.

The old gentleman was overwhelmed, but preserved a dignified composure, and tried to take it all as a matter of course, though he told Sanchez, confidentially, that he could not find words to express his gratitude—adding, in parenthesis, that he only regretted *not having a coat good enough for the epaulets.* He was sorry that, having sent all his animals off to the mountains, he could not acknowledge my gift on the spot by one of his best horses; but he intended to send some of his young men to Concepcion in the spring, and he would avail himself of the opportunity to forward me a suitable present.

This was but in accordance with established usage, for the Mapuchés are essentially a bartering people. Whatever present is made, or favor conferred, is considered as something to be returned; and the Indian never fails, though months and years may intervene, to repay what he conscientiously thinks an exact equivalent for the thing received.

The presents naturally led the old gentleman, who possessed an enlightened curiosity not common to his race, to inquire about the people who manufacture knives, guns, etc. He wished particularly to know if I had visited "*Lancatu-Mapu*" (the Country of Glass Beads). Supposing that he referred to Germany, I answered in the affirmative.

"Is it true," he asked, "that the beads grow upon trees in the land of the setting sun, and that they who gather them ride into the country at night on swift horses, and return laden before the rising of the sun, whose first rays would burn them to death?"

I felt indignant that any one, to enhance the value of his wares, should have told such a Munchausen story to the too credulous savage, and answered accordingly. But Sanchez dropped me a hint about "people in glass houses," and translated my reply in a manner not calculated to disturb the old gentleman's faith. He feared, perhaps, to endanger those who had fabricated the fable. It may be that he himself felt some interest in its promulgation.

We also gave the chief some tobacco, and handing it to his wife she soon returned with a pipe made of a dark stone (probably soapstone), with a straw inserted for a stem.

These people are excessively fond of tobacco, which they procure from the Chilenos, and, to some extent, from the Pehuenchés, who bring it from Buenos Ayres. Often to get the full benefit of a little, and to "make drunk come," they swallow the smoke, which produces stupefaction and a species of convulsions. The smoker while in this state, is allowed to lie for some time upon the ground; a drink of cold water is then given him, and he immediately recovers. Chewing is a degree of civilization to which the Mapuchés have not attained.

What with the effects of the pipe and the recollection of favors received, the old chief became more and more attached to the son of his old companion-in-arms: and when Sanchez told him that I desired to learn the language of his people and become as one of them, he promised to make me "*lacu*" (namesake) to one of his favorite sons, thereby adopting me into his family.

INDIAN MODE OF SLEEPING.

As night came on, several of my mothers and brothers *in prospective*—for all of whom there was not sleeping room in the house—began to huddle together on the divans with little other bedding than the clothes they had worn by day. For me, as a member of the family, *in posse*, they spread a hide near by. Upon this I made up my bed; but it soon appeared that my royal relatives were neither savory nor good-mannered—treating me with a brotherly familiarity well calculated to breed contempt—and jumping up, without stopping to dress, I started off for the tall grass, dragging my bed after me. A shout of laughter followed my precipitate flight, but I kept on, and finding Sanchez lying out in the open meadow, put down my bed beside him.

There was no reason to regret the change, for the night was beautifully clear, and the stars shone with that peculiar brilliancy which I have never seen equaled elsewhere than in the pure, dry atmosphere of Chili.

Next morning early, a bright, intelligent boy, about eleven years old, rejoicing in the title of "*Namcu-Lauquen*" ("The Eaglet of the Sea"), the name by which I was in future to be known, was brought up and introduced as my "lacu." I immediately ornamented his head with a brilliant handkerchief, and he started off for the sheep-fold, knife in hand, to kill a lamb for my use.

When the lamb was cooked, the boy's mother approached, and placed before me, on the ground, a huge wooden trencher containing one half the animal boiled. At the same time Mañin told me to accept it as a testimonial of lacuship from his son, who hoped to be able, at some future day, to set before me a larger animal, accompanied by wine, as a feast more worthy of the relationship established between us.

I had often heard that among the Indians it is a point of etiquette, the neglect of which is never pardoned, to eat all that is set before you; and as I looked first at the dish, then at the faces of the company, who were evidently expecting me to do something, I was sorely perplexed by the Brogdignagian meal that seemed inevitable. But Sanchez, seeing me in trouble, came to the rescue, offered to act as my proxy, seized the meat, and tearing it to pieces with his fingers, gave a portion to each one present. Soon after a rich mutton broth followed.

Having thus eaten myself into the family, I was presented to the women and children, respectively, as son and brother, and was greeted with the name of *Namcu-Lauquen*, or (as names are generally abbreviated by dropping one or two syllables) *Namculan.*

The giving of a name establishes between the namesakes a species of relationship which is considered almost as sacred as that of blood, and obliges them to render to each other certain services, and that consideration which naturally belongs to relatives.

Names among the Mapuchés were originally given, as among all primitive people, to designate certain traits of character and appearance, or they were derived from particular circumstances, as *Eupuelev* (The Winner of two Races), *Katri-Lao* (The Red Lion); but the necessity of distinguishing families caused the latter part of the father's name to be transmitted to the children, with some modifications to distinguish individuals. Thus arose such family names as *Hueno* (Heaven), *Coyam*, (Oak), *Lemu* (Forest), etc., analagous to names which will readily occur to any one in the various European tongues.

Still, though surnames are becoming more fixed

with time, national usage makes it optional with parents to transmit their own names to their children or not; and frequently, in a large family, no two will be found whose names bear any relation to each other.

My adopted father, supposing that in paying him a visit I had accomplished my only object, proposed to me, instead of continuing with the traders, to remain with him for a few days, at the end of which time he contemplated a visit to the frontier, and would conduct me on my way as far as San Carlos. The proposition rather puzzled me; but thanking him for the offer, I suggested that as he spoke no Spanish, and I no Indian, the inability to comprehend each other would prove a serious drawback to the pleasure that such an arrangement would otherwise afford. He appreciated the justness of the remark, and thought it better for me to accompany Sanchez, adding, that as I had become a Mapuché, the opportunity would be a good one to make the acquaintance of my countrymen.

CHAPTER XXIII.

Shaving.—Hair-pulling.—Katrilao.—Begging *versus* Taxation.—New traveling Companion.—Mule Doctoring extraordinary.—The good Omen.—Religion of the Mapuchés.—Sacrifices and Libations.—Christian Missions.

HAVING obtained, with so little difficulty, the coveted permission to go wherever we pleased, we started back to join the rest of our party at Chancay's.

On the road we stopped several times, and Sanchez lost no opportunity of recounting my story. I was gratified by the general disposition manifested to treat me with the consideration due to a "prince of the realm. There seemed to be no jealousy excited by the prospect of a foreign dynasty, nor any desire to question the validity of my title; and had I seen fit to settle down, I could no doubt have become the owner of unnumbered acres, and the lord of as many wives as I had the means to purchase.

Near the brooklet of Colyico, which gives its name to the surrounding district, we passed through an extensive field thickly studded with graves. The mouldering mementoes bore evidence of ages long past—it may have been the site of some sanguinary battle, whose name has perished with those alike of the victor and the vanquished. It may have been simply a burial-place for former generations: if so, it would imply a more dense population than that now found in the vicinity, as well as different customs from those which now obtain; for the modern graves in this neighborhood are found solitary, or in groups of two or three, and contrary to the practice farther to the north, generally near the house where the deceased formerly resided.

At one house where we stopped I saw an Indian, who, at first sight, seemed to be a white man, from the fact that his beard was grown as though unshorn for a week. He looked red and blotched, and was continually raising his hand to some part of his face—wearing all the while an expression of patient endurance. A closer scrutiny showed that he was engaged in shaving. These Indians pull out, or nip off the beard with small steel tweezers. This instrument was originally (as the Mapuché name signifies) a clam shell; but by intercourse with the whites, they have been enabled to procure a more elegant article. Every dandy carries his tweezers dangling from his neck, and at leisure moments amuses himself by smoothing his face to the taste of his painted mistress.

The arguments they adduce in defense of their treatment of the beard, are precisely those used by shavelings the world over, and their horror of hirsute appendages is not surpassed by John Bull's; but they are one step in advance of John, inasmuch as, not content with grubbing at the chin and lip, they also pull out the eyebrows, leaving only a narrow arching thread, which they paint black, in order to produce a more striking effect. Some of the young braves allow a very small fringe of hair to shade the upper lip; but the innovation is discountenanced by the older chiefs.

The Greeks, in the time of their degeneracy, are said to have cut the beard because in battle it afforded too good a handle for their enemies; but the Mapuchés are actuated by no such motive in baring the chin. On the contrary, while they cut the hair short on top of the head, it is purposely left long at the back and sides, that it may be easily grasped. To reproach an Indian with wearing short hair is equivalent to calling him a coward; and the common taunt among boys is not, as with us, "Come and wrestle if you dare!" but "Let us pull hair, if you are not afraid!"

Such a challenge is never refused. In an instant ponchos are whipped off, the chiripa is gathered up to give the legs free play, and the combatants stand face to face. A fair hold is taken of the long locks back of the ear, and the struggle commences; each tries to twist the other's head so as to destroy his balance, and bring him to the ground, in which consists the victory. Once down, there is no pommeling nor pulling, but the hold is immediately loosed, and again they confront each other. They rub the back of their necks for a moment, shake their heads defiantly, and the tussle is resumed. This continues until one of the two is fairly beaten out, after which they remain as good friends as ever.

We reached Chancay's house in time for supper, which I should have relished heartily if not for the never-failing *aji*, which is more used, if possible, by the Indians than by the Chilenos themselves; for not only do they saturate their food with it, but often when eating they hold in the hand a pepper pod, taking an occasional bite as a relish.

Next morning, as I was making my toilet, our hostess fell desperately in love with my fine-tooth comb and pocket looking-glass; so much so, that I promised on my return to present them to her—a promise which filled her heart with gladness. Her own comb, which she showed me, was a small bundle of bristles, made up like a paint brush, minus the handle. Mirror she had none, except the glassy surface of the spring, over which, as she descended every morning for water, she would hang to arrange her raven tresses, and paint her dusky cheeks.

After breakfast we started back to Mañin's. About half way we stopped at the house of a half-breed named Katrilao—a Christian in name, as was also his wife, who, though an Indian, had lived among the Chilenos long enough to learn Spanish and some of the ways of civilization. But the possession of a crucifix and a cheap lithograph of the Virgin Mary was probably the only difference between her Christianity and the heathenism of her neighbors.

Katrilao's lands were well tilled and fenced; and he seemed much better off than the great majority of the lower classes of the Chilenos. Immediately around his house was an apple orchard which, judging from the age of the trees and the regularity with which they were set out, must have been planted by Spaniards—probably by the Jesuit missionaries. The apple every where abounds in Southern Chili, and is found throughout the Indian country growing wild; yet that it is not indigenous, but owes its introduction to the Spaniards, seems clearly proved by the fact, that the Indians designate the fruit by the name of *manchana*, an evident corruption of the Castilian *manzana*.

We found Mañin-Hueno pretty much as we had left him the day before, except that he had laid aside his shirt, and wore instead an old, tattered uniform coat of antiquated pattern, profusely embroidered with gold, and bearing on the button the Spanish arms—a relic of the times when, under the auspices of the crown, he waged war against the republic. It boasted a stiff standing collar, and was made to button to the throat; but he wore it hanging open and loose for comfort, or for the display of his tawny breast and paunch, which were without covering.

Most of the women were absent, probably on begging expeditions; for we saw one of them returning, her horse loaded down with corn, potatoes, and a little of every thing else. As before mentioned, the chiefs levy no direct tribute; but when poor, and with large families, they frequently go the rounds of their subjects, complaining of bad crops, hard times, etc., and contributions, though not compulsory, are seldom refused to such powerful beggars. They also have a fashion of sending off the different members of the family on visits to friends; thus quartering them on people who are glad in the end to send them home with some present, in preference to enjoying their company.

For breakfast and provisions upon the road we bought two sheep, sending to one of the neighbors for the purpose, as required by the punctilious etiquette of the Mapuchés; for though our host, who had killed one animal for us on our first arrival (more than which their ideas of hospitality do not require), would not have killed another for us had we remained a month, yet the offer to buy a sheep from his fold would have smacked of rudeness, and been considered a reflection upon his generosity.

Besides the meat we were bountifully supplied with other things; for no sooner were we ready to start than the women came forward, each one with a dish of something under her cloak. One had boiled eggs; another a boiled fowl; but most of them brought toasted wheat and linseed ground together, of which I had already become fond, regarding the "ulpo" as not only a pleasant beverage, but almost as a necessity, in the absence of bread.

These presents were but returns for beads and trinkets received on our arrival. Those of the women who had children brought several different articles, saying, as each one was presented:

"To my son you gave a handkerchief; he sends you these eggs. To my daughter you gave beads; receive this flour in her name."

Katrilao, the half-breed, joined our party, and as a guide we carried one of Mañin's nephews, to whom the old chief intrusted us, with many injunctions as to our safety and his own conduct on the road. This gentleman, though a sprig of nobility of the first water, was an ungainly-looking rascal; thick, short, very dark, and with a large scar covering half his face, and distorting his mouth. Especially when excited, he was hideous; but he was good-hearted, honest, and possessed an inexhaustible fund of sport and deviltry. Having once been captive among the Chilenos, he spoke Spanish well enough to be useful as an interpreter, and altogether he was a general favorite.

His name was the same as that of his uncle, Mañin-Hueno; but as he had a perfectly Yankee fashion for swopping with every body, he had acquired the sobriquet of "*Trauque*" (literally a return made for a present received), a term commonly applied to each other by persons who have interchanged gifts.

With the accession of Katrilao and Trauque we numbered seven, and formed a very respectable cavalcade.

After crossing a beautiful brook which ran near the house, we headed to the south, and passing through groves of fine old oaks, soon came upon an undulating plain stretching as far as the eye could reach, and diversified by occasional clumps of trees.

Here the pack-mule, in jumping over a log, stumbled and fell. The *mozos*, instead of kicking and beating him, as is usual on such occasions, commenced unloading the prostrate animal, and placed the pack upon another, for he had broken his back, they said. When relieved of his burden, a few scientific wrings of the tail brought him to his feet. Sanchez then whipped out his knife, and laid open the poor brute's long ear with a gash, from which the blood flowed copiously. A handful of dirt was put upon the spot which the constant swaying of the pack had rubbed raw, and with a kick in the ribs he was sent limping off to join his companions. I thought this a queer cure for a broken back, but held my peace.

"It is a sad loss," said Don Panta, sheathing his knife; "the mule will be worthless for the future!"

But Don Panta was a shrewd jockey, and I suspect that, with a little fattening, the broken-backed creature brought full his original value.

This accident would have been considered ominous had we not soon been favored by a lucky sign. Suddenly our Indian companion, Trauque, put spurs to his horse and dashed forward, gesticulating wildly and shouting at the top of his lungs, while a small white eagle, frightened from its perch, soared majestically round us, and swept away to the far south.

This was the "Namcu," the eaglet whose name I had received but a few days before—and the fact of seeing the bird upon the right hand was deemed a peculiarly happy omen. The prayer—for such it was—addressed to the bird by the Indian struck me as beautiful:

"Oh, *Namcu!*" he cried. "Great being! look upon us not with thy left, but with thy right eye; for thou knowest that we are poor! Watch over our children and brothers; grant us happiness, and allow us to return in safety from our journey!"

The Mapuchés, like the ancients, argue much from the flight of birds, whether upon the right or the left hand. The kind of bird, too, is of great importance. The Namcu is, of all others, the bird they most venerate. In their dreamy notions of religion it ranks as a minor divinity, or, at least, as a heavenly messenger in direct communication with the Supreme Being. This is a strange coincidence with the attributes assigned to the eagle by many and divers nations; but not more strange than the almost universal existence of many other superstitions and customs among nations that could have had no connection with each other, except at a period of the remotest antiquity.

Far different from the Namcu, which is supposed to exert a benign influence over all, is a small black bird, whose shrill note resembles a mocking laugh. The Indian who, on setting out on some enterprise, hears that laugh of evil omen, as the malicious bird hides and dodges amidst the tangled thicket, upon his left, will go on with a desponding heart, or sometimes even turn back, whispering to himself, "Why should I go forward? Shall I not be unfortunate? Is not the Evil One mocking me?"

There are many other things which they regard as forewarnings of good or evil; for, like most ignorant people, they seek a supernatural agency in all things. If a horse stumbles, it portends evil; is there a nervous twitching in any part of the body, it is but the announcement of some good or ill about to happen.

What is the religion of the Mapuchés is an interesting question, but one which is difficult to answer. Ercilla says in his Araucana:

> "Gente es sin Dios, ni ley—aunque respeta
> A aquel que fue del cielo derribado;"

i. e. "They are a people without God or religion, but subject to the devil." But he would probably have said the same, or worse, of any people whose religious notions did not exactly tally with his own. Dobrizhoffer, in his history of the *Abipones* of Paraguay, says: "The savages of Chili are ignorant of the name and worship of God, but believe in a certain aerial spirit called *Pillan*, to whom they address supplications. The devil, which they call *Aloeé*, they detest with all their hearts."

According to Molina, God is called "*Pillan*" (The Thunderer). But *Alhué* means not simply the Prince of Darkness, but any hobgoblin or disembodied spirit whatever—something to be feared rather than detested.

In the Araucana we read of a class of

> "Predicadores
> Tenidos en sagrada reverencia
> Que solo se mantienen de loores
> Y guardan vida estrecha y abstenencia"——

a sort of Mapuché friars who make their living by preaching, and lead a life of austere self-denial. But if such a class ever existed elsewhere than in the brain of the poet, it is now extinct, for the Mapuchés have no priests. Owing to this want of any special expositors of religion, each one entertains his own ideas, which are more or less at variance with those of others. But, as far as I could learn, the belief is universal in the existence of a good and a bad spirit, like the Great Spirit and the Manitou of our own tribes—the one the origin of all good, the other the cause of all evil. Besides these, the Mapuchés have no other gods, though they believe in spirits of various kinds. They have no idols, nor do they worship the heavenly bodies, animals, or any other visible objects.

As they have no priests, so they have no temples, nor any fixed ceremonials of religion. The nearest approach they make to any formal public worship, is in the sacrifices sometimes offered at their national councils, and other great gatherings. An animal is slain, the blood is poured out as a libation, and the heart is borne round, upon a branch of the cinnamon tree, with dancing and a rude choral invocation. The meat is then eaten, and after the feast the bones are carefully collected and thrown into the nearest stream of running water, for being consecrated, it would be profanation to throw them to the dogs.

In time of war a prisoner is sometimes, though rarely, sacrificed. After being led to the place of execution upon a horse whose ears and tail have been cropped, he is called upon to dig a hole in the ground, into which he casts a number of sticks, naming, with each one, some of the celebrated warriors of his people, upon whom imprecations and ridicule are heaped by the spectators. He is then forced to fill up the hole, and having thus, as it were, buried the fame of his countrymen, his brains are dashed out with a club. The heart is torn from his breast, and, while yet palpitating, handed to the Toqui, who, after sucking a few drops of the blood, passes it to his officers that they may do the same. Flutes are made of the prisoner's bones; his head is placed upon a spear and borne round in triumph; and the skull, if not broken, is made into a drinking-cup to be used at their feasts.* But such sacrifices are not properly acts of religion, but rather of satisfaction to the manes of warriors who have fallen in battle.

At the entrance to one of the narrow defiles of

* Molina is responsible for these details; I neither saw nor heard any thing of these ghastly flutes and drinking-cups.

the Cordilleras, in which the Indians are often overtaken by violent storms, Sanchez told me that he had seen a large mass of rock with small cavities upon its surface, into which the Indians, when about to enter the pass, generally deposit a few glass beads, a handful of meal, or some other propitiatory offering to the "genius" supposed to preside over the spot and rule the storm. Other places there may be where certain local rites are performed, but he knew of none.

On receiving a plate of broth, an Indian, before eating, spills a little upon the ground; he scatters broadcast a few pinches of the meal that is given him, and pours out a libation before raising the wine-cup to his lips, as acts of thanksgiving for the blessings he receives, and of acknowledgment of his indebtedness to mother Earth. Thus the same rites by which the polished nations of antiquity returned thanks to Bacchus and to Ceres, serve the rude Indian of Arauco to testify his gratitude to a Supreme Being, whose attributes he seeks not to discover, but whom his untutored mind has learned to adore as the bountiful giver of all good things.

The Jesuits had extensive establishments in this country, the ruins of which are frequently met with; but of the Christianity they taught no traces remain. Probably they made but few true converts; for though respected as individuals, their influence as a body was dreaded, and though always treated with exemplary kindness, they were finally expelled by the Indians, who insisted upon their leaving the country entirely and forever. Other missionaries have since occasionally strayed into the interior, but the only evidences of their labors are a few Christian names, or the possession of medals and crosses, worn with other charms and amulets, and viewed with equal veneration.

At Valdivia, and a few other places on the frontier, there are missions, but their influence is limited to a narrow circle. These missions, of course, are all Catholic, for the government of Chili would tolerate no others. The devoted Gardiner, who afterward perished in his endeavors to carry the light of Christianity to the benighted Patagonians, at one time sought to establish himself among the Araucanians, but was unsuccessful.

Recently the Chilian government has imported a body of Italian friars, to be employed among the Indians, as a preparatory step toward colonizing their country with whites, but the result of the scheme remains to be seen. The Indians perfectly understand the system of tactics, by which a missionary post is made the nucleus for the formation of a town, soon to be followed by another more in the interior; and they will not fail to do all in their power to thwart the plans of the government.

CIDER-MAKING.

CHAPTER XXIV.

Camping Out.—Cider-making.—Plucking Wheat.—Potatoes.—Fingers *versus* Combs.—The Horse-thief.—Juan Yevul.—Regnaco.—Squabble.—The Cholchol.—Value of a Mustache.—Threshing Wheat.

ABOUT sunset we came to a deep gorge, through which ran a small stream; and as there was also fine pasture, and an abundance of apples, we determined to camp here for the night.

A fire soon crackles joyfully, half a sheep is spitted, and carefully planted to windward, so as to overhang the flame but avoid the smoke. José is scientifically adjusting a sheep-skin, wool down, preparatory to making cider; and Juan brings a poncho-full of apples (to my eye very green)—the load is emptied upon the skin, and kneeling upon the ground, these two worthies, with a couple of flexible "coligues," commence threshing lustily.

"*Illi inter sese magna vi brachia tollunt*," and quickly the apples are reduced to a pulp. A jug of water is brought and poured on, the whole is stirred together, and the "chicha" is ready.

As the *patron* I am entitled to the first attentions. A horn is placed on the ground, and José, plunging into the hide, fishes up a mass of pulp, which he squeezes between his long bony paws, converted into a temporary cider press. His hands might be cleaner, but it is useless to stand on trifles.

Such cider is somewhat coffee-colored, and rather sour; but I soon became fond of it, especially with the addition of a little toasted meal, which makes it much more palatable.

After a picnic supper one of the *mozos*, shouldering his saddle gear (his only bedding), started off to sleep upon the hillside as a look out; for though there were no houses near, some straggler, attracted by our fire, might be prowling around, ready to smuggle away any animal that wandered a little from our camp. The rest scattered about within hailing distance of each other, while I made up my bed under a wide spreading apple-tree, whose branches offered a shelter from the heavy dews. The ground was not quite so soft as the skins that the kind squaws had thus far always supplied for mattresses, but we were soon oblivious of the hardness of our beds. In such a balmy climate it is a luxury to sleep in the open air. There is a freshness, a sense of freedom from restraint, for the absence of which no in-door comforts can compensate.

Early in the morning we crossed the stream, which struck me as romantic: soon we reached another, running through a gorge; and an hour or two later, we came to still a third, winding through a deep valley. They were all small, clear streams, dancing over stony bottoms, and at the time not deep, though in the rainy season they swell and become rapid torrents.

The valley through which ran this last stream was very fertile, abounding with orchards and fields of grain. We saw houses scattered at short intervals from each other, evincing a comparatively dense population; and Sanchez informed me that it was thickly peopled throughout its whole extent. Such, indeed, is generally the case; the higher plains are mostly used for pasturage, while the houses are located near springs or running streams. At times a spring will dry up, and the neighbors move off to some more favored spot; for digging wells they do not understand —at least, they do not practice it.

Passing through a field, we met a troop of gayly-dressed boys and girls engaged in picking wheat—plucking each ear separately. Such was the original mode of gathering the crops prior to the introduction, by the Spaniards, of horses and European sickles; but it has gone gradually into disuse, until no longer remembered, except as a pastime for children and youths.

When thus engaged they pair off—a boy and a girl taking a small basket between them—and as they pass through the field, each one, as he (or she) plucks a head of wheat, rubs it upon the back of the other's hand, thus threshing out the grain, which falls into the basket beneath. They keep step to a monotonous cadence, to which also they sing, alternately, verses composed upon the spur of the moment—no very difficult task, as their strophes are without rhyme, or much pretension to measure. The burden of the song is generally love; and as the various parties become separated, each attending to its own affairs, opportunities are offered for the unfolding of many a hidden passion. Often is a coy maiden thus wooed and won.

The group we met were in a merry mood, and seemed much inclined to "chaff" us, criticising our appearance, and otherwise amusing themselves at our expense; until, turning our horses, we made a dash toward a body of damsels, whereupon they scattered in every direction through the bending corn, making the hills re-echo with their laughter as they fled.

Near the hill of *Huirlol* we rested for the siesta, in a spot where others had been before us, for there were still traces of a recent encampment; and, among other things, several small cane frames, about large enough for a man to crawl under, intended as a temporary protection from the inclemency of the weather; for by spreading ponchos over them, and lying beneath, a comparatively rainy night might be passed without getting wet.

Our fire soon procured us visitors; and among others came the son of a neighboring Cazique with most of his family. They brought a quantity of stewed potatoes that were excellent, not only in quality, but also as regarded the cooking. Nowhere in Chili, where the potatoes are always fine, had I seen better, though it is said that farther south, especially on the island of Chiloe, they are raised in still greater perfection. Throughout Chili and Peru, with every variety of soil and climate, from extremely wet to extremely dry, the potato is found of superior quality, and entirely unmolested by any of the diseases which have rendered the crop so precarious of late years in Europe and the United States. Would not a renewal of our stock from South America be the most effectual preventive of the rot.

The women of the company were positively ugly, with the exception of one bright-eyed little squaw, that was really quite pretty: but I was soon out of conceit with her; for as the men gathered about us to talk, the women drew off to one side, and having nothing better to do, began to perform for each other a service, in the absence of fine-tooth combs, highly conducive to comfort. It was a great damper to sentiment to see the pretty squaw thus engaged; but the climax was only capped when, pouncing upon some victim, she would toss him into her mouth, smiling coquettishly as she crushed him between her small white teeth. I experienced a squeamishness about the gastric region that threatened to revolutionize my breakfast. The sight afterward became familiar, but I never became quite reconciled to it.

The men were, as usual, inquisitive, and annoyed us by handling every thing—my gloves especially amused them, for they had never before seen any one, as they said, with "sumeles" (horse-skin boots) on his hands, and were at loss to understand how I could use my fingers. Some of the youngsters even asked me to pull them off, that they might have the pleasure of trying them on—a request that was flatly refused.

We got rid of our troublesome company by a liberal distribution of trinkets; but the Cazique's son held back to consult with Sanchez about some apparently important business; for they carried on a long conversation in low whispers. It seems that he had been helping himself to one of his neighbor's horses, and finding that there was a likelihood of being detected, and made to suffer (for the word of the great

Mañin had gone forth threatening vengeance upon all horse-thieves), he wished to avail himself of Panta's superior wisdom to find some way of smuggling the animal out of the country.

Though well disposed in most respects, these Indians, like all others, are addicted to horse-stealing, which has given rise probably to more quarreling among themselves and with the Chilenos than any other cause. Mañin having talked and counseled a long time in vain, had at length declared that he would make an example of the very next offender, and no one doubted that he would be as good as his word.

Resuming our journey, we rode for some time among the hills forming the western boundary of the plain, from the summit of one of which we, for the first time, descried the volcano of Claima—a beautiful double cone towering high above the surrounding mountains, and standing out, with its snowy mass, in bold contrast against the blue sky. Both the craters seemed to be emitting smoke, but owing to the distance it was not easy to determine.

On the road we met a party of young men—apparently Chilenos of the middle class—wearing the full European dress, without even the poncho, though, except in the cities, that garment is universally worn. We saluted them in Spanish, but were much surprised to receive an answer in the Indian tongue; for they were the sons of a neighboring Cazique named Juan Yevulcan.

This Juan Yevul (as he is generally called) is a chief of wealth and importance; and is much more intelligent than the most of his countrymen. Having lived among the Chilenos he speaks Spanish well, has acquired many European ideas, and lives somewhat like a Christian, although he keeps a seraglio of eight wives, and is desirous of adding as many more to the number. His lands, through which we passed, are extensive, and under better culture than any we had yet seen; and his house, which is large, is said to be furnished in a manner somewhat approaching to civilization. Sanchez and Trauque turned aside to pay the customary visit of ceremony; but, under the circumstances, it was prudent for me to keep out of sight, and I went on with the mozos without seeing the wonderful Indian, who is said to eat from a table and sleep between sheets.

We arrived about sunset at a place called Regnaco, on a stream of the same name. It is quite a little hamlet, there being six or eight houses within a stone's throw of each other ranged along the road, and forming the only approach to any thing like a village that we met in the whole country.

The Mapuchés all have an aversion to living in towns; but it is probable that this feeling arises, not, as has been supposed, from fear of the enervating influences of such a life, but from their necessities as an agricultural and pastoral people—each one desiring to be sufficiently removed from neighbors to cultivate his crops, and pasture his flocks without being encroached upon by others.

The house at which we stopped was that of a silversmith—a Chileno—a sort of renegade from justice, who had deserted his lawful wife and children to seek a refuge among the Indians, where he might live unmolested with a paramour, whose charms, by the way, hardly justified such a step.

During the night a mule was lost—a valuable animal—and we were delayed for two days in consequence. The time hung rather heavy on our hands; but we amused ourselves by bathing and chatting with the neighbors—a good-natured, lazy set, who would sit and gossip by the hour.

While here an incident occurred illustrative of the feeling existing between the whites and the Indians. A party of two or three traders, who had been buying cattle in the interior, arrived at the house, and were soon engaged in gambling at the old-fashioned game of pitch-penny. During the game one of the traders lost a quarter of a dollar. Having hunted for it in vain, he went on playing; but soon after a jauntily-dressed young Indian, pulling out a quarter of a dollar, offered it for a sixpenny harmonicon. The trader immediately claimed the coin as the one he had lost, and demanded its restitution. This was refused; whereupon he seized the young chieftain by the neck, threw him roughly to the ground, and planting a knee on his breast, jerked the money from his fingers. The Indian rose, his eyes flashing fire, his frame quivering with rage; but though a long knife glistened in his sash, and the unerring "laqui"* hung at

* The "laqui" (or "bolas" of the Buenos Ayreans) is a triple slung-shot, used as a missile weapon. In using it one of the shot is grasped in the hand, and the other two are whirled around the head until a sufficient impetus is attained, when it is thrown with great force and precision. It is no less efficient than the lasso in catching wild cattle; for it may be thrown so as to wind around the legs of a flying animal, and bring him instantly to the ground.

his waist, he pocketed the affront, and skulked off vowing vengeance upon his assailant.

Though the young Indian was the son of a wealthy Cazique, the others who were present looked on in silence without espousing the cause of their countryman. Like the Spartans of old, they thought the thief deserving of punishment, not for stealing, but for allowing himself to be detected.

The traders seldom hesitate to take the law into their own hand, though far in the interior, and completely at the mercy of the people whose feelings they often needlessly outrage. But, unless the circumstances of the case are extremely aggravated, the lookers-on seldom interfere; and if blood is sometimes shed, it is generally in fits of intoxication produced by the liquors introduced by the traders themselves. Yet this mild and inoffensive people are often described as turbulent and aggressive.

Leaving Regnaco we rode for some distance through a finely-wooded tract, and soon reached the Cholchol —the only stream we had met since crossing the Bio-Bio that could be dignified by the title of *river*. It was too deep to ford, and we were obliged to travel several miles down the stream to a place where the river was divided by islands into several broad channels.

Near the ford we drew up at a house where a number of Indians were collected. During the "talk" a burly fellow approached, and after scrutinizing me closely, laid his hand upon me, and commenced, as I supposed, an examination of my garments, to which I patiently submitted. But I soon noticed that all eyes were fixed on me, while the remarks of my examiner were received with laughter, in which Sanchez joined more heartily than any one. Not wishing to lose all the fun, I asked the cause of so much merriment.

"Oh, nothing," said Sanchez, "only he takes you to be a woman!"

The truth immediately flashed across my mind. As the sun was very hot I had covered my face, as is commonly practiced in Chili, with a handkerchief, leaving only my eyes and nose visible. This, coupled with a comparatively diminutive person, and a dress different from that worn by the rest of the party, had given rise to the suspicion that I might be a woman—a point which my friend was desirous of ascertaining. No farther explanation was necessary; and, under a sudden admonition from the spur, my horse plunged forward, sending the rascal reeling back among his countrymen, while drawing aside the handkerchief, I displayed my beard, much to the discomfiture of the astonished gentleman, who was met on all sides with shouts of derision.

Fortunately, I had disregarded the counsels of many friends who advised me to shave, in order to conform to the Indian custom; for as I was several times mistaken for a woman, despite a very respectable mustache, if clean shaven, who knows but in an unguarded moment I might have been carried off to become the unwilling bride of some amorous savage?

Beyond the river we were arrested by loud shouting and yelling ahead. Uncertain of the meaning of so much commotion the party halted, while Panta and Trauque went forward to reconnoitre, for much circumspection is needed in approaching an assemblage of Indians, for whatever purpose collected.

After a long palaver we were beckoned to come on, and found some twenty or thirty men, women, and children, engaged in threshing out wheat. The method adopted was that of treading out the grain with horses, as among the Chilenos. Half a dozen horsemen were in the ring reeking with sweat and dust, and bawling at the top of their lungs. When the horses were let out, the women turned in with twigs to sweep to one side the grain and chaff.

As usual, I became the centre of attraction, creating much surprise by my dress, gloves, and complexion, which last, though tanned by several months' exposure to the blazing sun, they were pleased to consider "passing fair." Such compliments are not received every day; but the effluvia which arose from these reeking men—to say nothing about the women—was so peculiar that I was glad to escape their admiration, though obliged to purchase freedom by a considerable outlay of Jew's-harps and thimbles.

CHAPTER XXV.

Singular Carvings. — Business Transactions. — The Boroans. — An Enigma. — Cancura. — Huilyiché Houses. — The Machitun. — Wives of Ayllal.—Weaving.—The Widow.

THE country between the Cholchol and the Cantin is fertile and thickly peopled. Burial-places are numerous, and we again noticed a difference in the method of designating the graves: each one, instead of being inclosed by rough-hewn boards, was marked by a single post, rudely fashioned and ornamented at the top; some by a figure somewhat resembling the European hat; others by what might, by one so predisposed, be constructed into a double-headed eagle.

What this latter carving is intended to represent I could not learn, but it is undoubtedly the same figure met with by the Spaniards when they first visited this region. By them it was hailed as representing the Imperial eagle of Austria, and is said to have suggested the name of *Imperial*, which was given to the city founded in this vicinity.

The double-headed eagle was a favorite symbol with the Spaniards at the time of the conquest, and may still be seen ornamenting many of the old churches and private dwellings throughout Chili. It is not strange, therefore, that they should have been quick to detect this fancied resemblance in the rude Indian carvings, and have drawn from it a favorable omen.

During the day we came across quite an extensive trench, such as are used throughout Spanish Chili for irrigation. Old apple-trees were planted in regular rows, and I even imagined that I could trace in places the furrows of the plow. I asked Trauque what these things meant, but he said he did not know, unless they were the work of the "Tityres"—a common name in Chili for the Jesuits.

We stopped for the night at the house of an Indian, upon the banks of the river Cantin. Our entertainer, though not a chief, prided himself on being a "ghelmen," and did not wish to be confounded with the vulgar herd.

A sheep was immediately killed for us, and dished up in the most approved style. Even the blood, which is generally considered a perquisite of the family, was served up to us, coagulated with salt to about the consistency of thick custard: the whole party pulled out their knives and made an attack upon the pudding. I myself, out of curiosity, ventured a mouthful; but, though not disagreeable to the palate, the idea of eating raw blood was enough to take away all appetite.

After the meal, the usual distribution of presents was made, and as the family was small, we were just congratulating ourselves on escaping cheaply, when in sauntered a neighbor, who was presented as "my brother;" he had hardly settled down to the enjoyment of his share of booty, when in dropped a bleareyed old woman, who proved to be "my aunt;" next followed a stately dowager, fair, fat, and forty, radiant with paint and silver ornaments, looking as innocent as though she had happened in by the merest accident in the world; she was "my sister;" and so it went on until we began to think our host's relatives were innumerable.

These relatives were scarcely satisfied, according to their various degrees of relationship, before the women from the neighborhood began to arrive. It seemed as though every body within a mile around had been telegraphed. They all brought concealed under their cloaks some present, or rather, something for sale. Each, after a salute and a short pause, advanced and placed at our feet her dish of meal or potatoes: the provisions were stowed away in our saddle-bags; a string of beads or a thimble was dropped into the plate in return, and smiling her acknowledgments the damsel withdrew to give place to another. But these presents poured in so fast that they were no longer acceptable, and Sanchez began to diminish the number of beads until his returns were scarcely considered equivalents, seeing which the last comers moved off, as silently as they had come, without so much as uncovering their wares.

One of the neighbors brought a poncho for sale: he asked six dollars for it, about six times its value. To my surprise Sanchez agreed to buy it at this exorbitant price, and pulling out his indigo bag he gave the man six spoonfuls, at one dollar each. The Indian went off satisfied that he had made a good bargain, though what he received was worth about seventy-five cents.

We crossed the Cantin in two branches, and soon after passed the Quepe. In neither case did we experience difficulty in fording. The intervening country was flat, and apparently thickly inhabited.

We were now within the confines of the warlike people of Boroa, concerning whom as many wonders have been related as of the fabled giants of Patagonia. Many of the best informed among the Chilenos believe that the *Boroaché* are a distinct race of *white Indians*, having golden hair and light-blue eyes. And even a distinguished foreigner of high scientific attainments, who, a few years since, passed over the coast-road from Concepcion to Valdivia, speaks credulously of the fair-haired and warlike children of Boroa, who, with ever-jealous eye, guard their borders against the approach of civilized man.

Strange have been the conjectures of those who have endeavored to account for the existence of so singular a race; but, unfortunately for the ingenuity of philosophers and the rhapsodies of poets, the Boroans are but Indians, as copper-colored, as ugly, as filthy, and as uncivilized as any of their neighbors. As among all the other tribes, an Indian may occasionally be met whose brown hair, light eyes, and fair complexion denote the presence of white blood. Such instances are more numerous among those living in and around Boroa than elsewhere, but not sufficiently so materially to affect the general appearance and character of the tribe.

The explanation seems to be simple. It will be remembered that, at the time of the destruction of the "cities of the plain," the inhabitants of the more northern towns were drawn off by the Spanish general, while those of Imperial, Valdivia, and Villa Rica, three important towns situated in this neighborhood, for the most part fell into the hands of the Indians.

The women and children were spared, and held as slaves in the families of their captors. Their descendents, if we may credit Molina, became the most formidable enemies of the Spaniards in after wars, and it is probable that their appearance, wearing the Mapuché costume, and fighting in the ranks of the Boroans, originated the belief in the existence of a tribe of white Indians.

With time the traces of Spanish blood have become effaced by intermarriage with the pure Indian race; and before long the blue-eyed warriors of Boroa will live only in story. Even the few that remain are only comparatively white, and could never be mistaken for members of the Caucasian race.

On the road we came across a Boroan who certainly showed none of the white man, and, strange to say, little of the Indian; but appeared to be a full-blooded African of the wooliest kind. This creature—for whether man or woman it was hard to tell—wore the male attire, and spoke in harsh accents; but the general appearance was that of a woman, which she doubtless was, though she had evidently a desire to render her sex uncertain. She was young, but exceedingly ugly, with an expression of mingled ferocity and cunning, and may have been an imitator, if not a disciple, of the celebrated female *machi* of Boroa, whose tripod she possibly hoped to inherit. She may have been crazy; but it is more probable that she had assumed the "celestial madness," which is somehow always connected with the idea of inspiration.

As we approached, this enigma addressed us with voice and words equally harsh; but feeling no desire to quarrel with so interesting a young lady, we kept on with merely a passing salute.

Leaving the Quepe we turned to the westward, passing a succession of gently undulating hills, parched and desolate in the extreme, until we reached Cancura, and stopped at the house of a Cazique named Ayllal.

The house, like all others in this region, was differently constructed from those farther to the north, having much the form of a boat turned upside down, and being built entirely of reeds and cane, presented, at a short distance, the appearance of a haystack. Its length was about a hundred and forty feet, and the width some thirty odd. The peak stood near fifteen feet from the ground, and the sides sloped down without any eaves. The customary shed of cane and twigs was ranged on one side, and in front ran the heavy cross-bar, within which no stranger presumes to enter without an invitation.

The interior reminded me of a ship's between-decks. On either hand stood a row of cane partitions, forming, as it were, state-rooms for the various members of the family—which was a large one, as several of the sons were married. Overhead were the usual provision-lofts, and down the middle of the cabin blazed half a dozen fires, each having an aperture above it in the ceiling, through which the smoke rose and found its way out through the chimney-holes left open in the centre and at each end of the roof. Large stones were ranged around the fires to support the pots used for cooking, and the ashes were allowed to accumulate as they fell—a custom adding nothing to the cleanliness of the ladies who were squatted round preparing the evening meal.

Where a family is small each wife has her own separate fire-place, and the polite manner of inquiring the number of a man's wives is to ask, "How many fires do you burn?" But where the number is large this is impossible, and, as in the present instance, several cook at one fire.

As the cooking goes on at all hours, these houses are always smoky, and it is probably owing to this cause that most of the old women are troubled with inflammation of the eyes.

One of the neighbors was dangerously ill, and during the night there was a grand *machitun* performed by the arch-exorcist, the medicine-woman of Boroa herself. I wished to be present, but Sanchez would not listen to such a proposal, insisting that we might expose ourselves to violence by appearing to interfere with this witch, whose hatred of the whites and influence over the natives are alike unbounded.

The night was black and threatening—well suited to her machinations. We could plainly hear the monotonous tap of the Indian drum and the discordant song occasionally rising with the frenzy of the moment into a shrill scream, then sinking to a low, guttural cadence, while all else was hushed as for very dread of the unhallowed rites. Suddenly the singing stopped, and there was a long silence, broken by the eruption of a wild troop of naked savages rushing around the house on horse and a-foot, brandishing fiercely lance and sword, and burning faggot, and blazing torch, and making night hideous with their demoniac cries. The frightened dogs howled in dismal concert, and again all was still. The evil spirit had been cast out and driven away. It only remained for the sick man to recover or die.

At Cancura we noticed some peculiarities in the dress of the females, especially in their method of wearing the hair, which, instead of being twisted serpent-like around the head, or allowed to hang down behind, was puffed out at the sides of the face, and hung in a couple of bead-twisted queues upon the breast.

Calling José's attention to this difference of fashion, our conversation naturally turned upon female dress, and without intending any disparagement to our fair entertainers, we compared them with the women we had seen at the house of Chancay. The women who were at work near by did not understand half a dozen words of Spanish; but with that intuitive perception which belongs to the sex, they were not long in discovering that our conversation related to themselves and their dress.

Immediately they held a council of war; and entering the house, they presently returned, each one bringing a net-bag full of trinkets. There were coverings for the head and breast composed of strings of beads of all colors, and dangling with brass thimbles and silver coins. There were rings and pendants for ears and nose; bracelets and anklets, collars and breast-pins of colossal proportions. These were held up for our admiration; and that we might more fully realize their wealth, the ladies proceeded to deck themselves with all their finery. They were at the same time jabbering at the top of their lungs, proving their own superiority to all other women, and appealing to us for a confirmation of their own good opinions.

Finally, the belle of the lot having ornamented her head, breast, and arms to their fullest capacity, stepped in advance of the others, and raising her dress as high as the knee, displayed, to our astonished gaze, a remarkably well-rounded piece of flesh and blood. Patting the calf with honest pride, and turning it about for inspection, she hung it round with beads, adjusted the many-colored anklets, and snapping her fingers contemptuously, poured out a perfect torrent of Mapuché. Unfortunately there was no one near to interpret this harangue, but, from her actions and the frequent repetition of the name Chancay, we gathered her meaning to be pretty much that, in whatever else the wives of Chancay might excel, she would defy them, or any one else, to produce a finer leg than the one before us.

We nodded assent, and reiterated "*Cumé! cumé!*" (Good! good!) But the injured fair ones were not to be appeased, and it was only when repeatedly summoned by the shrill voice of the *Unendom*, or first wife, who has authority over the rest, that they returned to their labors.

These women seemed to be constantly busied in various domestic duties. Some were cooking for their ever hungry lords. Some were hulling out the imperfectly threshed wheat by placing it in shallow wooden dishes, standing in which, they kept up a kind of shuffling motion, throwing up the grain on to one foot, and rubbing it with the other, alternating the feet in a manner that gave them the appearance of dancing in a butter-bowl. Others were winnowing the wheat thus hulled, by tossing it up into the air from small baskets.

Under the same shed where we were quartered, but separated from us by a low fence, were two rude looms, similar to those in common use throughout Chili. Upon these were manufactured all the woolen articles worn by the family, with the exception of a few bright-colored cloths purchased from the traders.

Many have supposed that the art of weaving was introduced among the Mapuchés by the Spaniards; and Ulloa states that, in his time, the Indians in the interior were said to wear no clothing. But the fact that the Mapuché language contains appropriate names for all their different articles of clothing, as well as verbs to express the making of such articles, would seem to prove the contrary. Their principal dye at present is indigo, which they obtain from the Chilenos. But they are probably acquainted with others, for Molina states that their favorite color was a deep bluish green.

At work upon the looms were two females—one a girl about fourteen years of age, the other a buxom widow more advanced in years, but still blooming. When there were no men about, these ladies favored us with a great deal of attention, talking and laughing with, or rather at us continually; and if their gestures were at all appropriate, much of their conversation was not over-delicate. Sometimes they would reach over the partition and attempt to pilfer from our luggage, and the widow, who was the bolder of the two, went so far as actually to pick my squire's pocket.

José being a man of few words, immediately seized the disconsolate widow, and, by gentle violence, compelled a restoration of his property. This she appeared to take in good part, exhibiting no signs of wrath; but we were afterward surprised to learn that, on the return of the men, she made a formal complaint, accusing my trusty follower of an attempt upon her virtue—a striking proof of the correctness of Mr. Weller's opinion, that "vidders are dangerous!"

This trick, it seems, is often resorted to for the purpose of extortion. But whether it was because the lady's veracity was doubted, or her virtue was below par, that no one took any particular interest in her wrongs, or that our party was, in their eyes, too respectable to be molested, certain it is that nobody espoused the quarrel; and the widow, controlling her grief, soon became as familiar and as troublesome as ever.

CHAPTER XXVI.

The Beggar's Dance.—Making Mudai.—Plain of Boroa.—The Volcanoes of Ketredeguin, Llayma, Llogoll, and Villa Rica.—Grinding Corn at Night.—Making Bread.

As I was sitting alone one day during Don Panta's absence, our host, Ayllal, who was not only a powerful chief, but moreover a good-natured soul, seeing me rather down-in-the-mouth, struck upon a plan which he thought could not fail to amuse me.

At his command three dirty little urchins, with very little clothing on, approached me; and after a profound salaam, fell affectionately about my neck. The first two kissed me upon the cheek, but the third, more considerate than the others, saluted me on the mouth. Rising, they began a frantic dance, leaping into the air, slapping their thighs, and screaming incessantly some words, of which the only one I could catch was the interrogative "*Chem?*" ("What?") which was constantly repeated.

When they were fairly out of breath they stopped, and repeated the kissing. After a moment's puffing, the dance was resumed. Then came another breathing spell, more kissing, and another dance.

The chief and others were applauding the boys, and encouraging them to renewed exertions, until I began to fear that my tormentors would never get through;

but José, who had been studying out their words, suggested that they were begging for something. I ordered him to open our pack, and no sooner did the red and yellow handkerchiefs appear than the dancing ceased as if by magic.

As the dancers capered around, each with a fanciful turban twisted about his head, the father seemed proud of his sons, but he was not quite satisfied; something was still wanting to complete his happiness, and after waiting some time, as if in expectation, he intimated, partly by signs, partly by a mixture of broken Spanish and Mapuché, that he was fond of music, and reminded me that I had not yet given him even a Jew's-harp.

In consideration of his importance I presented him with a brass harmonicon. No child could have been more pleased with the toy than was this gray haired chieftain, at whose command hill and vale for many a mile around would bristle with quivering lances, ever ready to do his behests.

While the females were engaged at their various avocations, one of them brought out a dish of meal, slightly moistened, and a small earthen jug, both of which she set down upon the ground. One of the girls approached, took a handful of the meal, and made it into a ball, which she stuffed into her mouth, and with both cheeks distended she returned to her work. Another followed, and another, until all, from the young children to the toothless old crones, wrinkled and blear-eyed, were busy munching and chewing, with their faces puffed out like balls, but still managing to keep up a ceaseless jabbering. In a few minutes the first returned, and lifting up the jug, emptied into it the whole contents of her mouth. She took another mouthful of meal and went off, chewing as before. The rest followed in due time, and so it went on until the meal was exhausted, and the jug was full.

Puzzled to comprehend such singular proceedings, I approached one of the women, and pointing to the jug, inquired, "*Chem túa*?" ("What is that?")

"Mudai!" she answered.

"What! Mudai?"

"Yes," she answered, and laughing at my surprise, she added, "*Cumé! cumé!*" ("Good! good!")

It was useless to seek further information in that

MAKING MUDAI.

quarter, and hunting up Sanchez I inquired of him what they were doing?

"Making mudai," he answered, composedly.

"What! mudai, the liquor I have been drinking for a month past?"

"The very same," he replied, and without noticing the nervous twitchings of my face, he went on to describe the process of manufacturing this beverage, which is a kind of beer, with a sub-acid, and not unpleasant taste.

A bushel or more of wheat is boiled over a slow fire for several hours, at the end of which time the decoction is strained off and set aside to cool. To this a jug-full of masticated grain is added, in order to produce a rapid fermentation. So soon as the fermentation commences, the mudai is considered fit for use.

A bumper of the *fresh brewed* was offered me before night, but I respectfully declined. This process of beer-making does not seem peculiar to the Mapuchés, for Herndon, in his "Valley of the Amazon," speaks of a native drink prepared in much the same way.

Cider is the only other liquor made by the Indians at the present time, for they procure all their wines from the Chilenos. But it is probable that they understood wine-making before the arrival of the Spaniards, for the wild grape is found to some extent in Chili, and the word *pulcu*, universally used to signify wine, is Mapuché.

From the hills of Cancura there was an extended and beautiful view. At our feet the plain, where may still be seen the ruins of the last Spanish outpost (Boroa), was rolled out like a map. The Cantin and Quepe, two threads of silver, were glistening in the sun; upon the far horizon the Cordilleras hung like clouds in mid-air, unconnected, as it seemed, with the plain; over which rose a vail of mist, severing the earth from the dim mountain-tops; and above all, a sight rarely to be met, towered four volcanoes, all plainly visible at the same time. First to the north stood Ketredeguin, black, desolate, and threatening; followed by the graceful, double peak of Llayma, clothed with a robe of purest white; then came the majestic Llogoll, clad in eternal snows, and far to the south glittered the cone of Villa Rica—Ercilla's

> "Gran volcan vecino,
> Frague segun afirman de Vulcano,
> Que regoldando fuego esta contino"—

whose untold wealth of hidden mines lured the greedy Spaniard to build an ill-fated city far in the depths of the wilderness.

Llayma and Llogoll were plainly active, pouring out columns of smoke, that, sweeping along in wavy masses, extended far to the north like an unbroken bank of clouds. At times the summit of Ketredeguin seemed wreathed in smoke, though the distance was too great to enable us to distinguish clearly; but Villa Rica, which is generally in a state of eruption, presented no signs of activity.

As there were several houses in full view, it was impossible at this time to take a sketch of the scene without exciting suspicion.

We were now near the southern boundary of the Araucanian territory, and another day's journey would have taken me to Valdivia, had I been willing to leave Sanchez and go forward with an Indian guide.

At another season of the year I would have done so, being desirous of visiting the southernmost provinces of Chili, having now sufficiently gratified my curiosity in regard to the world-renowned Araucanians; but as the season was arriving at which the heavy northwesterly winds prevail, rendering the passage to Valparaiso by sea difficult, I determined to return with Sanchez to Los Angelos, and preparations were accordingly made for facing to the north on the morrow.

About two hours after midnight we were awakened by a peculiar sound. The women were all engaged in the house, near by, grinding wheat.

The low, incessant rumbling of the mills was accompanied by a soft musical whistle, with which each one lightened her toil. All moved to the one monotonous cadence, which seems to embody their only conceptions of music, serving for every occasion, whether the burden of the song be joy or sorrow.

Occasionally some one would sing for a few minutes, and then drop the theme, to be taken up by another, improvising as they sang. Sanchez, who was lying near, translated for me a few of the stanzas. The song was simple, referring mostly to their labor. The following may serve as a sample:

"We are grinding wheat for the stranger
Who has come from a long way off.
May the flour be white to his eye
And pleasant to his taste,
For he has brought us beads;
He has given us bells to deck our hair."

As I lay gazing up at the tranquil light of the stars, long before the first gray streakings of the dawn, listening to that busy hum—the earliest pleasing sound of life and industry—my mind wandered to the far East, recalling the times when the daughters of Israel were wont to rise in the stillness of the night and grind their corn for the approaching day.*

Never before had I fully realized the import of that terrible denunciation against the children of Jerusalem—"I will take from them the sound of the millstones, and the light of the candle."

The mill used by the Mapuchés in no way differs from that already described as in common use among the country people throughout Chili. It is the same as that used by the Mexicans, as also by the ancient Hebrews, and is doubtless the original patent taken out by Adam when first doomed to eat his bread in the sweat of his brow.

Though the Mapuchés generally use wheat in the form of meal mixed with water, or boiled in broth, they also understand the making of bread, which they call "covqué." We did not see any of it; but probably it is not unlike the unleavened "pan de graza" of the Chilenos—a species of bread made by kneading the flour with lard. We saw several of their ovens, which were simply excavations in banks of earth.

* We learn from modern travelers that this custom still prevails among the Oriental nations, and that the stranger is often awakened at an early hour by the sound of the mills busy in grinding corn to supply the daily wants of the family.

CHAPTER XXVII.

We begin our Return.—Graves of the Huilyichés.—Fording Rivers.—Collecting Cattle.—The Rule of Three.—Ruins of Imperial.—A Miracle.—Cattle-Driving.—The troubles of Trauque.

After taking an affectionate leave of Ayllal and his many wives, we started on our homeward way.

As we were obliged to stop at various places to collect the animals already bought, we wandered considerably from the beaten trail, and saw much that was new and interesting.

We had several fine views of the volcanoes; and taking advantage of a moment when no one was in sight, I drew, as well as the restiveness of my horse would permit, a hasty sketch on a blank leaf of my note-book.

As we came down into the plain, Trauque, who rode some distance ahead, commenced shouting, "*Namculan! Namculan!*" beckoning to me in great glee. Not knowing what to expect, but nothing doubting, I put spurs to my horse, and galloped to the spot where the Indian stood laughing immoderately, and applying to his "Huilyiché" brethren a choice selection of epithets, both Mapuché and Spanish. The object which called for so much merriment and contempt, was the burial-place of some departed hero and his eight or ten wives.

Over each grave was planted an upright log, ten or twelve feet high, rudely carved to represent the human frame. The chief—for such he must have been—stood in the centre of the group with no other clothing than a hat and a sword, while on either hand were ranged the wives "*in puris naturalibus.*" However the sculptor may have fallen short in other respects, he had succeeded admirably in distinguishing the sexes, which seems to have been his principal aim.

These figures, however rude, require more than ordinary skill, and the few Indians who devote themselves to this branch of the fine arts, reap an abundant harvest; for a carved tombstone, which is considered indispensable for a grandee, will bring a fat ox or two, according to the size of the figure and the elaborateness of the finish.

These were the only carved representations of the human figure, or of any other animate object that we met among the Mapuchés, for they have no idols, neither do they mould earthenware vessels into the forms of men and animals, as was customary among the Peruvians.

The Quepe and Cantin were forded without accident, but the Indians experienced some difficulty in getting the animals across. What with their unwillingness to enter the stream, their unruliness in fording, and their capers on reaching the opposite shore, the passage of a large drove of cattle over one of these rapid streams forms an amusing and exciting scene. Here a wild young heifer is rushing back up the bank, followed by a flaunting red poncho, and a cataract of oaths. In the middle of the river an unruly bull wheels about with a show of fight, throwing the whole herd into confusion, while a half-naked savage dashes about in the water swinging his lasso, and hurling at the belligerent a volley of gutturals, hard enough to break every bone in his body. Meantime, on the farther shore, the animals as they land scatter in every direction over the boundless plain.

For the night we stopped at the house of our old friend the Ghelmen, upon the shores of the Cantin.

As we rose in the morning a beautiful sight presented itself. The sun, just about to rise, tinted the eastern sky with the most brilliant hues, forming a gorgeous background, upon which the two volcanoes, Llayma and Llogoll, stood out in bold relief—so distinctly that we could perceive the curling of the smoke jets as they rose from the craters.

The day was spent in collecting the animals which had been bought in the neighborhood. They had all been paid for at the time of making the bargain, and left to be claimed on our return, yet there was no delay, nor any attempt to defraud in giving them up; and whenever a question arose as to the particular animal that had been agreed upon, the trader was allowed to make his own selection. It happened so throughout the journey, though, in several instances, nearly a month elapsed between the purchase and the delivery.

The capture of a particular animal from a herd, with a range of pasture utterly unbounded, except by mountains and rivers, is often difficult, and gives rise to many exciting chases and ludicrous scenes. Even when taken, the captives are not easy of management —their attachment for old associates manifesting itself in frequent attempts to return.

One particular bull gave great trouble. He was a noble fellow, of spotless white—such a one as bore the beautiful Europa through the waters of the Phenician deep, or such a one as might be worshiped upon the shores of the Ganges.

After a long pursuit he was lassoed, and the horseman, who had literally taken the bull by the horn, started off complacently to lead him to the place of gathering. But his bullship did not take the going as a matter of course, for with a mad bellow he charged upon his captor, who, seeing a very formidable pair of horns dashing toward him, started at full gallop, still holding fast the lasso, which he in vain tried to keep "taut." The horse was jaded, and old Whitey was fast gaining. Another Indian bounded forward, and dexterously throwing his lasso, caught the unoccupied horn, bringing up the pursuer with a round turn. The bull was not yet conquered. After plunging and pawing, bellowing and tossing, for a while, he changed his tactics. Making a rush and a feint at one of his annoyers, he wheeled about suddenly, and nearly succeeded in catching the other on his horns. Things were becoming more complicated than ever, when, as the infuriated animal stood head down, with his tail stuck out at an angle of forty-five degrees, a third horseman came to the attack, and whirling his lasso, with a jerk, caught the "caudal extremity" in a running knot!

Thus the two men at the sides were safe, provided

the man behind kept his lasso strained. But a question in the "rule of three" now arose: "If three men catch a bull, one by each horn, and one by the tail, and all pull in different directions, which way can the bull go?"

No one seemed able to work out the answer; but Katrilao was a man ready for all emergencies, and dismounting, he started to the assistance of his companions, armed with a long lance and a red poncho. Running before the bull, he threw the poncho on the ground, a few paces in front; the man behind slackened a little, and the bellowing captive made a desperate plunge at the red cloth. A jerk on the tail stopped farther progress until Katrilao, picking up the poncho on the tip of the lance, tossed it several yards in advance. There was another slackening, another plunge, another jerk, and so on until the "critter" was brought to the desired spot.

The next trouble was to loose the captive. Sundry scientific pulls brought him to the ground, and Katrilao springing forward slipped the lassos from the horns. But another remained on the tail. That, no one would venture to untie, for the bull had risen, and stood glaring frantically around. An Indian, unsheathing his long knife, ran full tilt at the extended tail, and with one blow severed the greater part of that useful member from the body.

This last was the "unkindest cut of all." The poor brute was fairly conquered. He stood with head hanging, eyes glaring, the tongue lolling from his frothing mouth, his once spotless coat defiled with foam and dirt, while the drip, drip, drip of the warm blood upon his heels, rendered the abjectness of his misery complete.

In one of his rides, in this neighborhood, Sanchez came upon the site of the ancient Imperial. He did not inform me until it was too late to turn back, but he assured me that nothing remained except the grass-grown traces of the streets and houses, such as I had already seen at Colhué.

This town, which was the most important of the Spanish settlements in Araucania, was subjected to frequent attacks, and several times narrowly escaped destruction. On one occasion, if we may believe Ercilla, it was saved only by divine interposition.

To make a long story short, while the Indians were encamped within a short distance of Imperial, the Devil appeared, riding on a fiery dragon with twisted tail and forked tongue, and urged them on to the destruction of the city, which he represented as unable to withstand their overwhelming force. Influenced by this counsel, they took up their march, when suddenly the heavens opened, and a beautiful woman, more resplendent than the sun, descended, accompanied by a venerable old man. Addressing the savages mildly, she advised them to turn back, for God had given them into the power of the Spaniards, any rebellion against whose authority would subject the offender to the divine wrath.

Saying thus, she ascended, leaving her hearers in stupid admiration. They of course followed her advice in preference to the Devil's, and returned to their homes.

The date of this undoubted miracle, which, says

the gossiping old chronicler, was attested by many eye-witnesses, was the 23d of April, 1554.

For what reason the divine protection was afterward withdrawn, we do not learn; but the almost obliterated ruins of Imperial bear silent witness that when the too long oppressed savages again arose in their might, no miraculous hand was stretched out to ward off the impending destruction.

Our drove was continually receiving additions, and as many of the cattle were perfectly wild, we had a number of little episodes that served to enliven the journey.

Many was the long chase, and great was the whirling of lassos, and the brandishing of pointless lances as some refractory animal would wheel about and make a bee line for the South Pole.

At the first thicket of *coligue* I procured a long, quivering cane, and thus equipped enrolled myself in the ranks, dashing off with the rest whenever there was a stampede, entering into the wild excitement of the chase, and feeling as though there were no life more noble and inspiring than that of the untrammeled Guacho coursing over the boundless pampas in the full flow of joyous animal spirits, and in the proud consciousness of power.

My horse, too, caught the infection. Pricking up his ears he bounded off, without waiting for the admonition of bit or spur, snorting in exultation, and displaying a degree of enthusiasm of which I had not thought him capable.

The Indian, Trauque, who had always shown a liking for me, was delighted as I galloped about lance in hand. Not a moment passed that he did not shout my name, *Namculan! Namculan!* at the top of his lungs, waving his hand in encouragement, and declaring that I needed but a slight acquaintance with the language to become a perfect Mapuché.

He even wished to instruct me in the use of the *laqui;* but as the tyro is apt to rap himself about the head and shoulders, I did not take many lessons. While thus engaged, I noticed that two of the stones of his laqui were enveloped in several folds of leather, while the third was left entirely naked at the sides.

"When I fight with a *friend*," said Trauque, showing one of the covered balls, "I use this; but when I fight with an *enemy*, I strike him with that!" pointing to the bare stone.

Our progress was necessarily slow and uncertain, and we passed several nights far from any house, in the most quiet and sheltered nooks that could be found. We made no fires for fear of attracting visitors who might be thievishly inclined, and consequently could cook no supper. On such occasions we had to fall back upon the provisions that our saddle-bags afforded, and more than once we passed the whole twenty-four hours with no other food than green apples and toasted wheat.

Strange to say, with this vile diet we all enjoyed the most robust health, and I became convinced that daily exercise on horseback, and living, as we did, entirely in the open air, will enable a person of naturally good constitution to eat any thing with impunity.

At a house upon the road we were unexpectedly detained until late, and we determined to stay there for the night. Meantime Trauque, who had been requested to go on for a few miles and await us, was broiling in the hot sun for half a day, without food or company, and was, moreover, robbed of his tobacco and his Jew's-harp by some Ishmaelites, who, finding him alone in the fields, signified their partiality for smoking and music, at the same time making a hostile display of knives and laquis.

No one remembered the poor fellow's situation until reminded of it by his returning at night, looking five times more black and scowling than ever. Throwing himself on the ground, he sat wrapped up in his poncho, unwilling to listen to excuses, and answering only in angry monosyllables. Seeing him in this humor, I said nothing to him, but was turning away, when, looking up at me, he said,

"*Namculan, won't you speak to me?*"

His voice was tremulous with emotion; and as I saw the big tears standing in his eyes, I could have hugged the black rascal—had he not been so dirty.

There was no earthly reason why this Indian should have formed such an attachment to me; but the likes and dislikes of the untutored savage, like those of a child, are unaccountable and uncontrollable. To be left upon the plains to starve, or to be beaten like a dog, and he a *Ghelmen*, was an insult that his fiery spirit could not brook; but to be treated with indifference by one from whom he expected sympathy, was wounding to the finer chords of his nature, and he felt as does a child when treated with coldness by those from whom he would seek consolation in his sorrow.

But a good supper and a pipeful of tobacco had a soothing effect upon the nerves of our *Ghelmen*, and in the morning he was in as good-humor as ever, seeming to forget his misfortunes of the day before.

CHAPTER XXVIII.

Arrive at Mañin's.—Nachi.—The Game of Pelican.—Gambling.—Avas.—Teetotum.—Sumeles.—A new Sister.—Sad Parting.—Rheumatism.—Budeo.—Good-by to Arauco.

WHEN we arrived at Mañin's house the old gentleman was not at home, and we determined to wait twenty-four hours in order to see him.

Our Trauque immediately went to his own house, and soon after invited us to come and partake of a sheep, which he had procured for our entertainment. We obeyed the summons, but were surprised to find the sheep not yet dead, for our friend intended to give us the extra treat of a dish of *ñachi.*

This dish, which is considered a great luxury, is essentially Mapuché, and the method of its preparation is interesting.

The animal is hung up by the fore feet instead of the hind, as usual. The operator then carefully cuts the windpipe, down which he stuffs, by the handful, a mixture of red pepper and salt. This done, the jugular is severed, and pulled out sufficiently to turn the mouth of the vein into the windpipe, down which the blood flows, carrying the pepper and salt into the lungs. The poor writhing creature is soon swollen up, and dies in exquisite agony.

When the sheep is opened, the lungs are found distended with blood, pepper, and salt, the whole forming one coagulated mass. This is the *ñachi*. It is carefully extracted, cut in slices, and served up warm from the still quivering animal!

Early in the morning we saw a number of boys engaged upon the fine lawn in front of the house, in planting out twigs at short intervals, thus forming an alley about forty feet wide, and some three hundred long. They were preparing for a game of *pelican*. Others were blowing a long horn (formed by the insertion of a cow's horn into a hollow cane), to the tones of which came back answering notes, as though a rival band were approaching over the hills. The night before we had heard the same challenge to the neighboring youths, and the same echoing reply, but more faint and distant.

At last the enemy was seen emerging from the woods; a shout of welcome arose; there were many salutations, a "big talk," and all put themselves in readiness for the great trial of skill.

The game of *pelican* differs but little from the *hockey*, or *shinty*, so common with us as a school-boy game. It is played with a small wooden ball, propelled along the ground by sticks curved at the lower end. The two sides have their bases at opposite extremes of the alley. The ball is placed in a hole half way between the bases, and over it two boys are stationed, while the other players are scattered along the alley, each armed with a stick. When all is ready, the two boys in the middle strike their sticks together in the air, and commence a struggle for the ball, each striving to knock it toward the opposite party. The object of every one is to drive the ball through his opponent's base, or, in defense of his own, to knock it sideways beyond the bordering line of twigs, in which case the trial is put down as drawn, and recommences. Each game is duly notched on a stick, and the party first tallying a certain number gains the victory.

There was much shouting and scuffling, many a cracked shin, and an occasional tumble—but the greatest good-will reigned throughout.

Some thirty players were engaged in the game—mostly naked, with the exception of a poncho about the loins. I was much disappointed by their physical development, which was not as fine as I had expected to see. They struck me as inferior to the laboring classes in Chili, both in muscle and in symmetry, though possessing the same general features. Neither was their playing remarkable, either for skill or activity; and, if they were a fair sample, it would be an easy matter to select from many of our large schools or colleges a party of young men more than a match for the same number of picked Araucanians, at their own national game of *pelican*.

As the heat of the sun increased, the game of *pelican* was given up, and the players scattered about in groups under the shady trees. The game of *avas* now commenced. This is somewhat like dice, and is played with eight beans marked on one side, and ten small sticks used as tallies.

Upon the ground is spread a poncho, upon which the players sit facing each other. Alternately they take up the beans, shake them in the hand, and throw

MAPUCHES GAMBLING.

them down upon the poncho: the spots turned up are counted, and the one first reaching a hundred wins.

While thus engaged they caress the beans, kiss them, talk to them, rub them upon the ground and on their breasts, gesticulating wildly, and shouting at the top of their lungs, imploring good luck for themselves and evil for their opponents with as much sincerity as though, with Pythagoras, they believed that beans have souls.

The air resounded with a discord of wild voices. Shirts, ponchos, laquis, and knives were staked, rapidly changing hands; and more than one of the players returned to his home with little other covering than that dame Nature had furnished him.

Besides the *avas*, they have a game of chance played with a four-sided teetotum. They are also said to play several games of skill, and among others, one somewhat resembling chess.

Like all uncivilized people, they are excessively fond of gambling, in which they indulge habitually. Many a Mapuché has staked his all upon the turn of a bean—the fate of prisoners of war has often depended upon the caprice of a teetotum; and more than once, when disputes have arisen in the national councils, grave questions of policy have been decided by a game of *pelican*.

Many of the young bucks, drawn together by the prospect of sport, were dressed in their finest toggery, and from one of them I bought a new pair of *sumeles*.

These horse-skin boots, which are worn by the Guachos of Buenos Ayres, as well as by the Indians, are made without peg or seam, as follows: When a horse dies, the owner strips off the skin from the hind leg of the steed and, yet reeking, draws it on to his own. The top is folded and tied at the knee, and the bottom, if too long for the foot, is cut off. It is worn until dry, when it is taken off, scraped, rubbed, and again drawn on. By repeated rubbings it becomes as soft and pliable as buckskin.

The skin of the horse's knee readily adapts itself to the wearer's heel, and that which covered the shin shrinks in drying, and takes the exact form of the foot; while at the point the boot is left open as a matter of convenience to the Indian, who in riding always takes a grip with the big toe on his small triangular wooden stirrup.

These boots are very comfortable when riding, for which purpose alone they are used—for the Indians at other times go barefooted. The cowhide sandals and moccasins often worn by the poorer classes in Chili and Peru are unknown to the Mapuchés.

In the evening Mañin, my adopted father, arrived. He had been off on a begging tour, collecting a tithe of corn and potatoes among his distant vassals. He congratulated us on our speedy return, and charged us with many friendly messages to the Intendente at Los Angelos, as well as to my supposed father, Vega.

With him also came the daughter of Juana, the white wife, and for the first time I became acquainted with my only grown-up sister. She was about fifteen, and quite pretty, with a rich complexion, the bright Spanish blood glowing warmly through the dark olive of her cheek. She was decked with a profusion of barbaric ornaments; and though modest and retiring, possessed an air of pride that did not ill beseem a daughter of the haughtiest of the Araucanian chiefs.

I gave her the only remaining musical instrument, with which she seemed highly delighted, and doubtless, to the present day, the remembrance of her *Huinca* brother is inseparably connected with a penny whistle.

Our Trauque seemed really sad at the prospect of being separated from us, and exacted from me a promise to come and see him the very next time I visited Los Angelos. But a present of the jack-knife which I had carried on the journey did something toward assuaging his grief; and, without impeaching the disinterestedness of his affection, I fear the promise of a striped cotton shirt and a pair of fringed drawers, to be sent from Los Angelos, almost reconciled him to our departure.

Several days later we reached the Kaillim, and stopped for the night at the house of Kilal.

Borrowing a hide, I made my bed upon it, and retired. About midnight I awoke, feeling unpleasantly cold, and found myself lying naked in the wet grass, with a strong sou'wester blowing furiously over me. The wind had blown off the bed-clothing, and as we were upon a side-hill, I had managed to slide down gently, off the slippery hide, without waking.

I crawled back and made up my bed again as well as I could, but when morning came every bone in my body had a separate ache of its own, and I found myself in pretty much the condition of Sam Slick's horse, that was "so weak in the joints that he could'nt stand up, and so sore in the ribs that he could'nt lie down." In addition, I had a violent headache and a high fever, which almost disabled me from proceeding, for I felt at times as though I should fall from my horse.

There was a long and tedious ride before us, but it was fortunately our last day's journey, and I resolved to hurry on, for I feared a serious illness; and there was something horrible in the very idea of being sick in the midst of these barbarians.

For the first time, I yearned to be once more among civilized men, and it was with heartfelt joy that I looked down from the brow of the last hill into the little valley of Budeo, just as the sun was setting. True, we were still in the Indian country, but those scattered huts were the haunts of white men, and seemed to form a connecting link with the civilized world.

Panta's family were rejoiced at our return. To me they were very kind, and did all in their power to make me comfortable.

In the morning, though better, I still suffered from severe rheumatic pains, and it was not till the second day after arriving at Budeo, that we went on toward Los Angelos.

It was already night when we reached the ferry on the Bio-Bio, and the last boat was returning, giving us the cheering prospect of a night among the desolate sand heaps around us. But by screaming and informing the captain of the barges that we were "commissionados," and in great haste to see the Intendente, he at last consented to send another boat for us.

Bidding adieu to the land of Arauco, we embarked, and on reaching the opposite shore I felt as if once more among my fellow-creatures.

CHAPTER XXIX.

San Carlos.—Doña Pablita.—A Damper.—Los Angelos.—A Peripatetic Government.—Town of Rére.—Palm Sunday.—Concepcion.—Visit De la Vega.—Kindness of Friends.—Conclusion.

AT San Carlos we lodged, as before, at the house of Panta's "compadre." The kind-hearted people were very glad to see us back, and none more so than the fair Pablita, who sympathized deeply with me in my distress; but added that I should be thankful for having returned at all—a piece of good fortune that she attributed solely to St. Joseph, with whom she had interceded daily in our behalf.

My little friend made me up a clean, soft bed with the best the house could afford, and after a month's roughing on bull-hides, with nothing overhead but the blue canopy of the heavens, the white sheets and sheltering roof were perfectly Sybaritic; but on retiring I could not sleep. I missed the soft radiance of the stars. I felt stifled for want of air, and after dozing for a few minutes, would wake with a sense of pressure upon the chest, restraining the freedom of the lungs, and making me long for my hard bed on the boundless plain.

The house, like most of the Chilian ranchos, was full of cracks, through which the wind circulated in a manner that any where else would be thought intolerable; but the change was too sudden for my fastidious lungs. All confinement was irksome, and it was fully a week before I could sleep with comfort under a roof, even with doors and windows wide open.

Early in the morning Doña Pablita was at my bedside with a fragrant maté. Then there was no looking-glass in the house (for my own now gladdened the heart of the "Oak-that-buds-in-the-Spring"), and she insisted upon combing my hair and tying my cravat. Her little attentions were so sisterly, and she treated me so much like an invalid, that I began to feel as though I ought to wait a few days and recruit; then my linen was dreadfully in need of repair, and would afford a good excuse for repaying, in a solid manner, the kindness I had received. There, too, was my old friend the commander of the garrison; it would be too bad to go off without seeing him. In fact, I had quite a notion of remaining a few days at San Carlos, and hinted as much.

The intimation produced quite a flutter among certain laces and ribbons that were growing, under the needle, into some inexplicable article of coquetry, and the fair sewer was ere long whispering confidentially to her god-father (Sanchez). He soon took the opportunity of informing me that Doña Pablita was on the eve of being married; and that my stay in the house, however well meant, might cause some uneasiness to the bridegroom.

Now I had no reason to be vexed; I certainly would not begrudge the young couple their happiness (which after all was problematical); a cottage by the shores of the Bio-Bio, even though illuminated by the constant smile of a pretty face, had never been my ambition. But the announcement was unexpected, and it did feel too much like taking a shower-bath. However, with as good a grace as possible, I ordered my horse to be immediately saddled, and after congratulating the blushing bride, and promising to send her a bridal present, I mounted and started at full gallop for Los Angelos.

There was a delightful sense of freedom in being able, once more, to course over the familiar plain, alone, unrestrained, and with no lurking apprehension of encountering some wandering savage. But despite all this I was continually haunted, not by a wild Mapuché, but by somebody's pretty face, and I fear that, before reaching the journey's end, my horse's ribs suffered many severe inflictions that were intended for some one else—not a horse.

Los Angelos was in an uproar of excitement, growing out of the expected visit of the President: for Don Manuel Montt, following the example of the great Prince-President of the model French Republic, had undertaken the tour of his dominions. Not only did His Excellency travel, but with him the whole government became peripatetic; there were the heads of all the departments with their clerks, and every town and village along the road became, in turn, the Capital. Decrees were scattered broadcast; hospitals, churches, bridges, and school-houses were every where erected—on paper, and the joy of the people was unbounded—at least so said the official journals.

Early in the morning a courier dashed through the streets, announcing that the President might be momentarily expected. Drums beat, trumpets sounded, and the garrison—horse and foot—turned out, and formed along the principal thoroughfare. The squads of militia from the surrounding district then came pouring in. Mounted on the most wo-begone animals, armed with long "coligue" lances tipped with iron, their red flannel ponchos begrimmed with dust, they presented but a sorry appearance; yet these men, with a little training, make the best soldiers in Chili. As the natural effect of climate they are more hardy than the people to the north, and the land not being (as in other provinces) completely monopolized by the few, the most of them are small land-owners, having a spirit of independence unknown to the servile "peon," and consequently possess that *morale* which in the composition of an army is of far more importance than the mere *physique*.

The people, too, were all out in their best. Flags streamed from every house, and triumphal arches spanned the street. But hours rolled on: the poor soldiers were broiling in the sun, and it was not till near sunset that the booming of a gun announced the approach of the procession.

First came an escort of dragoons; then the Government, riding in ten or a dozen gigs. All were enveloped in a cloud of dust, and his Excellency was undistinguishable from the rest. The bands played; the troops presented arms, and the cavalcade moved slowly up the street, but few were the cheers that arose. There was no outburst of enthusiasm. The people were sullen, and even of the soldiers that formed the procession, there were probably few who would not have joined the ranks of any bold conspirator against the man whom they were assembled to honor.

Two or three days having been spent in reviewing troops, straightening out the affairs of the province, and decreeing a number of things that *ought* to be done, the President and his cortége moved on to Nacimiento; and Los Angelos, after enjoying the short-lived glory of being the seat of government, relapsed into its former insignificance.

Engaging a mozo, I set out for Concepcion by a road different from that which I had before traveled.

Night overtook us before we reached the Laja, and it seemed that we should be obliged to sleep supperless on the plain; but the barking of a dog directed us to a house where we procured a "casuela," and an abundance of grapes and new wine.

Soon after sunrise we reached the river, but we had missed the ford, and though piloted by a countryman, we had much difficulty in crossing, for the bottom was full of holes and quicksands. A little farther on we passed the Rio Claro, and again came upon the dreary waste of volcanic sand which skirts the northern bank of that river.

Over this we rode for two or three hours until we reached the foot of the hills forming the coast range. So far we had experienced no difficulty in guessing the way, but amidst this wilderness of hills we were soon lost. Neither the servant, who was worthless, nor I myself knew any thing of the road; and we wandered about at random, only seeking to keep in the general direction (about northeast) of our destination, and acting on the axiom that "every road must lead somewhere." But even the most self-evident propositions are not always true, and more than once we climbed to the summit of a hill only to find our advance stopped by an impassable gulley, washed down by the recent rains.

By dint of blundering and guessing we reached the little town of Rére during the afternoon. I had a letter to deliver to a lady in this place, who kindly invited us to remain until the morrow, and treated us with that frank hospitality which in Chili is always extended to the stranger who comes well recommended.

The town of Rére, though small, is one of the prettiest to be met in the country. The houses are generally built of adobe, and roofed with tiles; and we saw none of those unsightly hovels which generally disfigure the outskirts. The church, built by the Jesuits in their palmy days, is tasteful, and boasts a fine bell, which is said to owe its mellow tones to a large proportion of silver in its composition. Near the church a stately palm towers high in air—a beautiful and striking object.

Our route the next day still lay among the interminable hills, but after riding an hour or more we came upon the main road, which was familiar, for it was the same I had pursued in going to Yumbel.

We met many country people in their best attire going toward Rére, and we could not but notice the beauty of the mountain lasses with their rosy cheeks and clear white complexions, such as are rarely met with among the lower classes in other parts of Chili.

It was not until our attention was attracted by the little crosses and twigs of evergreen that each one bore that we remembered that the day was Palm Sunday. There was something beautifully impressive in the sight of these gayly-dressed crowds moving along the highway with green branches in their hands, to commemorate the triumphal entry of Our Saviour into Jerusalem.

Having reached Concepcion, one of my first cares after getting comfortably settled at my old quarters under the ample roof of our ever-hospitable countryman, Don Pablo ——, was to seek out the Señor De la Vega, whose name I had so unceremoniously usurped as a passport to the good graces of Mañin.

He turned out to be a little smiling Catalonian, the owner of a small store, and well to do in the world. He was much amused by my story, laughing heartily at the success of the ruse, and assured me that I should be perfectly welcome to retain the name, and that he would be most happy to acknowledge me as his son.

He consented to receive whatever presents the lordly Mañin might see fit to send in return for favors received, and to give a favorable account of Namcu-Lauquen. It is to be hoped that before this some noble animal—the pride of the pastures of Chacayco—has been sent to gladden his heart, and reconcile him to the departure of a son whose existence even he had never suspected, and who was found only to be again lost.

Many were the congratulations received from those whom my protracted absence and long silence had led to fear that some accident had befallen me in the prosecution of what they deemed a rash adventure, and many were the polite attentions I received during my stay in Concepcion. Pleasure-parties and rides, excursions to Penco and Landa, Bella Vista and Collen, followed each other so uninterruptedly, that the days glided swiftly away; and when the time came for departure, it was with regret that I found myself compelled to say good-by to friends from whom I had received so much kindness.

There are few places associated in my mind with such pleasing recollections as Concepcion—none to which I shall always revert with feelings of more unalloyed gratification. But even had I been willing longer to encroach upon an unbounded hospitality, the season forbade, for the rainy months were setting in, and traveling either by land or sea would soon be difficult.

Fortunately I was able to procure a passage in a vessel bound to Valparaiso, at which port I intended to embark in the British steamer for Panama.

It was a fine day when we set sail, and as we glided down the noble bay of Talcahuano, the familiar spots along the shore looked more beautiful than ever; but fairly out upon the ocean, it was with a thrill of pleasure that I saw the goodly vessel pointing to the north; for at last I found myself fairly started for my native country, which an absence of four years had rendered doubly dear.

THE END.

www.ingramcontent.com/pod-product-compliance
Lightning Source LLC
LaVergne TN
LVHW020212110826
845151LV00003B/689